THE LEGISLATIVE PROCESS IN OKLAHOMA

UNIVERSITY OF OKLAHOMA PRESS: NORMAN

THE LEGISLATIVE PROCESS
in Oklahoma

Policy Making, People, & Politics

by
Samuel A. Kirkpatrick

By Samuel A. Kirkpatrick

Urban Political Analysis: A Systems Approach (with David R. Morgan; New York, 1972)

The Social Psychology of Political Life (co-editor with Lawrence K. Pettit; California, 1972)

Quantitative Analysis of Political Data (Columbus, 1974)

American Electoral Behavior: Change and Stability (editor; Beverly Hills, 1976)

The Oklahoma Voter: Politics, Elections, and Political Parties in the Sooner State (with David R. Morgan and Thomas G. Kielhorn; Norman, 1977)

The Legislative Process in Oklahoma: Policy Making, People, and Politics (Norman, 1978)

Kirkpatrick, Samuel A.
  The legislative process in Oklahoma.

  Bibliography: p.
  Includes index.
  1. Oklahoma. Legislature. 2. Legislators—Oklahoma.
      I. Title.
JK7171.K57   328.766   77-26641
ISBN: 0-8061-1421-5

FOR DOROTHY M. KIRKPATRICK,
participant and teacher

Preface

The process of lawmaking is the most vital element of a democratic system. It is through representative government that public policy is enacted in the United States. Yet, the processes associated with it are little understood by the citizenry. Indeed, the average voter has only passing knowledge of legislation, and the subtle complexities of the process are usually beyond his understanding and interest. In Oklahoma, as in other states, the legislature is a key institution about which the electorate has only modest knowledge. This book is dedicated to the purpose of closing that knowledge gap and to reinforcing the linkage between the represented and the representatives.

The following chapters attempt to cohere as a text on the legislative process in Oklahoma useful to the average citizen, more active participants in politics, and college and secondary school students, as well as to novice legislators and those who aspire to legislative service. The range of subjects treated includes all aspects of the legislative process, with an emphasis on political actors, the politics they engage in, and the ways they make policy. Other themes are the institutional, legal, and formal aspects of lawmaking and the more informal and personal components of the process. These emphases reflect the author's contention that a full understanding of policy making must take into account the behavior and attitudes of lawmakers, in addition to the institutional characteristics of the legislature. If these goals are achieved in the eyes of readers, it will be the most comprehensive treatment of any lawmaking body in the American states.

The content of the book reflects the above commitment, as it treats the following subjects: rules and procedures, the personal and political characteristics of legislators, attitudes about lawmaking and "rules of the game," roll call voting, and empirical data on legislative effectiveness. Analysis sections employ the most current empirical procedures available in the social sciences, yet those which require little previous knowledge of research methodology. I have drawn heavily from lengthy interviews and verbatim accounts

vii

by legislators, yet such material is analyzed in the context of other research literature on the state legislative process, available social science theory, and systematic data on other states. While some popular materials are included and normative evaluations addressed, the text is neither a polemic nor a product of journalistic sensationalism.

The organization of the book attempts to address a wide range of topics in orderly sequence, beginning with a basic description of the legislature: formal powers; the characteristics of office; the sequence of events in each legislative session; and the changing political, social, and economic characteristics of legislators and their districts. The second chapter departs from more formal considerations to address the personal aspects of legislative life: the legislator's perspective on his job; satisfactions and frustrations of lawmaking; personal ambition and involvement; and the way individuals adapt to a legislative career. Chapters 3 and 4 treat the process of public policy making from two fundamental perspectives: first, the components of the legislation-enacting process and the individuals, agencies, and procedures associated with it; second, the variety of internal and external influences on roll call voting. Chapter 5 continues an emphasis on informal aspects of lawmaking by examining norms or "rules of the game" adopted by legislators vis-a-vis their political party and the multitude of daily legislative tasks. Chapter 6 moves beyond the legislative institution and its members to examine external relationships with constituents, interest groups, and the press. The concluding chapter addresses the normative issue of legislative effectiveness, the status of Oklahoma in comparison to other states, reform proposals, and factors influencing effectiveness of the institution. The book also contains student-oriented appendices with study guides on legislative rules for each house and a glossary of legislative terms.

A number of individuals and agencies have played a key role in this project. The American Political Science Association (through the Ford Foundation) provided an initial grant to the Oklahoma State Legislative Service Project, for the specific purposes of assisting the Legislative Council in conducting presession legislative conferences and developing a legislative manual which could serve as a basic resource document for both new and experienced legislators. The American Political Science Association recognized that the legislatures are playing an increasingly vital role in the American federal system, while the demands of legislative life are growing in number and complexity. The legislator must perform a variety of functions in a relatively short and intense period. Information-seeking and priority-setting are crucial elements of legislative decision making, yet the immediacy of the lawmaking process and the time demands upon it require extensive familiarity with legislative life if lawmakers are to "get on with their business." When it takes one term or so in office for the legislator to develop a firm grasp of the process, the business of lawmaking and representation inevitably suffers. With rectification of these problems in mind, the Association provided funds for presession conferences and the development of *The Legislative Process in Oklahoma: Preliminary Foundations For a Legislative Manual* (coauthored with Gary L. Cathey) which served as a foundation for this more comprehensive text. The project was expanded and extended through funds made available by the Bureau of Government Research and the H. V. Thornton Memorial Fund after the author recognized that citizens, as well as new legislators, must have a good working knowledge of the legislative process.

In this more extended effort I have relied heavily upon the assistance of Gary L. Cathey, Research Assistant on the State Legislative Service Project, who aided in the collection of basic data and their analysis. The 1972 Oklahoma Legislative Study conducted with Lelan E. McLemore and the staff of the Bureau of Government Research, through funds provided by the H. V. Thornton Memorial Fund, enabled the collection of data on legislators' perceptions of their job and informal rules of the game. I have relied heavily on subsequent work by McLemore and am highly indebted to his persistence and intellectual encouragement. Furthermore, research conducted by various political science doctoral students at the University of Oklahoma enabled an extensive treatment of various topics: Richard D. Bingham on legislative reapportionment, E. Lee Bernick on legislative roll call voting, and William Lyons on legislative rules and procedures. The research and encouragement of faculty colleagues has also played a vital role. I am especially indebted to Professor David R. Morgan, Associate Professor of Political Science and Associate Director, Bureau of Government Research; Professor F. Ted Hebert,

Associate Professor of Political Science; and Professor John W. Wood. Many of these former students and current colleagues also made possible the publications contained in the Bureau of Government Research, Legislative Research Series, from which this text draws heavily.

I have also relied on a variety of individuals outside the University who have provided resource documents, data, manuscript comments, and other forms of valuable assistance: Jack Rhodes, James Johnson, Ronald Stewart, and James Croy of the Legislative Council; Lee Slater, State Election Board; Richard Huddleston and Louise Stockton, House of Representatives staff; and Anna Walls, Oklahoma Department of Libraries. I am also indebted to the members of the Oklahoma House and Senate who kindly participated in various interview projects, and especially to the assistance of Senator James Hamilton, former Representative C. H. Spearman, Senator Lee Cate, and the late Senator Phil Smalley. Evron Kirkpatrick and Walter Beach of the American Political Science Association were particularly helpful in providing support for the Oklahoma State Legislative Service Project, as were other Fellows who have shared their ideas, especially Dr. Lawrence K. Pettit (Montana) and Professor Charles Wiggins (Iowa). In addition, the staff of the Citizens Conference on State Legislatures kindly provided supplemental materials on legislative effectiveness and permission to reprint Figure 5. The entire project would also not have been possible without the diligent assistance of efficient secretaries: Pat Stermer, Debbi Bass, and Judie Grove. Finally, I have dedicated the book to my mother, Dorothy M. Kirkpatrick, who has more than passing interest in the legislative process and who provided an early environment which stimulated my interest in practical politics.

S.A.K

Norman, Oklahoma

Contents

                                                                    page

Preface   vii

List of Tables   xv

List of Figures   xviii

1. The Legislative Setting in Oklahoma: An Institution and
   its Members   3
   The Legislator in Oklahoma Politics   3
   Formal Legislative Powers and Restraints   6
   Legislative Organization and Composition   7
     Sessions   8
     Qualifications, Responsibilities, and
       Compensation   8
     Legislative Officers   10
   Entering the Legislature   11
     Presession Activities   13
     Convening the House and Senate   15
     Oath of Office   15
     Election of Legislative Officers   16
     Message from the Governor   16
     The First Week of Activities   16
   Political and Social Composition   18
     Party Membership   20
     Background Characteristics of Legislators   22
   Urbanism and Legislative Reapportionment   35
     Reapportionment in the Oklahoma House of
       Representatives   40
     Senate Reapportionment   46
   The Changing Shape of the Legislative Universe   49

2. Personal Aspects of Legislative Life: Lawmakers'
   Perspectives on Their Job   52
   How the Legislator Sees His Job   53
     Legislative Roles   53
     Role Conflict   56

Purposive Roles 59
Satisfactions and Frustrations with Legislative Life 67
Job Satisfaction 70
Frustrations 70
Legislative Efficacy 72
Perceptions of Power and Privilege 74
Career Perspectives 77
Tenure and Turnover 77
Political Ambition 81
Legislative Activity and Involvement 85
Styles of Adaptation 88

3. Enacting Public Policy 93
Information Inputs and the Development of Legislation 93
The Oklahoma Legislative Council 94
Oklahoma Department of Libraries 100
Attorney General's Office 101
Other State Agencies 103
The Course of Legislation 104
Types of Legislative Measures 109
The Committee System 120
Committee Functions 123
Number of Committees 125
Committee Assignments 128
Appointment of Committee Chairmen 130
Powers and Duties of Chairmen 131
Committee Procedure 132
Interim and Special Committees 134
Committee Jurisdiction 134
The Components of Policy Enactment 135

4. Legislative Behavior and Roll Call Voting 136
Internal Forces on Decisions 137
Party Influences 138
Cue Taking from Colleagues 140
External Forces on Roll Call Voting 141
Constituency Influences 142
The Environment of the Legislative System 142
Interest Groups 143
Gubernatorial Influence 143
The Mix of Internal and External Forces 144

Influences on Roll Call Voting in Oklahoma 145
Partisan Factors and the Role of the Governor 146
Non-Party Influences on Party Support 152
Constituency Influences in Oklahoma 155
Legislators' Political Beliefs 160

5. Informal Rules of the Game: Legislative Norms 162
Norms in the Oklahoma Legislature 167
Partisan Norms 170
Procedural Voting 172
Substantive Bill Voting 174
Committee Action 175
Floor Behavior Norms 176
Publicity 177
Floor Speaking 179
Freshman Floor Speaking 180
Dealing in Personalities 180
Legislative Specialization 181
Expertise Specialization 182
Number of Bills Introduced 184
Interest Groups and the Governor 185
Interest Groups 186
Gubernatorial Support 187
Awareness of Shared Beliefs 189
Norm Sanctions 191
Norm Awareness 193
Norm Monitoring 194
Rewards and Punishments 195
Sanctioning Agents 197

6. External Legislative Relationships: Constituents, Interest
Groups, and the Press 199
Constituent Relationships 199
Representational Roles 203
Organized Interests 211
Lobbyists 213
Regulation of Lobbying Activities 216
Media Relations 219

7. Oklahoma in Comparative Perspective: A Postscript on
Legislative Effectiveness 225

Measuring Legislative Effectiveness 225
  Functionality 226
  Accountability 227
  Information Handling Capability 227
  Independence 228
  Representativeness 228
How Oklahoma Fares 228
Factors Influencing Legislative Effectiveness 235
Public Policy Linkages 241

Appendices
  Appendix A: Senate Rules Study Guide: Selected
                Review Questions on Senate Rules 247
  Appendix B: House Rules Study Guide: Selected
                Review Questions on House Rules 260

Notes 275

Glossary of Legislative Procedure 285

Bibliography 287

Index 297

List of Tables

page

1 Party Membership in the Oklahoma House of Representatives 21
2 Party Membership in the Oklahoma Senate 22
3 Average Age of Oklahoma Senate and House Members,by Party: 29th-35th Legislatures 23
4 Average Age of Oklahoma Senate Members, by Party: 29th-35th Legislatures 24
5 Percentage of Republican State Senators Elected From Metropolitan/Urban and Rural Districts 25
6 Average Age of Oklahoma House Members, by Party: 29th-35th Legislatures 26
7 Education Levels of Oklahoma Legislators, 29th-35th Legislatures 27
8 Education Levels of Oklahoma Senate Members, by Party: 29th-35th Legislatures 27
9 Education Levels of Oklahoma House Members, by Party: 29th-35th Legislatures 28
10 Proportion of Native-Born Legislators in the Oklahoma House and Senate: 29th-35th Legislatures 28
11 Occupational Representation in the Oklahoma Senate, 29th-35th Legislatures 30
12 Occupational Representation in the Oklahoma House, 29th-35th Legislatures 30
13 Religious Affiliations of Oklahoma State Senators, 29th-35th Legislatures 34
14 Religious Affiliations of Oklahoma House Members, 29th-35th Legislatures 34
15 Influence Indices for Metropolitan Members of the Oklahoma House Before and After Reapportionment 38
16 Influence Positions Held by Metropolitan House Members Before and After Reapportionment 39
17 Influence Positions Held by Metropolitan Senate Members Before and After Reapportionment 40
18 Influence Indices for Metropolitan Members of the

Oklahoma Senate Before and After Reapportionment   41
19 Purposive Role Orientations in Oklahoma and Four Other
     States   61
20 Ritualist Attitudes in the Oklahoma Legislature   63
21 General Perceptions of Job Satisfaction in the Oklahoma
     Legislature   69
22 Frustrations With the Legislative Process in Oklahoma   71
23 Feelings of Legislative Efficacy   73
24 Perceptions of Power and Privilege in the Oklahoma
     Legislature   75
25 Composition of the 34th Oklahoma Legislature (1973-74)
     by First Year of Most Recent Continuous Service   79
26 Career Attitudes and Perceptions of Oklahoma
     Legislators   82
27 Legislative Activity and Involvement in Oklahoma   86
28 Styles of Adaptation to a Legislative Career   89
29 Frequency of Legislative Measures (Bills and Resolutions)
Introduced in the Oklahoma House and Senate:
     1959-1976   112
30 Percentage of Bills Considered by the Oklahoma House
     and Senate Relative to the Total Number of Legis-
     lative Products: 1959-1976   114
31 Percentage of Resolutions Considered by the Oklahoma
     House Relative to the Total Number of Legislative
     Products: 1959-1976   116
32 Percentage of Resolutions Considered by the Oklahoma
     Senate Relative to the Total Number of Legislative Pro-
     ducts: 1959-1976   117
33 Percentage of Bills Enacted by the Oklahoma House and
     Senate Relative to the Total Number of Bills Consi-
     dered: 1959-1976   118
34 Number of Standing Committees in the Oklahoma House
     and Senate: 1959-1976   126
35 Range in Size of Oklahoma House and Senate Standing
     Committees: 1959-1976   127
36 Universe of Content and Scale Analysis Results for 1970
     Oklahoma House of Representatives and 1959 Okla-
     homa House of Representatives   148

37 Relationship Between Party and Five 1970 Roll Call
   Scales   149
38 Effect of Office Holding on Legislative Party Support
   Scores   153
39 Effects of Residency, Experience, and Competition on
   Legislative Party Support   154
40 Summary of Mean Relationships Between Urban-Rural
   Cleavages and Roll Call Categories and Proportion of
   Curvilinear Relationships in the 1970 Oklahoma House   156
41 Levels of Legislative Interaction and Observation in the
   Oklahoma House and Senate   166
42 Optimal Partisan Norms in the Oklahoma Legislature   174
43 Optimal Floor Behavior Norms in the Oklahoma
   Legislature   178
44 Optimal Specialization Norms in the Oklahoma
   Legislature   183
45 Optimal Norms for Relations with Interest Groups and
   the Governor   187
46 Representational Role Orientations in Oklahoma and
   Four Other States   205
47 Legislators' Attitudes About Representation   209
48 A Comparison of Oklahoma's Legislative Effectiveness
   with Selected Environmental Indicators   239
49 A Comparison of Oklahoma's Legislative Effectiveness
   with Selected Policy Consequences   242

List of Figures

1 A Simple Role Model of the Legislative System   56
2 Course of a Bill Through the Oklahoma Legislature   106
3 A Model of Influences on Roll Call Voting   138
4 Major Focal Points for Legislative Norms   168
5 Regional Distribution of Legislative Capabilities —
   Final Ranking   232
6 A General Political System Model for Oklahoma   236

THE LEGISLATIVE PROCESS IN OKLAHOMA

CHAPTER 1

The Legislative Setting in Oklahoma: An Institution and its Members

Many observers of state politics have noted the relative decline in the powers of the legislative branch that has accompanied a decrease in state powers relative to the federal government during this century. There is recent evidence, however, that states are playing a more crucial role in a newly revitalized federal system. Furthermore, the change in the status of state legislatures is far from absolute. They deal with matters of great importance, spend more money than ever before, are more active and productive, and considerably better than their nineteenth-century counterparts. This is part of a larger trend for states to perform more services, spend more money, and employ more people than in previous periods. The Oklahoma legislature is no exception to these trends. While the job of a legislator is not drastically different now from what it was at the time of statehood, important changes have occurred since then. The number and complexity of demands placed on the legislature have increased significantly, demographic changes and reapportionment efforts have literally changed the face of the Oklahoma lawmaking body, and modern technology has altered the nature of relationships between constituents and their representatives. These changes have occurred at a time when state legislatures have been characterized as the "emerging nations" of American politics; at a time when state legislatures face serious challenges and crises. Undoubtedly the Oklahoma legislature is not alone at an important crossroads in American political history.

THE LEGISLATOR IN OKLAHOMA POLITICS

There is obviously more to a legislature than its history and institutional framework. Organizational characteristics, powers, and responsibilities are all part of the legislative scene and they require our immediate attention in this chapter. Yet, the legislative institution is composed of individuals gathered together for common tasks. Public policy emerges from a conglomeration of individual styles, personalities, capabilities, and backgrounds. Since laws are fashioned by men and women within a formal institutional setting, those men and women and their perceptions are keys to understanding the legislative process.

In addition to characteristics of the legislature as an institution, this chapter deals with individual background attributes of lawmakers and the various jobs that they are called on to perform. The legislator's emergence from a successful electoral contest in November is quickly followed by a complex set of new demands often requiring major adjustments in his life style and work schedule. For both the new and experienced legislator alike, many demands are unexpected, and many roles and jobs are dismayingly complex. Out of this complexity emerge several basic functions of legislative life which occupy a majority of lawmakers' time.

One of the primary and most visible jobs of the legislator is that of lawmaking. While the executive branch has primary responsibility for administering government, and the court system serves as an adjudicator of conflicts in the political system, the distinctive responsibility of the legislature is to make public policy. The constitutionally defined realm of lawmaking is quite broad in scope—a typical legislative session will produce bills that appropriate monies, regulate individual and governmental activity, protect individuals, and allocate a variety of resources and powers within Oklahoma. Unlike most other legislative bodies, the state legislature may exercise any legislative power unless limited by the state or federal constitution.

The lawmaking function, however, is closely tied to another basic job of the legislator—that of representative. In a democratic society elected representatives serve the people's interests and needs, and the legislature as a whole is supposed to represent and act for the entire community. In any state or community there are many voices to represent—individuals, towns, organizations, and the state as a whole. One of the most difficult jobs of the legislator is deciding how to represent effectively a variety of individuals and a variety of interests, as well as his own conscience and commitments, in best service to the state.

Because of the diversity of interests and viewpoints, the legislator plays a third major role in Oklahoma: counseling, advising, and resolving conflicts. Lawmaking and representation are certainly not simple notions, and the key to legislative success is often dependent upon priority setting and compromise. The determination of solutions to public problems involves a capacity to resolve conflicts growing out of a diverse society.

Another major job of the legislator is oversight of the administrative branch. Laws are enacted to achieve certain agreed-upon ends, and the administration of legislative intent is of vital interest to most representatives. In a complex set of government structures, very important implementation decisions are not made by the legislature or elected executives or judges—but by civil servants. While complex bureaucracies are inescapable in modern society, the legislator has a responsibility to monitor its operation and protect and represent citizens' interests, when those citizens' most frequent contacts are with a seemingly impersonal set of governmental policies.

While lawmaking and representation are relatively distinctive functions of the legislator, the other two primary jobs—oversight and conflict resolution—are often shared throughout government. This shared responsibility, which is more informal than legal, grows out of the everyday demands of legislative life, and it makes the job of the legislator particularly complex. For example, while the executive branch has primary responsibility for administering laws, the legislature eventually becomes involved in aspects of this administration. Similarly, the courts are constitutional arbiters, yet arbitration, negotiation, and conflict resolution are also vital daily components of legislative work. This work is also subjected to involvements and interpretation by the courts, which in reality are not far removed from politics and lawmaking. Since the executive branch also makes legislative proposals and formulates programs, there is even further sharing of responsibilities.

The legislative job that emerges from these shared responsibilities is therefore complex by definition. But in addition to primary functions, the job is riddled with related roles that comprise legislative life. The legislator is expected to serve the public interest, engage in public debate, uphold the constitution, introduce bills and vote on matters before the legislature, study legislation, serve on committees, submit constitutional amendments to the people, serve his political party and its program, and effectively exercise his legislative powers toward a solution of public problems. In performing these jobs, the legislator's day is full, and the pressures of time are serious. In any one day he may begin with a breakfast meeting, attend morning committee meetings, do research and read legislation, visit constituents and answer letters, debate bills and vote, and attend evening conferences and meetings.

FORMAL LEGISLATIVE POWERS AND RESTRAINTS

In addition to the general legislative functions cited above, the legislature has a variety of specific powers which it may exercise under the constitution. The exercise of these powers, however, is often controlled by constitutional restraints and limitations.

One of the most basic and specific legislative powers is taxation. The legislature may levy inheritance, production, excise, gross revenue and graduated legacy, succession, collateral, and income taxes. These taxation powers are constitutionally defined so as to prevent contracting away or surrendering responsibility by the legislature. The constitution allows property tax exemptions when educational, religious, charitable, and certain other public purposes are involved, and it empowers the legislature with the right to extend taxation powers to cities, towns, school districts, and counties. An important restraint on taxation powers requires that taxes be uniform when applied to the same class of subjects.

The Oklahoma legislature also has powers and duties relevant to initiative and referendum proposals. It may submit constitutional amendments, constitutional convention calls, or measures to incur indebtedness to the electorate. The legislative route for state questions is more frequently used than the initiative petition, and it has a considerably higher rate of success. If legislators fail to attach an emergency clause to a bill, it is subject to popular petition for a ninety-day period and a majority vote in a referendum election. The legislature may also refer statutes to a popular vote if it so desires.

Powers and restraints related to indebtedness and state expenditures are important components of lawmaking in Oklahoma. Generally, the constitution places broad constraints on legislative power to borrow on credit (exceptions include credit financing for defending the state in time of war or for controlling invasions or insurrections). For the most part, debt powers are vested in the electorate, with a few residual powers remaining with the governor or administrative agencies (for example, the governor may issue deficiency certificates to prevent serious problems in public services and several administrative agencies, such as the Turnpike Authority and the State Regents for Higher Education, may issue revenue earning bonds). The 1941 budget balancing amendment plays a major role in this series of constitutional constraints. It regulates powers of appropriation and short-range debts by providing that expenditures (not appropriations) may not exceed collected revenues. Furthermore, the legislature may not authorize appropriations in excess of anticipated revenues during the following fiscal year.

In addition to the general oversight function cited earlier, officials in the executive branch and courts are subject to legislative impeachment. Both impeachment and legislative approval of executive officers are part of the complex system of checks and balances present in the Oklahoma constitution.

As we have seen above, many legislative powers are accompanied by sets of restraints on those powers. In summary, the constitution places four major limitations on lawmaking:

1. All bills must be concerned with one single subject, clearly expressed in the title, except for general appropriation bills and those which adopt a code, digest or revision of existing statutes.

2. General appropriation bills must be confined to expenses of the legislature, executive, and judicial departments, or to interest on state debts; other appropriations must be made by separate bills which state the amount and object to which it is applied.

3. General laws shall operate uniformly throughout the state, and special laws may not be passed if a general law can be made to apply; local or special laws cannot be considered unless prior published notice is given in the political area affected.

4. Revenue bills must originate in the House, although subject to Senate amendment, and no revenue bills may be passed during the last five days of the session, thus excluding the use of the governor's "pocket veto" on revenue measures.[1]

LEGISLATIVE ORGANIZATION AND COMPOSITION

The Oklahoma legislature is a bicameral or two-house legislative system consisting of a House of Representatives and a Senate. By constitutional definition, both houses must act in order to pass any law or joint resolution. Since reapportionment efforts began in the

1960's, particularly the *Reynolds* v. *Simms* decision of 1964, population serves as a criterion for representation in both houses of the legislature. Members of the House are elected for a period of two years, while the Senate term is four years, with one half of the body elected at each general election. Legislators in both houses represent a single or multicounty district. The size of both houses has varied over the years: the Senate began with 44 members and increased to 48 in 1965 after court-ordered reapportionment; the House began with 109 representatives in 1907, dropped to 92 in 1921, increased to a high of 123 in 1953, until it reached its present level of 101 members following reapportionment in 1971.

Sessions

Until the voters approved a constitutional amendment in 1966, the legislature met every two years in regular session. Since that date, annual legislative sessions, which are not limited to any particular substantive business (such as budgetary matters), meet for a maximum of ninety legislative days. The regular session begins on the first Tuesday after the first Monday in January of each year at 12:00 noon. The constitution also provides for the calling of special sessions by the governor to consider only such matters as he recommends. It is also possible for the governor to call the Senate alone into session, primarily for action on appointments requiring Senate approval. Although the legislature determines its own date of adjournment (unless it is deadlocked on a date), neither house alone can adjourn for more than three days without the consent of the other house. Following adjournment, those bills which remain unresolved at the end of the first regular session are carried over to the second session of the biennium, and their progress status achieved during the first session is maintained.

Qualifications, Responsibilities, and Compensation

The constitutional definition of qualifications for a state legislator prescribes both age and residency requirements. Members of the House of Representatives must be 21 years of age at the time of election, and a state senator must be 25 years old. Members of both houses must also be qualified voters in and residents of the district they represent. In addition, a legislator may not be an officer of the state or national government or receive compensation for such a job while he serves in the legislature. Other restrictions prescribe that any person convicted of a felony may not serve, that a member may not be appointed to a newly created office (or one for which the salary is increased during his term), and that a legislator cannot have a vested interest in any public contractual arrangements which are authorized by law during his tenure and for two years thereafter.

In addition to qualifications and regulations on behavior, formal sanctions of the legislative body are available to enforce the proper conduct of legislative affairs. Both houses may punish members for disorderly conduct or expel them from service. Expulsion requires a two-thirds vote of the membership, and if one is expelled for corruption, he is ineligible for any further legislative service. Since each house is the judge of elections, vote returns, and qualifications of members, it also has exclusive powers. Either house may refuse to seat a person, despite claims that he is duly elected, by a simple majority vote.

The availability of sanctions and the prescription of qualifications is complemented by certain privileges, immunities, and compensations for legislative service. Immunity from arrest appears to be broadly defined to exclude arrest while attending or traveling to and from session, except in instances involving treason, a felony, or a breach of peace. An immunity is also granted when a legislator engages in floor debate: he cannot be questioned or held accountable for remarks made in debate on the floor of the legislative chambers.

Legislative salaries and amenities are regulated by the Board of Legislative Compensation. Travel expenses are provided for one weekly trip to and from the meeting place of the legislature while it is in session, and members residing outside the capital city receive per diem support for each day of the session spent in Oklahoma City. During the interim, legislators may receive a per diem and mileage for up to twenty legislative meetings, with possible extensions approved by the Council Executive Committee. Other benefits and compensations include a legislative office and secretarial assistance, telephone and mailing allocations, an official immunity card identifying the individual as a legislator, gallery passes for constituents, a life and health insurance program, and a retirement plan. The speaker, president pro tempore, majority leaders, and minority leaders receive additional compensations in conjunction with their official positions relevant to legislative business.

Legislative Officers

Oklahoma's organization of legislative leadership is similar to that of most other state legislatures. The selection of officers is usually a party function for the majority party (in caucus), and it is accomplished before the session begins, although the formal election itself occurs at the outset of the session. The House caucus selects candidates for speaker and speaker pro tempore (to act in the Speaker's absence), as well as floor leaders and assistant floor leaders. The speakership is a prominent position in Oklahoma government, both formally and informally. For example, the speaker presides over the House, appoints committees, decides rules of order, certifies bills and resolutions, recognizes members on the floor, calls members to order, assigns committee rooms, controls privileges to the chamber and galleries, serves as chairman of the Legislative Council every other biennium, appoints House members to the Council Executive Committee, and is responsible for printing and publishing session laws. The job of the floor leader and assistant floor leader is to mobilize legislative support for the party's position. The minority party also elects floor leaders, but sometimes it does not offer candidates for all leadership posts in both houses. In addition to formal party officers, the House employs related support officers, including a chief clerk, journal clerk, calendar clerk, reading clerk, enrolling and engrossing clerk, auditor, and sergeant-at-arms.

On the Senate side, the chief presiding officer and president is the lieutenant governor. He may not cast a vote except in instances where there is a tie. The elected officer of the Senate is the president pro tempore, who becomes president if the lieutenant governor is absent, dies, assumes the governorship, or is impeached. In recent years, the duties of the presiding officer tend to be performed by the elected officer of the Senate, and in many ways they correspond to powers of the speaker on the House side. An additional power (or honor) for the Senate presiding officer is his responsibility for presiding over joint sessions. The party caucuses also elect a majority and minority floor leader, assistant floor leaders, and whips.

A set of additional officers and clerks exists on the Senate side of the legislature, and their titles and responsibilities correspond to the House officers.

ENTERING THE LEGISLATURE

Legislators in Oklahoma, like their counterparts in the other forty-nine states, are elected primarily to enact laws. Yet we have noted that this function is only one of the many integral and extensive duties that must be performed by the legislator. Apart from being a lawmaker, he is also a committee member, caucus participant, researcher, and colleague, just to name a few of his roles. The job of legislator is difficult and demanding, and each person finds himself engaged in activities which are peculiar to his district and constituents, as well as those activities which have no direct relation to the "people back home." The job requires energy, intelligence, and the capacity to learn from experience. For the returning legislator, there is already a reservoir of experience from which to draw, but for the freshman the legislative arena is a unique experience. Some information and aid will come from past experiences—from professional experience, such as law, or from other forms of public officialdom—but in general the freshman legislator enters a new world full of traditions, rules, informal norms, and unique work tasks.

In order to cope with their new world, legislators must have a means for "learning the ropes," conforming to norms and informal rules of the game, and developing attitudes about legislating and representing. Furthermore, they must acquire cognitive skills relevant to sources of information and learn the procedural complexities necessary for lawmaking. Various agents perform crucial roles in this learning or socialization process. While some prefer to speak of an "inner club" of tenured members and party leaders as the primary agents of socialization, a study of the Michigan House indicates that the primary agents are informal groups within the legislature.[2] The primary task of these agents is to limit conflict and promote cooperation. In Oklahoma, this is often seen as the responsibility of prominent legislative leaders. The advice from such a source may be more formal and diffuse than cues rising from day to day contact with peers and informal work groups, yet the nature and content of advice is substantially the same.

In advising new members of their tasks, one legislative leader recently suggested eight major points that all legislators must take seriously:

(1.) Probably the greatest challenge that we will have is to make a maximum effort individually and collectively to restore faith to the people in the legislative process, faith in the government, and its institutions. I might point out to you that it will not be an easy task because being a good legislator is not a simple thing to do. There is no royal road that I know on which we can travel that will give assurance that we are going to do a good and capable job.

(2.) The second suggestion that I am going to make you might find a little difficult because it's going to take a lot of work....study bills. The more you study bills, the more knowledge you are going to have concerning that particular piece of legislation....You will know a little more about government, your knowledge will improve and the greater knowledge that you have, the better vote you should be capable of making....Keep up with the reading of the bills. You should learn to read the bills at the beginning of the session because you will find as the session progresses more and more bills will be introduced, your committee assignments will become heavier, and as a result, you just don't have time to read the bills.

(3.) Do not commit yourself to vote for or against a piece of legislation until you first have the opportunity to read it.

(4.) Make every effort to attend session and committee meetings.

(5.) Rome was not built in a day....have patience. You will find out that some of the programs you know must be approved aren't nearly as important to some folks as it might be to you, so have some patience in getting things done.

(6.) You've got to compromise....but along with that compromise I suggest that we have integrity and sincerity of purpose not to compromise the principles and fundamentals of government, because when we compromise principles and fundamentals of government the price is too high regardless of what the conclusion might be.

(7.) Your title is State Representative or State Senator....You want to represent your people that sent you to the legislature with dignity and honor, but again your title is State Representative or State Senator. You are supposed to be able to look at the problems of all of Oklahoma and then try to do a good job not only for your people but the whole state.

(8.) Keep your word. If you want to be respected and gain stature in the House and stature in the Senate, and if you want to win friendships that really count, you must honor every commitment that you make even if it takes a great sacrifice....If you want to feel lonesome, you'll never feel more lonesome when you've got a piece of legislation that you have commitments on and you look around and those who made the commitments are out or they forgot commitments that they made.

Presession Activities

The job of being a legislator begins immediately after the November election. There is little time for rest, as the legislator will be involved with such tasks as talking and visiting with his constituents, making and receiving phone calls, making appointments, planning various types of meetings, and gathering a variety of information to aid him in his job. For the most part, these duties are nonpartisan and are performed by each legislator.

After a legislator is elected in November he may want to visit with a number of his constituents. Aside from being "good politics" to keep in personal touch with the people back home, the legislator finds it beneficial to speak with his constituents prior to the legislative session. Such presession meetings aid him in plotting his future course and stands on bills and issues. The legislator is always aware that his constituents not only elect him but also are valuable sources of information in aiding and directing his program interests.

During the weeks prior to the regular legislative session the legislator may also want to make appointments with registered lobby groups and news media representatives. Meetings with lobby groups will help develop rapport with various interests and aid the legislator in future dealings with such groups when the time arises. Knowledge and familiarity with the news media is also useful in developing rapport with newspaper, television, and radio reporters. The advantages of knowing who to talk to are known by the veteran legislators and are realized quite soon by freshmen.

Aside from the regular duties and functions of receiving and meeting individuals, the legislator also participates in presession caucus meetings. This is one of the more important duties to be performed by the legislator prior to the regular session. The caucus meetings are a rather unique experience, and parallel situations are seldom found outside the political arena.

The primary purpose of the caucus meeting is the unofficial election of legislative officers. Since the Oklahoma constitution provides that all legislative officers are to be elected on the first day of the first regular session of the biennium, the presession caucus meetings select officers-designate. The importance of the caucus meetings cannot be overemphasized as they allow each party in each house to meet prior to the official election of legislative officers so that problems can be resolved and the "best man" elected. The caucus meetings allow each party to join in unanimous support for their respective legislative leaders.

Aside from the unofficial election of legislative officers, there are other important and useful functions performed at the party caucus gatherings. First, freshman legislators become acquainted with their colleagues. During the campaign a freshman legislator may have had an opportunity to become acquainted with one or several of his future colleagues, but the party caucus provides an opportunity for each legislator to make new friends, increase his visibility, and see firsthand the politics of party gatherings. The returning legislator also finds such meetings beneficial, as he will meet new colleagues and renew old friendships. Another function of the presession caucus meeting is to allow each legislator an in-depth view of, and participation in, party organizational activities. Since each party's caucus gathering reflects and exposes party leaders, the legislators find such organizational gatherings beneficial as a means of learning the practical application of party rules and procedures.

The caucus meetings held prior to the first regular session are called formally by the Democratic and Republican caucus chairmen, but in practice the legislator who has sufficient votes to be elected speaker of the House or president pro tempore of the Senate calls the caucus meeting. Without exception the majority party elects the speaker, speaker pro tempore, and Senate president pro tempore, while both parties elect floor leaders and whips. Although the minority party does not or cannot elect one of its members to the presiding offices, the organizational importance of the presession caucus is not negated. Both parties find it beneficial to elect those members who will best serve their respective parties on and off the floor of the legislative chambers. The caucus gatherings may be held at any time after the primary elections and prior to the regular session, but in recent years the general trend has been to hold the caucus meetings several days following the primary elections. Later in the year, usually in mid-December, freshmen and various experienced members have an opportunity to learn legislative procedure and new issues of public policy by attending the Presession Legislative Conference jointly sponsored by the Legislative Council and the University of Oklahoma.

Convening the House and Senate

The Oklahoma constitution provides that the legislature "shall meet in regular session at the seat of government on the first Tuesday after the first Monday in January of each year, beginning at twelve o'clock noon...." (Article 5, Section 26). Each house convenes separately, followed by a joint meeting of the House and Senate. The initial separate meetings provide an opportunity for the formal election of officers; however, a swearing-in ceremony for all members usually takes place prior to the session and shortly after the general election. The subsequent joint meeting takes place in the House chamber as it provides the largest area in which to seat the members of both houses comfortably. The primary purpose of this joint session is to hear a message from the governor, and hear the secretary of the State Election Board present the result of the previous election. Generally, the first day, though official, is primarily a day of eliminating those items of business that must be acted on before the business of enacting laws can be initiated.

Oath of Office

Before any legislator takes official command of his job, he must receive the oath of office. The official oath is administered in separate Senate and House conclaves, usually prior to the session. The oath is administered in two parts—a verbal recitation and a signing of the oath form. Officially the oath may be administered by any judge, but traditionally this duty has been performed by the chief justice of the Oklahoma Supreme Court. Prior to the recitation, the oath forms are obtained from the secretary of state's office and dispersed to each legislator. Each form is placed at the temporary desk of the legislator to facilitate signing. After the oath has been verbally administered by a judge, each legislator signs the oath form, at which time they are collected and placed on file by authority of the secretary of state.

Election of Legislative Officers

On the first day of the first legislative session, the presession party caucus actions are given full status by each legislative branch. This action is simply a formality, as the officers to be elected have already been chosen during the organizational party caucus held several weeks earlier. The formality of the election of legislative officers is necessary because the constitution of Oklahoma requires that on the first legislative day all officers in the state legislature are to be elected.

Message from the Governor

The governor has the obligation of speaking before the joint legislative session. There are no set rules as to the type of speech to be given, but traditionally the governor presents his State of the State message. It is seen as an opportunity for legislators to hear the plans and proposals of the executive branch. More detailed proposals are usually presented later in the form of a budget message to a joint session. An outline of the governor's plans allows the legislators an opportunity to know in some detail what types of legislation the governor will be seeking. In addition, the governor will receive needed feedback from the legislature concerning the major thrusts of his plan.

The First Week of Activities

Immediately after the first joint legislative session the legislature devotes itself to the tasks of adopting rules, organizing committees, selecting committee chairmen, vice chairmen, and members, and other similar duties. The first week is seldom devoted to the business of lawmaking, since each member must settle into his new office and organize his surroundings for the task of legislating.

The assignment of committee chairmen, vice chairmen, and members usually takes place during the first few days of the first legislative session. The actual selection of committee chairmen and vice chairmen may take place sometime after the general election, but the official designation of chairmen and vice chairmen takes place during the first week of the legislative session.

The task of making committee appointments is difficult and requires much deliberation by the speaker and president pro tempore. In order to aid the leader in his selection, committee preference forms are sent to each member. Each legislator fills out the questionnaire listing desired committees in order of preference. In practice, the leaders attempt to seat each member on a certain percentage of the committees he prefers. No single factor predetermines the selection of chairmen and vice chairmen; the presiding officer relies upon several determinants in aiding his selection. First, the type of committee is of primary importance. For the more important committees the leader will appoint legislators who (a) have long years of legislative experience; (b) actively support the leadership's interest; (c) are of the same political party as the leadership; or (d) have a particular interest in serving on a committee which has a direct impact upon their home districts. Appointments to other, less important committees may be made on the basis of informational expertise, loyalty to the speaker, party affiliation, legislative experience, or district interest.

The assignment of offices to members is determined by the leadership, and it usually occurs prior to the first week of activities. A variety of guidelines are followed in the assignment of offices. First, attempts are made to assign committee chairmen and vice chairmen to the same office. A primary consideration in this dual assignment is the compatability between the chairman and the vice chairman. Second, a freshman is usually placed in an office with the committee chairman and vice chairman of a committee on which the freshman serves. The intent is to familiarize the freshman with his committee duties and to facilitate a close working relationship with the committee chairman or vice chairman. Third, office preference by members may also be taken into consideration. Finally, the type of committee, the number of committees, and seniority are factors which may aid the leadership in assigning specific offices to members.

POLITICAL AND SOCIAL COMPOSITION

In addition to a perspective emphasizing formal powers and constitutional limitations, the Oklahoma legislature can be viewed from the individual level focusing on the personal characteristics of legislative composition. The men and women who shape public policy vary in their social and political backgrounds and, as we shall see later, in their attitudes about politics and lawmaking. They achieve the status of "legislator" through a complex recruitment process which shapes composition. While all political systems must perform the basic recruitment function of selecting political leaders, the mechanisms for that recruitment vary widely throughout the world. In a democracy, the political system is characterized by a heavy emphasis on popular election and the circulation of political leaders throughout all levels. In the United States, political leaders obviously do not rise or "grow from" the masses without the aid of a complex set of intermediary institutions which serve as recruiting agents.

The most important recruiting agencies for state legislatures are constituencies and political parties.[3] The mass public in a legislative constituency generally sets broad standards of acceptability for state legislative recruitment—standards which reflect the social characteristics of the constituency and the local political culture. This force in recruitment tends to select candidates reflective of the constituency demographic characteristics, such as class, race, ethnicity, education, and religious background. The second major recruiting agency is the political party, as well as some nonparty groups. One of the primary functions of all parties is to recruit leaders and to set more specific leadership criteria within the broad boundaries defined by constituencies. On the whole, parties look for political talent and ambition, and ideological comradeship, yet leaders must also be capable of compromising and preventing a damaging party primary fight. Since there is a substantial amount of elite involvement in political party recruitment, and because of some popular social myths held by constituents, state legislators

recruited in service to the party tend to "rise above" the median
rungs on the socioeconomic status ladder of the legislator's district.
Historically, the characteristics of Oklahoma legislative districts
and the state as a whole have influenced the general shape of
legislative composition. That composition has varied somewhat
over the years since statehood, especially with regard to age composition, education levels, sex and racial characteristics, and occupational prestige.

The political, social, and economic climate of Oklahoma immediately preceding and following statehood had an important impact on early Oklahoma legislatures. In some respects, the early
period was very much a picture of the "old West," with a population consisting primarily of white settlers, their families, and In-
dians representing the Five Civilized Tribes. Most of the early settlers located on sparsely populated land which had been "staked
out" during land rushes prior to statehood. The Indian population
was more concentrated with a large number in eastern Oklahoma.
The mix of political cultures during this early period has had a
lasting effect on contemporary Oklahoma politics. Many of the
state's ties stretched to the Middle West and upper Middle West,
largely characterized by a populist movement. This populism was
closely tied to agricultural interests which were clearly predominant
during the early period. Remnants of influence are still visible today in many sections of the State constitution and in early statutory
provisions. In addition, both the House and Senate were
predominantly oriented toward agricultural interests until the contemporary period, which is characterized by an increasing tendency
toward urbanism and efforts at legislative reapportionment. Today, the Middle Western populist influence has been translated into
a form of political conservatism characteristic of wealthier, wheat-
farming regions in the north and northwest parts of the state.

The nature of migration patterns has also contributed to an interesting blend of political perspectives and cultures in Oklahoma.
In this respect, the state takes on many characteristics of other
"border" states. The deep South influence and its particular brand
of political conservatism is most obvious in the southeastern section of the state in more deprived rural areas such as "Little Dix-
ie." As a result, the contemporary political climate in Oklahoma,
while primarily traditionalist, reflects early populist elements, con-

temporary wealthy farming perspectives, plus liberal social welfare concerns on the part of the rural poor.[4]

Party Membership

Political parties in Oklahoma contribute to the most important and obvious aspects of legislative composition: the partisan affiliation of state legislators. Indeed, the single most important factor shaping recruitment throughout the American states is the level of partisan competition within a given state.[5] The level of competition ranges from that of ten deep South states with firm Democratic control over governorships and the state legislatures to that of ten more diverse states where neither party has legislative or gubernatorial control on a regular basis. One of the most striking characteristics of American state legislatures is the general lack of party competition; a majority of states in the contemporary period are either one-party or limited two-party states. Oklahoma falls in next to the lowest category of partisan competition; by all standards it is considered a one-party dominant state, sharing sectional influences and migration patterns with border states that are similar historically and demographically.

Previous studies have shown that party organization is more important for recruitment in competitive states, whereas in other areas candidates are more likely to be self recruited, tied to various interest groups, and more likely to run for higher office without first having "worked up" the hierarchy of political positions.[6] While these nonpartisan forms of recruitment are obvious in Oklahoma, the feature of one-party dominance ensures more fierce battles within the majority party at the primary election level, and thereby reinforces the importance of party in the electorate. While Oklahoma state legislators are infrequently handpicked by party organizations, their recruitment is highly influenced by partisan activities among the Oklahoma electorate at the primary level. Indeed, most of these recruitment decisions are made prior to general elections.

Because of one-party Democratic dominance, Republicans have never enjoyed wide success as politicians in Oklahoma. A large percentage of members in nearly all Oklahoma legislatures have been Democratic partisans, and legislative control has fallen into

TABLE 1.—Party Membership in the Oklahoma House of Representatives

Years	Total Members	Number of Democrats	Percent of Total	Number of Republicans	Percent of Total
1959-60	119	110	92.5%	9	7.5%
1961-62	121	107	88.4	14	11.6
1963-64	120	95	79.2	25	20.8
1965-66	99	78	78.8	21	21.2
1967-68	99	74	74.7	25	25.3
1969-70	99	76	76.8	23	23.2
1971-72	99	78	78.8	21	21.2
1973-74	101	75	74.3	26	25.7
1975-76	101	76	75.2	25	24.8

the hands of Republicans in only two instances: once with a majority of House members elected in 1920, and once with a Republican speaker chosen by a coalition of Democrats and Republicans in 1929. At the same time, although Republican gains in recent years are most obvious at the senatorial and gubernatorial level, the party has not been without success in contemporary state legislative battles. The recent history of this partisan composition is reflected in Tables 1 and 2.

Table 1 shows a slow increase in the proportion of Republican House members during the last fifteen years to a high point in 1973. The largest increase in Republican membership occurred between the 1961-62 and 1963-64 legislatures, and is somewhat reflective of urban Republican gains in Oklahoma. Gains in the Senate (Table 2) are comparable, but of slightly lesser magnitude. In spite of these increases, however, Oklahoma remains a one-party dominant state, as it has been since statehood.

In general, it has only been in the last ten years that Republicans have been able to garner one-fourth of the seats in the House and one-fifth of the seats in the Senate. A portion of this change is due to court-ordered legislative reapportionment, which has had an impact detrimental to the Democratic party. For example, during the 1967-68 legislature, six of the nine Republican state senators were elected from metro-urban districts. Indeed, several of the

TABLE 2.—Party Membership in the Oklahoma Senate

Years	Total Members	Number of Democrats	Percent of Total	Number of Republicans	Percent of Total
1963-64	44	38	86.4%	6	13.6%
1965-66	48	41	85.4	7	14.6
1967-68	47	38	80.9	9	19.1
1969-70	48	38	79.2	10	20.8
1971-72	48	39	81.3	9	18.7
1973-74	48	38	79.2	10	20.8
1975-76	48	39	81.2	9	18.8

Republican seats in districts in Oklahoma County and Tulsa County appear to be quite solidly Republican. Nevertheless, if every Senate seat held by a Republican were safe, their strength would amount to only one-fifth of the entire body. These gains are therefore marginal, and there is no reason to expect substantial Republican strength in state chambers in the near future. An increase in Republican strength will undoubtedly continue to manifest itself at the gubernatorial and senatorial level, more so than in the state legislature.

Background Characteristics of Legislators

American state legislatures tend to be composed of individuals of higher socioeconomic status, who are generally unrepresentative of the population as a whole. Minorities and women are not represented in proportion to their numbers in legislative districts. Throughout the nation, state legislators tend to be long-term local residents (although the population as a whole is highly mobile), and tend to come from higher status families and more prestigious occupational groupings. Less than 10 per cent of all state legislators have occupations the same as those held by a majority of workers in the United States.[7] There are particular occupational biases toward professional and technical backgrounds (especially law),

TABLE 3.—**Average Age of Oklahoma Senate and House Members,
29th-35th Legislatures**

Years	Senate	House
1963-64	50.0 (41)	48.1 (111)
1965-66	45.4 (45)	47.0 (96)
1967-68	46.9 (44)	47.6 (95)
1969-70	46.7 (44)	47.4 (94)
1971-72	47.6 (45)	47.1 (94)
1973-74	48.1 (46)	46.2 (97)
1975-76	45.2 (48)	43.4 (98)

proprietors and managers, and farmers. Educational levels are also considerably higher than constituency averages. It has been suggested that such forms of elite stratification indicate that voters want both the typical and atypical in their state representative.[8] There is a tendency for legislators to reflect religious, racial, and ethnic characteristics within their constituency, but to be a notch higher on the socioeconomic status ladder defined by education, occupation, and income. In other words, legislators tend to match their constituents in terms of ascribed status, but to be higher in levels of achieved status. Since these general trends hold for Oklahoma, there is reason to believe that constituents reward success within the limits of their own religious, ethnic, and racial groupings. These and other trends are evident as we examine social composition by age, urbanism, educational attainment, place of birth, occupation, religious affiliation, sex, and race.

One of the most obvious effects of the legislative recruitment process in the United States has been a decline in the average age of congressmen and state representatives. Older, more established legislative elites tend to be replaced by younger cohorts—a phenomenon that is larely associated with age shifts in the total population and increased urbanism. Yet state legislators tend to be considerably older than the population as a whole, and Oklahoma is no exception. The contemporary period evidences a concentration of legislators in the 45-55 age category, whereas the median age

THE LEGISLATIVE PROCESS

TABLE 4.—Average Age of Oklahoma Senate Members, By Party: 29th-35th Legislatures

Years	Democrats	Republicans
1963-64	49.7 (35)	51.8 (6)
1965-66	45.4 (38)	45.3 (7)
1967-68	48.1 (35)	42.0 (9)
1969-70	47.5 (34)	43.5 (10)
1971-72	48.8 (36)	42.8 (9)
1973-74	50.6 (36)	38.9 (10)
1975-76	47.1 (39)	37.1 (9)

for the entire Oklahoma population was 30 in 1960 and 29 in 1970.[9] From 1963 to 1976 the average age for senators and House members declined approximately five years, and while that decline is not precipitous, it is somewhat reflective of the urban impact on age composition within both houses. Recent reapportionment efforts have shifted the legislative balance toward urban areas, and the accompanying age shifts are reflective of general population differences between urban and rural areas in Oklahoma.

Table 3 presents data on the average age of Oklahoma House and Senate members for the contemporary period.[10] A major shift toward younger candidates occurred in the Senate in the mid 1960's, with a tendency toward a slight increase in age during the remaining decade. While few drastic changes are evident for the House, it is characterized by a more constant and linear age decrease. However, both houses witness a decline in average age for the most recent legislature under obversation. On the whole, drastic shifts in age composition have already occurred throughout the Oklahoma legislature, and the immediate future will probably see a gradual change.

Although aggregate shifts in both houses have not been substantial, they tend to mask important differences between the political parties. As Table 4 shows, the average age for Senate Democrats in 1975 was 47, whereas the average Republican senator was approximately a decade younger. A large proportion of the age differences can be accounted for by the election of younger Republicans from

TABLE 5.—Percentage of Republican State Senators Elected
From Metropolitan/Urban and Rural Districts

Years	Metropolitan/ Urban	Rural	Total N
1963-64	50.0%	50.0%	6
1965-66	85.7	14.3	7
1967-68	77.8	22.2	9
1969-70	80.0	20.0	10
1971-72	77.8	22.2	9
1973-74	90.0	10.0	10
1975-76	100.0	0.0	9

more urban districts. The table shows that for all but one of six legislatures, the average Republican was younger than his Democratic colleague. Most important, however, is the more pronounced decline in the average age of Republican senators (almost fifteen years) compared to Democratic members. Republican voters appear to have begun a trend in the early 1960's toward electing younger individuals to serve in the Senate. Changes in Senate composition by age are especially reflective of increasing youthful Republican gains in urban areas. Table 5 shows that the majority of Senate Republicans were elected from metropolitan or urban districts throughout the period, and that by 1975, all of them came from districts with at least one city over 10,000 in population.

Average age differences between Democratic and Republican House members follow closely those found for the Senate (see Table 6). In 1974, the average age for House Democrats was 49, whereas Republican members were eleven years younger on the whole. While the mean age for House Democrats subsequently dropped to 44, thereby narrowing the partisan age gap, the overall decline for Republicans is sharp (although less pronounced than in the Senate). The most substantial age shift occurs for Republicans elected to the 1973-74 legislature following important reapportionment changes. Those changes appear to have had the immediate effect of reducing the average House Republican age by about ten years.

While it is difficult to isolate the precise causes of age shifts

TABLE 6.—Average Age of Oklahoma House Members, By Party:
29th-35th Legislatures

Years	Democrats	Republicans
1963-64	47.6 (86)	49.8 (25)
1965-66	46.3 (75)	49.5 (21)
1967-68	47.8 (70)	47.0 (25)
1969-70	47.7 (71)	46.4 (23)
1971-72	46.6 (73)	48.1 (21)
1973-74	49.0 (72)	38.4 (25)
1975-76	44.2 (74)	40.6 (24)

described above, the shift toward youth is heavily dependent upon growing Republican urban strength. However, other factors are obviously at play in the recruitment process. Republican strength in and around urban areas is usually located within sections of larger Oklahoma cities that are more powerful socially and economically, plus the suburbs. Republicans tend to be recruited from these areas, which are growing in strength, and since Republicans are normally of higher socioeconomic status, the trends are mutually reinforcing. Furthermore, a small minority party, such as the Republicans in Oklahoma, is more likely to recruit younger leaders in a state dominated for years by the older majority party. The increased upward mobility of Republicans, plus their higher socioeconomic status, and disproportionate location within urban and suburban areas, are all factors which have contributed to important age changes.

In addition to age, one of the most fundamental social factors affecting the recruitment process is level of educational attainment. Almost by definition, political elites in the United States are drawn from upper educational strata and are very unrepresentative of the population as a whole. Since these education levels are steadily increasing, we expect almost commensurate shifts over time in the Oklahoma legislature. Table 7 displays the level of educational attainment for state senators and representatives over a fourteen-year period. For the most recent sessions, over three-fourths of the senators were college graduates, many with advanced professional degrees, and almost two-thirds of the House members held college

TABLE 7.— Education Levels of Oklahoma Legislators, 29th-35th Legislatures

	Senate			House		
Years	College Graduate	Some College	High School or Less	College Graduate	Some College	High School or Less
1963-64	73.2% (30)	19.5% (8)	7.3% (3)	50.4% (57)	16.8% (19)	32.8% (37)
1965-66	77.8 (35)	11.1 (5)	11.1 (5)	55.2 (53)	19.8 (19)	25.0 (24)
1967-68	79.1 (34)	11.6 (5)	9.3 (4)	53.2 (50)	25.5 (24)	21.3 (20)
1969-70	77.2 (34)	11.4 (5)	11.4 (5)	59.6 (58)	20.2 (19)	20.2 (19)
1971-72	77.8 (35)	13.3 (6)	8.9 (4)	58.5 (55)	22.3 (21)	19.2 (18)
1973-74	76.0 (35)	19.6 (9)	4.4 (2)	61.9 (60)	22.7 (22)	15.4 (15)
1975-76	76.0 (35)	19.6 (9)	4.4 (2)	64.3 (63)	25.6 (25)	10.1 (10)

TABLE 8.— Education Levels of Oklahoma Senate Members, By Party: 29th-35th Legislatures

	College Graduate		Some College		High School or Less	
Years	Democrats	Republicans	Democrats	Republicans	Democrats	Republicans
1963-64	74.3% (26)	66.6% (4)	20.0% (7)	16.7% (1)	5.7% (2)	16.7% (1)
1965-66	76.3 (29)	85.7 (6)	10.5 (4)	14.3 (1)	13.2 (5)	6.0 (0)
1967-68	76.4 (26)	88.9 (8)	9.3 (4)	11.1 (1)	9.3 (4)	0.0 (0)
1969-70	73.5 (25)	90.0 (9)	9.1 (4)	10.0 (1)	11.4 (5)	0.0 (0)
1971-72	75.0 (27)	88.9 (8)	13.9 (5)	11.1 (1)	11.1 (4)	0.0 (0)
1973-74	69.4 (25)	100.0 (10)	25.0 (9)	0.0 (0)	5.6 (2)	0.0 (0)
1975-76	70.2 (26)	100.0 (9)	24.3 (9)	0.0 (0)	5.5 (2)	0.0 (0)

TABLE 9.—Education Levels of Oklahoma House Members, By Party: 29th-35th Legislatures

Years	College Graduate		Some College		High School or Less	
	Democrats	Republicans	Democrats	Republicans	Democrats	Republicans
1963-64	48.9% (43)	56.0% (14)	19.3% (17)	8.0% (2)	31.8% (28)	36.0% (9)
1965-66	58.7 (44)	42.9 (9)	18.7 (14)	23.8 (5)	22.6 (17)	33.3 (7)
1967-68	56.5 (39)	44.0 (11)	23.2 (16)	32.0 (8)	20.3 (14)	24.0 (6)
1969-70	60.5 (43)	56.5 (13)	19.7 (14)	21.7 (5)	19.7 (14)	21.7 (5)
1971-72	60.3 (44)	52.4 (11)	21.9 (16)	23.8 (5)	17.8 (13)	23.8 (5)
1973-74	61.1 (44)	64.0 (16)	23.6 (17)	20.0 (5)	15.3 (11)	16.0 (4)
1975-76	62.2 (46)	70.8 (17)	27.0 (20)	20.8 (5)	10.8 (8)	8.4 (2)

TABLE 10.—Proportion of Native-Born Legislators in the Oklahoma House and Senate: 29th-35th Legislatures

Years	Senate			House		
	Natives	Born out of State	Total N	Natives	Born out of State	Total N
1963-64	70.7% (29)	29.3% (12)	41	67.3% (76)	32.7% (37)	113
1965-66	66.7 (30)	33.3 (15)	45	71.1 (69)	28.9 (28)	97
1967-68	75.0 (33)	25.0 (11)	44	63.5 (61)	36.5 (35)	96
1969-70	84.1 (37)	15.9 (7)	44	71.9 (69)	28.1 (27)	96
1971-72	80.0 (36)	20.0 (9)	45	71.3 (67)	28.7 (27)	94
1973-74	67.4 (31)	32.6 (15)	46	69.1 (67)	30.9 (30)	97
1975-76	69.6 (32)	30.4 (14)	46	76.5 (75)	23.5 (23)	98

degrees. While the table shows a higher percentage of college graduates in the upper chamber, approximately equal proportions have attended some college classes. The tendency for Senate membership to be drawn from upper educational strata is not atypical of Oklahoma; it occurs in many other states and at the national level, where the Senate chamber is viewed as the more prestigious body.

There are several important changes in educational levels which have occurred over the period under consideration. The House has shown a gradual increase in the number of college graduates, from one-half to nearly two-thirds of its membership. The House also has a noticeable increase in the proportion of members attending college without receiving a degree and a marked decline in the number of members with educational attainment at the high school level or less.

While levels of education have remained high and quite stable in the Senate, other patterns are evident from a partisan perspective. For the fourteen-year period, it is not unusual for 70 to 75 per cent of the Senate Democrats to hold college degrees (Table 8). The most significant shifts have occurred for Senate Republicans; the period increase is from two-thirds of the membership to 100 per cent with college degrees in 1975. Furthermore, in only one of six legislatures shown in Table 8 did Senate Democrats have a higher proportion of college graduates than the Republicans.

The data in Table 9 do not reveal the same high educational levels for House Republicans as shown for their partisan cohorts in the upper chamber. Slightly over two-thirds in 1975 had received a college education. Similar figures for Democrats indicate that House Republicans are not necessarily better educated. The table also suggests that change over time is a bipartisan phenomenon, with relatively commensurate decreases in the proportion of less educated members in both parties.

In sum, the data indicate that better educated legislators are attracted to the upper chamber; that levels of education have increased throughout the legislature, especially the House; and that the most drastic shifts have occurred over time for Senate Republicans. These effects of recruitment are not common only to Oklahoma, however. Studies of other legislative systems have concluded that a disproportionate representation of upper education levels is

TABLE 11.—Occupational Representation in the Oklahoma Senate, 29th-35th Legislatures

Years	Attorney	Insurance	Farming/ Ranching	Real Estate	Other
1963-64	40.0% (16)	15.0% (6)	20.0% (8)	0.0% (0)	25.0% (10)
1965-66	40.9 (18)	15.9 (7)	9.1 (4)	4.5 (2)	29.6 (13)
1967-68	44.2 (19)	9.3 (4)	9.3 (4)	7.0 (3)	30.2 (13)
1969-70	43.2 (19)	11.4 (5)	11.4 (5)	6.8 (3)	27.2 (12)
1971-72	44.5 (20)	8.9 (4)	13.3 (6)	8.9 (4)	24.4 (11)
1973-74	46.7 (21)	13.3 (6)	11.1 (5)	2.0 (1)	28.8 (12)
1975-76	50.0 (24)	6.3 (3)	10.4 (5)	12.5 (6)	20.8 (10)

TABLE 12.—Occupational Representation in the Oklahoma House, 29th-35th Legislatures

Years	Attorney	Insurance	Farming/ Ranching	Real Estate	Other
1963-64	16.7% (18)	6.5% (7)	26.8% (29)	4.6% (5)	45.4% (49)
1965-66	23.7 (23)	8.3 (8)	18.5 (18)	8.3 (8)	41.2 (40)
1967-68	21.1 (20)	10.5 (10)	20.0 (19)	8.4 (8)	40.0 (38)
1969-70	25.3 (24)	5.3 (5)	20.0 (19)	6.3 (6)	43.1 (41)
1971-72	25.5 (24)	4.3 (4)	25.5 (24)	7.5 (7)	37.2 (35)
1973-74	23.7 (23)	4.1 (4)	15.5 (15)	10.3 (10)	46.4 (45)
1975-76	20.4 (20)	3.1 (3)	16.3 (16)	6.1 (6)	54.1 (53)

widespread throughout the United States.[11] The pattern for Oklahoma is most striking when we consider the average educational levels within the state population as a whole. The census figures for 1970 show that the median school years completed for persons over fourteen years of age is 11.9 years, or slightly less than a high school education. Furthermore, only 8.4 per cent of those Oklahomans over fourteen have completed four years of college or more, and 29.5 per cent of Oklahomans over the legal recruitment age (25 years for the Senate) have the equivalent of an eighth grade education or less.[12]

Oklahoma legislators typically attend college within the state, they tend to be long-term residents with close ties to local communities, and for the most part they are native-born. In recent years, the percentage of Senate members born in other states varied from 16 to 33 per cent, while House composition ranges from 28 to 37 per cent who are not native-born (Table 10). In addition, there have been no significant shifts in the predominance of native Oklahomans within either house of the legislature. While we have no direct information on the length of district residence, a cursory examination of legislative careers suggests that most lawmakers are long-term residents of their district, as well as of the state. Again, this pattern in Oklahoma is not atypical of other legislatures. In a study of four states, Wahlke and his associates found that over 50 per cent of state legislators are residents of their districts for over thirty years.[13] Voters not only tend to view long-term residents with favor, but the process of elite recruitment through party machinery is more likely to tap natives with family ties in the state.

As we suggested earlier, agricultural interests tended to dominate early Oklahoma legislatures. This situation has been altered considerably during the contemporary period as we see an increase in the presence of various professional and other nonagricultural occupations. Tables 11 and 12 display the occupational breakdowns of state senators and representatives to the 29th through 35th legislatures. Both tables indicate that the predominant occupational representation comes from the ranks of the attorneys. This pattern is most evident in the state Senate, where nearly half of the membership reflects the legal occupation over the last fourteen years. While lesser in number, there are almost equal proportions of insurance men and farmers in the Senate. The most drastic shifts have occurred in agricultural and ranching occupations during the contemporary period—largely a reflection of reapportionment efforts and increased urban representation.

The proportion of attorneys in the House has also been relatively stable over time, yet the total percentage is about half of that in the Senate. On the average, the House typically has about twice the proportion of farmers that the Senate does. Again, this reflects the latest reapportionment efforts which have resulted in a decline of agriculture-related occupations in the latest legislative sessions. Another distinguishing feature of the House (Table 12) is the greater variety of occupational representation. The lower chamber has a significantly larger proportion of "other" and miscellaneous occupations—students, teachers, automobile dealers, reporters, engineers, housewives. Two factors appear to account for this higher level of heterogeneity in the House: smaller legislative districts and the larger size of the lower chamber.

Legislators who make a living in the fields of insurance and real estate account for a relatively small proportion of House membership, yet their importance as interest group representatives cannot be dismissed lightly. As a group or bloc, these two occupational categories are a powerful force, along with miscellaneous oil-related interests. These occupational categories are far better represented in the legislature than other interests in Oklahoma, such as teachers and laborers. Indeed, explicit labor representation is weak and diffuse, with few members considering themselves working men and women. This absence of labor legislators is further indication of the tendency for a legislative elite to represent upper socioeconomic strata in the population as a whole. Yet it does not follow that such lower status occupations are not represented, nor that there is an absence of labor sympathy among legislators. To the contrary, organized labor often finds a sympathetic voice in the legislature, especially among metropolitan Democrats. This pattern is not uncommon to Oklahoma, yet it tends to be more pronounced in other states with better organized labor interests.

The tendency for some occupations to reflect specific political and social interests raises a variety of issues about "inside lobbying." Such lobbying is obviously one of the rewards of legislative life, and few representatives sense any conflict of interest about their roles. It is common for inside legislator-lobbyists to contend that they are merely bringing their own expertise to bear on lawmaking.[14] While it is true that many lawmakers have specialized occupation-related knowledge, it is frequently difficult to draw the line between technical assistance and self-interest promotion. Such conflicts of interest are most obvious for legislators with business occupations, yet lawyers, on the whole, are not immune to such pressures.

There is lively debate over the extent to which attorneys use their privileged position to further interests of their profession. There are contentions, for example, that lawyer-legislators fashion the law to increase dependency upon specialized legal skills—such complaints usually coming from the ranks of nonlawyer legislators.[15] Some scholars have attacked this issue directly by examining the extent to which lawyers form legislative voting blocs. In a comprehensive study of the Indiana legislature, Derge[16] was not able to find such an identifiable voting bloc, and further concluded that lawyer legislators are not second-rate professionals who take up legislative careers because of failure in private practice. By definition, attorneys have training more relevant to the legislative process than other representatives, and the importance of such expertise is apparently held in high esteem by the electorate. One veteran political scientist/legislator suggests that few legislators consciously attempt to complicate statutes in order to create legal disputes, yet the possibilities for unconscious representation of particular interests are always present. Lockard[17] suggests that as long as the job of the legislator is necessarily part-time, there will always be difficulties in separating a legal career and a private practice from the more general jobs of representation and lawmaking. The problem will obviously be a constant one in legislative life since the potentially conflicting needs for representation and expertise will always be present.

Unlike occupations, the religious composition of the Oklahoma legislature is much more representative of the population as a whole. While legislative membership from a religious perspective has less direct ties to policy making than the nature of occupational recruitment, there are times at which issues become sufficiently important and visible to legislators to have a bearing on lawmaking. Recent examples include efforts to repeal prohibition, institute liquor by the drink, and pass legislation regulating abortion. The most important impact of religious affiliation, however, is not ex-

TABLE 13.—Religious Affiliations of Oklahoma State Senators, 29th-35th Legislatures

Years	Baptist	Methodist	Disciples of Christ	Presbyterian	Episcopalian	Other Protestant	Roman Catholic	Other	Total N
1963-64	30.0%	32.5%	7.5%	12.5%	5.0%	10.0%	2.5%	0.0%	40
1965-66	28.9	24.5	17.8	13.3	2.2	8.9	2.2	2.2	45
1967-68	29.5	22.7	15.9	15.9	2.3	11.4	2.3	0.0	44
1969-70	25.0	25.0	18.2	15.9	2.3	11.3	2.3	0.0	44
1971-72	32.6	23.3	16.3	11.6	0.0	13.9	2.3	0.0	43
1973-74	31.1	20.0	15.6	17.8	0.0	11.1	2.2	2.2	45
1975-76	30.4	17.4	17.4	19.6	2.2	6.5	6.5	0.0	46

TABLE 14.—Religious Affiliations of Oklahoma House Members, 29th-35th Legislatures

Years	Baptist	Methodist	Disciples of Christ	Presbyterian	Episcopalian	Other Protestant	Roman Catholic	Total N
1963-64	34.3%	31.4%	6.7%	9.5%	4.8%	10.5%	2.8%	105
1965-66	28.4	30.7	14.8	10.2	3.4	8.0	4.5	88
1967-68	27.0	28.1	13.4	15.7	2.3	11.2	2.3	89
1969-70	21.8	32.2	10.3	11.3	6.9	16.1	1.2	87
1971-72	20.7	28.7	12.7	11.5	9.2	16.1	1.1	87
1973-74	25.0	27.2	10.9	7.6	11.9	14.1	3.3	92
1975-76	28.7	22.3	21.3	9.6	6.4	8.5	3.2	94

plicit. Religious ties establish a milieu and place boundaries on the nature of policy making. This more implicit and general impact in Oklahoma is frequently tied to the Bible belt characteristics of the state as a whole. Knowledge of Oklahoma's religious morals suggest that Bible belt areas are not only fundamentalist in perspective, but also politically conservative. Religious perspectives, therefore, contribute to the over-all political culture of the state and tend to influence lawmaking indirectly.

Tables 13 and 14 present data on the religious affiliations of Senate and House members for a fourteen-year period. They display striking similarities between both chambers and a high degree of continuity over time. Baptists and Methodists comprise the two largest religious groups in both chambers—typically over half of the membership—and the composition tends to parallel religious preferences throughout the state. Typically, "higher" nonfundamentalist Protestants, plus Catholics, form a religious minority in the legislature. In other states, and especially the U.S. Senate,[18] nonfundamentalist Protestants tend to be over-represented, but in the Oklahoma legislature religious affiliation is more reflective of the fundamentalist religious dominance throughout the state. Catholic underrepresentation is more uniform across the United States, and there are some indications that Catholics in Oklahoma have difficulty achieving elected office. This appears to hold for the state legislature as well as recruitment to national office. The overwhelming defeat of John F. Kennedy's presidential election bid in 1960 is often cited as an example of this phenomenon in Oklahoma, although anti-Catholic sentiment was prevalent in many other states during that period.[19] There is difficulty in making judgments about such sentiments in Oklahoma, however, since the recent period has seen the election of a Catholic governor and his subsequent rise to the U.S. Senate.

URBANISM AND LEGISLATIVE REAPPORTIONMENT

Some of the most profound changes in the social composition of the Oklahoma legislature reflect a gradual urban growth throughout the state, accompanied by reapportionment efforts altering the proportion of urban representation and the balance of party strength. Many of the larger cities and towns have grown rapidly over the recent decades, and cities nonexistent thirty-five years ago have appeared within metropolitan areas. Such urban growth reflects migration from rural areas—a trend not uncommon to other states. The growth of urban areas is less dependent on intrastate and sectional migration than on interstate shifts in population. The three most recent decennial census reports for Oklahoma reveal a substantial gain in population for all urban counties and some rural county decreases.[20] This recent trend toward urban and metropolitan growth and rural outmigration has had visible impacts on the composition of the Oklahoma legislature, especially for the Republican party as noted earlier. In addition, the small minorities of women (three) and blacks (four) in the 34th legislature came entirely from metropolitan districts.

Legislators are well aware that any change in the composition of the chambers can bring about alterations in basic functions and lawmaking. In earlier periods, legislatures were not only controlled by Democrats, but by predominant rural interests. This dominance in the Oklahoma House and Senate led to rural-oriented policies and a subsequent deemphasis of urban interests. Since the balance of representational strength has now shifted to urban and metropolitan counties, a recent study of the legislature in the early 1970's made specific inquiries about the impact of those shifts.[21]

Although the effect of reapportionment on the passage of important legislation cannot be determined precisely, the first recently reapportioned legislature (1965) produced some noticeable results relating to urban areas. Probably the most significant act permitted municipalities to levy a one-cent sales tax. The legislature also passed the Inter-Local Cooperation Act authorizing local governments to enter into cooperative agreements in metropolitan areas. Soon thereafter metropolitan councils of government were established in the Oklahoma City and Tulsa areas. Additional legislation permitted cities and counties to create joint park and recreation commissions (previous legislatures had authorized city/town consolidation for libraries and health services). And finally, the state highway department was required to share equally with local units of government the costs of acquiring right-of-way for interstate highways traversing incorporated areas. Considerable savings resulted for municipalities, since right-of-way costs had previously been the sole responsibility of the locality.

A good argument can be made that urban areas may never attain their full potential for influence in the legislative arena until they begin to acquire their proportionate share of key committee chairmanships and other leadership positions. While an analysis of these factors cannot deal directly with the actual exercise of power, it treats the potential for influence that inheres in leadership position and provides more in-depth knowledge about urban impacts than is otherwise reflected in social composition changes. In order to measure a variety of influences, comparisons were made between the two major metropolitan areas (Oklahoma City and Tulsa) and the balance of the state. Subsequently, three indices of influence were developed: (1) a membership/population index which measures population representation parity by dividing the percentage of urban members in each chamber by the percentage of urban population; (2) a population influence index which measures the percentage of influence positions held by urban legislators in terms of the percentage of urban population; and (3) a legislative influence index reflecting the percentage of influence positions held by urban legislators in terms of the percentage of urban membership in each house. Influence positions are defined as chairmanships or vice-chairmanships of the following key committees: agriculture, appropriations, education, finance and commerce (previously banks and banking), judiciary, revenue and taxation, roads and highways, and rules; plus the following legislative leadership positions—speaker of the House, speaker pro tempore (House), and majority floor leader (Senate).

The 1963 legislature, which was the last one prior to the first major apportionment, will be compared with that of 1969-70, the third legislature following first reapportionment. Table 15 presents the summary indices of these two sessions for the Oklahoma House of Representatives.

As expected, the largest change occurred in the ratio between the percentage of metropolitan members in the House and the percentage of metropolitan population in relation to the state's population. From 1960 to 1970, Oklahoma and Tulsa counties increased their proportion of the state's population only slightly (from 33.7 per cent to 36.3 per cent), while metropolitan House members went from 11.7 per cent to 34.3 per cent following reapportionment. This, of course, was the dramatic change that reformers had long

TABLE 15.—Influence Indices for Metropolitan Members of the Oklahoma House Before and After Reapportionment

Years	Membership/ Population Index	Population Influence Index	Legislative Influence Index
1969-70	.94	.44	.46
1963	.35	.28	.81
Net Change	+.59	+.16	—.35

insisted upon; the one that could be mandated directly by the courts. Influence positions, on the other hand, are beyond the reach of judicial action and would be expected to change more slowly as, indeed, Table 15 indicates. Reapportionment brought about a slight increase in influence positions per population for House members from the state's two largest urban areas. In fact, only one new influence position in the House was gained by the metropolitan areas, as indicated in Table 16, which shows the actual number of key legislative positions held by metro House members and the percentage increase before and after reapportionment. The .44 population influence index for the two large counties (Table 15) still falls considerably short of the ideal figure of 1.0. This means that the percentage of metropolitan House members in 1970 was still less than half of what it would have been if these urban legislators held leadership positions proportionate to the population of their districts (compared with the balance of the state).

The most striking development revealed by Table 15 is the relative loss suffered by metropolitan area legislators with respect to the legislative influence index. This index dropped from .81 to .46 despite the net gain of one metropolitan legislator in an influence position. Thus, in proportion to the overall net gain in metropolitan membership, there were fewer leadership positions held by metropolitan lawmakers following the first major reapportionment. In order for this index to reach 1.0, the percentage of influence positions held by metropolitan House members would have

TABLE 16.—Influence Positions Held by Metropolitan House Members
Before and After Reapportionment

Years	Number of Key Influence Positions	Number Held By Metropolitan Legislators	Percentage
1969-70	19	3	15.8%
1963	21	2	9.5
Net Change	−2	+ 1	+ 6.3

to equal the proportion of metropolitan members in the House as a whole.

The overall gains for the two major metropolitan areas in House influence positions as a result of reapportionment must be judged as modest at best. In addition, during the six years in question, the powerful speaker of the House, who had represented an Oklahoma City district for over twenty years, was defeated at the polls and replaced as speaker by a representative from rural areas.

Turning to the Oklahoma Senate, Table 17 indicates changes in the actual number of influence positions held by upper-house members from Oklahoma and Tulsa counties before and after reapportionment. Table 18 reveals the various influence indices for metropolitan senators as they appeared before and after reapportionment. Basically, the data reflect the same pattern for the Senate as for the House. Reapportionment brought almost perfect population representation for the upper chamber (slightly better than in the House), but little improvement resulted for the metropolitan areas with respect to the influence indices. Despite the acquisition of three new key positions by metropolitan senators, the leadership changes proportionate to the total number of senators from metropolitan areas show a rather large loss. Actual legislative leadership parity for big county senators (compared to their proportion of the Senate) would require that at least two more senators from either Oklahoma or Tulsa counties be elevated to formal positions of authority. Despite this relative loss, the senate reflected a higher index of metropolitan legislative influence (.61) than the

TABLE 17.—Influence Positions Held by Metropolitan Senate Members
Before and After Reapportionment

Years	Number of Key Influence Positions	Number Held By Metropolitan Legislators	Percentage
1969-70	18	4	22.2%
1963	20	1	5.0
Net Change	—2	+ 3	+ 17.2

House (.46) after reapportionment. It is also worth noting that the 1969-70 president pro tempore of the Senate was a Tulsa county delegate, whereas prior to reapportionment the position had been held by a nonmetropolitan senator.

In conclusion, reapportionment produced almost exact legislative equality (based on population) for the two largest urban counties in both legislative chambers. Yet, comparable gains in legislative positions of influence were not forthcoming. In fact, proportionate losses in leadership positions on the part of metropolitan officials (compared with their newly acquired numerical strength) were noted for both House and Senate. The upper house retained a better relative position on the influence indices than the lower chamber. There were, nonetheless, slight numerical increases in leadership positions held by large county legislators following the first major reapportionment. Steady gains may still be possible for legislators from metropolitan areas, as evidenced in more recent reapportionment efforts, yet it is obvious that the greatly increased legislative power for large urban areas that many thought would result from reapportionment was not realized by the early 1970's, and significant changes have not occurred since that time.

Reapportionment in the Oklahoma House of Representatives

The original apportionment plan for the Oklahoma House was the

TABLE 18.—Influence Indices for Metropolitan Members of
the Oklahoma Senate Before and After Reapportionment

Years	Population Index	Population Influence Index	Legislative Influence Index
1969-70	1.00	.61	.61
1963	.13	.15	1.19
Net Change	.87	.46	-.58

product of drafters of Oklahoma's constitution. As written in
1907, it was the sole basis for reapportionments until various sections were repealed in the mid-1960's. The original plan was designed to give each of Oklahoma's seventy-seven counties at least one
House representative.[22] Several counties were apportioned as bi-
county districts and one tri-county district was created. This plan
brought the membership in Oklahoma's first House to eighty (one
for each of the seventy-seven counties and three additional districts
in Tulsa and Oklahoma counties). All population figures
employed in 1907 were from the 1900 decennial census; subsequently the 1911 legislature apportioned the House on the basis of 1910
census data. It has been reported that from 1911 to 1921 the apportionment of the House "fully respected all constitutional
provisions."[23] In 1931 the legislature again apportioned the lower
chamber, but this time lawmakers ignored certain population
alterations or shifts. Eight counties had fallen below the population
figure required for representation, and instead of joining these
eight counties with others or combining them into new districts, the
legislature simply retained the status quo; they allowed the eight
counties to be overrepresented.

    Following the 1940 census the legislature again apportioned the
House, accepting virtually in toto the 1931 plan. This was the second time the legislature had ignored population/representation
discrepancies and passed on legislation furthering an already acute
apportionment situation. The action in 1941 precipitated the first
court case involving the Oklahoma legislature, *Jones* v. *Freeman*.

The case was reviewed by the Oklahoma Supreme Court, and the resulting decision retained the 1931-status-quo malapportionment. The legislature again tried in 1951 to correct some of the existing problems, but the end product saw many remaining instances of unequal representation. Malapportionment continued unchecked during the 1950's and the first few years of the 1960's. Then in 1962, the famous *Baker* v. *Carr* decision was handed down by the United States Supreme Court; an historic decision which was to serve as the central force responsible for correction of malapportionment.

How badly was Oklahoma malapportioned? In response to this inquiry, Bingham comments as follows:

Using representation as it existed on March 26, 1962, the date of the historic *Baker* v. *Carr* decision, Glendon Schubert and Charles Press used a measure of skewness and kurtosis in an empirical study of state by state variations in malapportionment. With perfect representation being indicated by a score of 100.0, Massachusetts ranked high with a score of 96.3 and Indiana low with a -4.3. Oklahoma was very close to the bottom—ranking forty-seventh in the nation with a score of only 9.5. This history of malapportionment and disregard for constitutional provisions may in fact explain the vigor, bordering on impatience, of the Federal Court in Oklahoma when dealing with apportionment.[24]

The Oklahoma legislature was not immediately disposed to redistrict the House in accordance with the *Baker* v. *Carr* decision. Furthermore, voters defeated two referendum measures aimed at reapportionment in the early 1960's. By June 1962 the Tenth Circuit Court of Appeals handed down a decision declaring inoperative all of Oklahoma's apportionment statutes. The decision, *Moss* v. *Burkhart*, was reached five months prior to November 1962, thus allowing the legislature sufficient time to reapportion the House before the general election. Since no plan was adopted before the election, the Court was prompted to fix a March 1963 date as the final deadline. At this point, the legislature was under court order to reapportion House districts using as a base the principle of "substantial numerical equality." The following series of events resulted in other court actions and eventual reapportionment plans adopted by the legislature. The federal district court responded to the court-ordered plan of March 1963 by declaring it unconstitutional. The legislature had not apportioned the House (or Senate) in accordance with the principles of substantial numerical equality. Therefore, the court itself undertook to reapportion the House and Senate, relying on a plan designed by the Bureau of Government Research at the University of Oklahoma. This action was hampered due to further litigation, and in June 1964, the attorney general submitted an apportionment plan with two basic points: to utilize the principle of equal population, and to maintain county boundry integrity. The legislature's response to the attorney general's plan was rather cool, if not hostile. It was obvious that any plan based on the principle of equal representation would dilute rural interests. However, a modification of the attorney general's plan was approved by the District Court, and the immediate effects on the August and November elections in 1964 were far-reaching—more than 50 per cent of the incumbents did not return to their legislative seats.

The forced reapportionment of the House in the 1960's reduced some of the conflict over attempts to reapportion in 1971 and established important guidelines for later action. It was evident to most legislators that reapportionment was not only an inevitable occurrence, but that it was necessary. The courts would accept nothing less than equal representation for all citizens: one man, one vote. Prior to efforts in 1971, the legal services division of the Oklahoma Legislative Council sent a memo to the Committee on Constitutional Revision and Regulatory Services. Through this process, the House received directives which "outlined the requirements, permissible factors, and prohibitions of the Oklahoma constitution and the apportionment decisions."[25] The basic reapportionment norms to be followed included: (1) any reapportionment plan must be based upon the principle of one man, one vote (*Reynolds* v. *Simms*); (2) as population variations occur between districts, these departures from equal representation must be substantially justified (*Swan* v. *Adams*); (3) the courts would allow minor inequalities in one house if the balance could be made up in the remaining house; and (4) attempts by a legislature to balance urban and rural representation would not be permitted (*Davis* v. *Mann*).

In an in-depth study of efforts in 1971, Bingham concluded that the above constraints were in the forefront of any decisions regarding reapportionment. The sentiment of the courts was that the "fundamental principle of representative government in this country is one of equal representation for equal numbers of people without regard to race, sex, economic status, or place of residence within a state."[26] This meant that each state had the responsibility of developing its own reapportionment plan encompassing all the principles set down by the courts. An additional constraint was placed on the Oklahoma House in the form of a constitutional provision. By 1971 the constitution required the legislature to apportion itself within sixty days after convening following each decennial census. If the legislature failed to accomplish this task, an apportionment commission would carry out the plan. Bingham notes that because the courts had allowed broad discretion in regard to how legislative districts should be drawn, that political considerations would play a major role in House reapportionment efforts.[27] The subcommittee on reapportionment was thus faced with legal constraints and political considerations, all of which made the task especially complex. It was decided that reapportionment should be the responsibility of each house and that the end product would have to be acceptable to the other chamber. This effort made reapportionment an "in-house" function rather than a duty of the legislature. Once the preliminary working constraints had been recognized, the House subcommittee had the arduous task of compiling the necessary maps for designing new districts. The maps were to be used in conjunction with census divisions, and it was soon evident that virtually every house district would have to be redrawn. Efforts at estimating populations proved ineffective, prompting the House subcommittee to implement a basic computer assistance program.

The final method chosen by the House was to use the computer as a large storage device, with information on each county, census tract, population, and current legislative district assignment. With this information it was possible to shift parcels of land from one district to another while trying to achieve near perfect population distribution (25,339 people per district). The final result yielded 101 House districts, only three of which had a population variance of one per cent. The use of a computer in 1971 should not convey the idea of a purely mechanical process. The computer aided in the speedy and accurate transferral of population from district to district and from plan to plan. The decision as to which parcels to move and where to move them was made by legislators, primarily members of the subcommittee. The results took account of political considerations, and a legislator's present and future districts. If two incumbents ended up in the same district, the decision as to which would survive was based on political considerations. When decisions had to be made which would adversely affect a Democrat or Republican, the general rule was to let the minority party suffer the consequences.

However, as Bingham notes, even in a one-party dominant state, the interests of majority party members are not always followed: "In a one-party state, conflicts between power blocs within the majority party replaced inter-party conflicts. The controlling faction within the majority party will obtain maximum results by suppressing the minority faction."[28] This rule is based on the capacity of majority party elites to punish party "mavericks" or dissidents. In the Oklahoma House, the speaker is the most powerful and influential legislator. His influence can be seen in most areas of House activity; he appoints committee chairmen, and even though the allocation of chairmanships is influenced by seniority, the speaker still has the power to place legislators as heads of committees. To chair an important committee a legislator must have seniority and/or be an active supporter of House leaders, and seniority without a close working relationship with others can amount to an almost complete lack of power. Bingham notes that the politically powerful House members usually have a great deal of seniority and chair important committees, and that they "are unquestionable supporters of the Speaker of the House as he appoints them."[29]

During the course of reapportioning the House, six members banded together to oppose the plan. Bingham refers to these legislators as the "frustrated six."[30] Earlier in 1971, the six representatives had openly opposed reelection of the speaker—they instead offered their own candidate for the leadership position. Their efforts failed, and subsequently none of the six legislators chaired any standing committee or held positions on any important committees. As Bingham notes, "these six individuals were given last consideration when it came to district boundaries."[31] Two of the "frustrated six" were placed in districts with other incumbents. One of the six was to face a powerful senator in the upcoming election, and sure to lose. The remaining four were given districts made up of what was left over from those districts around them. The "frustrated six" openly opposed the reapportionment plan, but their efforts were ineffective. They had fallen from "political grace," and for all intents their political futures were insecure. Although other forces opposed the reapportionment plan, no other bloc was as politically disregarded as these six.

The final report of the subcommittee was accepted by the House on the basis of a lopsided vote, seventy-seven to fifteen. Seven Tulsa representatives opposed the House plan, desiring more influence in the creation of their districts, yet they abstained from voting rather than casting negative votes. The Oklahoma House had reapportioned itself and had remarkable success in creating districts with near perfect population parity. By 1973, it had complied with the basic principles of representative government and one man, one vote as enunciated by the U.S. Supreme Court.

Senate Reapportionment

The first Senate apportionment plan as written in the original constitution made provisions for thirty-three districts. This part of Oklahoma's constitution remained unchanged for over fifty years. Despite increases in the state's population and shifts in county population, the Oklahoma Senate was not reapportioned until the early 1960's. Although the constitution required reapportionment of the Senate after each decennial census, the letter of the law was virtually ignored.

According to the constitution, reapportionment was to follow each census, and if an increase in the number of senatorial districts was required, they could be added during the reapportionment of the entire senate. Instead, the legislature "followed a policy of erecting additional districts when they believed it expedient to do so."[32] Starting in 1911, the legislature approached reapportionment of the state Senate as if the task were "illegal." The law was disregarded by the legislature in 1911, and this response continued for many years. The situation was quite different from the condition in the lower chamber, since the House of Representatives was reapportioned soon after statehood.

The creation of the Senate's additional districts began in 1910 and continued into the 1920's and 1930's. These actions were piecemeal attempts at best, and in 1946 the state Supreme Court concluded that the simple creation of new senatorial districts was unconstitutional. However, there was no mandate from the court to force the Senate to be reapportioned on the principle of equal representation.

The inequalities which existed in the Senate during this period far exceeded the unequal representation found in the House. The lower chamber had been reapportioned several times, thereby minimizing the malapportionment problem. In 1951, for example, the six counties composing senatorial districts 4,7, and 36 were rural counties, and each of these districts had an average population of 20,000. This is an example of the overrepresentation of rural Oklahoma, especially when compared with the underrepresented districts. Yet underrepresented counties were not necessarily urban centers. For example, each of three semirural districts (11, 23, 34) had over three times the average population per district (65,000 to 90,000 people) compared to the overrepresented areas. If the 1951 Senate had been reapportioned on the basis of equal population, each senator would have ideally represented approximately 50,000 persons. Instead, the senator from District 11 represented over 89,000 people, while the senator from District 4 represented less than 20,000 individuals. An even more extreme condition held for urban areas. District 31, Tulsa, with 250,000 people, was represented by one senator. On the other extreme, District 26 (Love and Marshall counties) was also represented by one senator in 1951, yet the district had only 16,000 residents. These two extremes point to the power held by rural counties in the state Senate as late as 1951. But the time was soon approaching when this power would be split, and more equal representation would be achieved.

Preceding the historic *Baker* v. *Carr* and *Reynolds* v. *Simms* decisions, the Senate was in no position to rely upon what had become an outdated part of Oklahoma's constitution. The original article and sections (Article V, Sections 9a and 10b) did not apply to Oklahoma in the 1960's. As with the House, the Senate had for too long relied on makeshift attempts to provide representation to the state's citizens. The entire court system, from the Supreme Court of Oklahoma to the U.S. Supreme Court, began to hand down decisions which would make reapportionment a matter of fact for the Senate. A number of citizens in Oklahoma appealed to the courts in the early 1960's in hopes of finding legal relief from the discriminating practices of over- and under-representation. By 1963, efforts in the legislature were underway to reapportion the Senate on the basis of equal representation for equal population.

The work by the legislature in regard to reapportioning the Senate was done coterminously with actions to reapportion the House. Both chambers were under legal constraints to act quickly to alleviate the malapportionment problem in the state. However, the Senate had historically remained secure in a closed system whereby all actions of reapportionment were "in-house" decisions. The opinions of the public, the courts, study committees, and urban interests appeared to be of little consequence to the majority of Oklahoma state senators. Therefore, forced reapportionment was generally viewed with resentment and hostility. In view of the composition of the Senate, these negative feelings and a general unwillingness to accept the dictates of the courts were understandable. It was evident that some senators would necessarily compete with other incumbent senators in upcoming elections.

A pattern of equal representation was established in the 1963 reapportionment plan. When the 1970 census records were made available it was again evident that substantial population shifts had occurred to warrant another sweeping effort. This time the Senate was better prepared to cope with the situation. The events in 1963 and 1964 had left a series of scars on the upper chamber, but there was an apparent resolution to move more effectively in 1971. When the latest reapportionment began, both the Senate and the House set out to achieve nearly perfect numerical balance between districts.

The courts had made emphatic rulings making the principle of one man, one vote the necessary criterion to be observed in the reapportionment of both chambers. The courts, however, did not elaborate on how the districts should be drawn. By this omission, the Senate was able to devise its own plan which would maximize the wishes of powerful and influential senators, while still seeking a near perfect numerical division between districts. The practicalities of politics were observed, as the senators who wielded the most influence had the largest impact on the 1971 plan. There were attempts to minimize the creation of districts which would force incumbents to run against each other. When this situation could not be avoided, those incumbent senators forced to compete against each other were the least powerful and were minority party members. Since the Democrats controlled the Senate by a large majority, it was to their advantage to pit Republicans against each other whenever possible. If this could be done without serious attacks upon the intent of the Senate by the public, the press, or the courts, the end result would be two incumbent Republicans facing each other in an election where one must lose. Looking further down the road, Democrats could perceive a possible increase in the number of Democratic senators. As on the House side, the often harsh realities of practical politics were manifested in the Senate's reapportionment plan of 1971, yet the end result was almost perfect numerical equality between senatorial districts.

THE CHANGING SHAPE OF THE LEGISLATIVE UNIVERSE

This chapter has focused on two primary factors which shape the character and style of a legislative body: formal powers and individual attributes. The fundamental duties and powers discussed above define the boundaries of individual action within which lawmakers' characteristics vary, and they are relatively enduring in their effect. Yet the social and political characteristics associated with individuals vary more widely across time and space, and these demographic shifts in the composition of the legislature have literally changed the face of the institution in the contemporary period.

The social composition of the legislature is only generally reflective of constituency characteristics in Oklahoma. As in many elected institutions in the United States, its composition more accurately reflects the characteristics of elites in those constituencies; the entire recruitment process is related to societal stratification in Oklahoma. While the United States is often seen as a classless society in comparison to other countries, there tends to be substantial socioeconomic variation between the mass public and elected representatives, and this variation is greater than that among lawmakers themselves. Indeed, legislative composition is skewed toward higher socioeconomic, educational, and occupational levels in Oklahoma society.

Changes in composition are also reflective of shifts in the larger society along these dimensions, especially in terms of age, education, and urbanism. More specifically, gradual age changes characterizing the legislature have been affected by growing urban strengths, reapportionment efforts related to those strengths, and by recruitment differences between the two major political parties, which have produced substantially younger Republican lawmakers in comparison to their Democratic counterparts. Educational levels of lawmakers are high vis-a-vis the population as a whole, and are generally on the increase, especially among Senate Republicans. The bulk of legislators are also native-born Oklahomans, long-term residents of their district, and lawyers by occupation. Shifts in occupational characteristics are most notable for farmers and ranchers, whose representation has been eroded with occupational changes in society and resultant reapportionment efforts. Many of these changes have occurred coterminously for both the House and Senate, yet the lower chamber tends to be slightly more heterogeneous, largely a reflection of smaller districts and greater chamber size.

Changes in religious, racial, ethnic, and sex composition have been less pronounced than the changes more directly associated with socioeconomic status, and in the aggregate the legislature is more representative of Oklahoma society in those respects. Indeed, on status dimensions which are *ascribed* to the individual, such as sex, race, and often religion, lawmakers with characteristics similar to their constituents will be elected to office. On the other hand, statuses which are *achieved* tend to be more elite in character. In other words, those characteristics which are most susceptible to change by the individual—largely through initiative and mobility—such as education and occupation, tend to be rewarded by an electorate which holds success dear in our society.

While partisan composition shifts have been gradual in the legislature, with slight increases in Republican strength in both chambers, the most profound influences are associated with growing urbanism in the state. This factor has produced partisan, educational, age, and occupational changes; has had an impact on the type of legislation produced; and has resulted in a greater proportion of metropolitan legislators. After a long, arduous and complex path of reapportionment as discussed above, the legislature has finally achieved substantial population parity for metropolitan areas. The leadership effects of reapportionment, however, are less noticeable. Such legislative leadership parity is obviously more difficult to change since a variety of complex factors are at work, such as tradition, seniority, and individual personality. The passing of time and the socialization of new leaders will result in more gradual changes in the character of the legislature. General socioeconomic shifts are also likely to be subtle in the decade ahead in comparison to the tumultuous times of the immediate past.

CHAPTER 2

Personal Aspects of Legislative Life: Lawmakers' Perspectives on Their Job

The Oklahoma legislature is an institution which authoritatively makes laws for our citizenry, but it is also a human work group composed of various individuals with different perspectives on politics who must work together in the public interest. The total activity of any legislator—what we refer to frequently as *legislative life*—is all encompassing and highly diverse. In many respects, a lawmaker lives his work, and the resulting public policy reflects individual feelings as much as the formal procedures which guide the path of a bill. Standardization of rules does not imply a lack of diversity in beliefs and actions. Indeed, formal organization, committee rules, floor procedures, and leadership are necessary because of the diversity in any large group—they serve as a mechanism of social control to insure an orderly policy making process. As we have seen, the economic, social, and political backgrounds of legislators vary in any single session. Although this variation is not as great as in the Oklahoma population as a whole and tends to represent a narrower class from which elected officials are recruited, the attitudes, feelings, and behavior of legislators include a substantial range of possibilities. The more informal and individual characteristics of the legislature have an enormous impact on lawmaking, although these human aspects are often hidden from sight and obscured by procedural machinations.

Some legislators' approach to their job varies considerably from others, they view their tasks differently, they come to the legislature through different career paths, and their future ambitions are different. Similarly, the processes of lawmaking and its tangible products depend upon the dissatisfied, frustrated, and conflicted legislator as well as upon those more successful at adapting to the complexities of legislative life. In order to treat these human aspects of lawmaking, this chapter investigates individual perspectives on the job of the legislator, the satisfactions and frustrations associated with that job, political ambitions, commitment to the institution, and the various styles of adaptation characterizing Oklahoma lawmakers. Subsequent chapters will go beyond these basic orientations to offer a more in-depth examination of informal rules and norms governing behavior, as well as factors shaping roll call voting and other individual perspectives.

HOW THE LEGISLATOR SEES HIS JOB

While the formal powers and legal functions of the legislature establish the boundaries governing a legislator's behavior, there is considerable flexibility in how a lawmaker sees his job. His definition of the task at hand in everyday life on the floor of the legislature, in committee meetings, and in contacts with constituents is shaped by a network of relationships with other political actors in the lawmaking body. Each legislator therefore takes a variety of roles based upon a coherent set of norms which define one's job. These norms are shaped by expectations of behavior in the legislative arena and are influenced by the daily interactions with other decision makers. Certain behaviors are expected of occupants of legislative positions, and one's role reflects how those expectations are perceived. In other words, the job of the legislator is not only shaped by formal powers and by his status, position, or office in the legislature, but also by conceptions in legislators' minds. Indeed, a substantial portion of legislative behavior is role behavior—sometimes referred to as role playing or role enactment. The variety of legislative actions required on the part of members is highly related to members' conceptions of their roles.

Legislative Roles

An executive officer or bureaucrat in an Oklahoma agency has his primary roles formalized into a position with an explicit job description; however, the legislator's job is both more complex and less clearly defined. Any legislator must consistently relate to a variety of clienteles, interests, and pressures which shape a set of multiple roles: he makes laws, serves constituents, relates to the governor and the executive branch, and to his political party. As a decision maker, he may take one or a number of *purposive roles* reflecting his conception of the basic characteristics of his job.[1] He may see his purposive role as a defender of the people (*tribune*), as a staunch supporter of the formal rules and procedures of the legislative body (*ritualist*), as an *inventor* or innovator, or as a *broker* having major responsibility for working out legislative compromises. In his role as a *representative*, the legislator may see himself as a free agent primarily responsible to the dictates of his conscience (*trustee*), as a *delegate* of his constituency who represents their interests and wants, or as a *politico* who fashions his job on the basis of a mix between his own conscience and the actual or perceived interests of his constituency. The legislator is also likely to adopt a particular *areal role*, whereby his behaviors are governed by primary orientations to his district, to the state as a whole, or to a combination of those orientations. He may also fulfill a variety of roles relevant to his *structural position* in the legislature: as expert, leader, committeeman, or friend.

In addition to roles internal to the legislature and those relevant to a constituency, the legislator relates with and adapts to three important sets of groups: interest groups, bureaucratic groups, and political parties. His conscious relationship with interests groups may be close and friendly (*facilitator*); knowledgeable and aware, yet hostile (*resister*), or he may have little knowledge or feeling about outside interests (*neutral*). Since the job of a legislator also involves interaction with the executive branch of Oklahoma government, he learns to adopt a particular *bureaucratic role* whereby he may be most concerned with his relationships with the governor and other top officials in the executive branch, or with his ties to a particular bureaucratic agency or set of agencies, which reflect either his substantive interests in legislation or the interests of his constituency. Finally, any legislator has an orientation to the important group through which he was elected and which subsequently serves as an organizing force for the legislative body: his political party. In this regard, we find that some legislators prefer to see their party role either in terms of strict adherence to party procedures and wishes (a *party man*), or as one who is fundamentally *indifferent* to party leadership and desires, or as a *maverick*, casting out on his own and sometimes being hostile to his party organization.

Since a legislator's roles shape a considerable amount of his behavior and a variety of aspects of legislative action, it is logical to inquire about the sources of legislative roles or those factors which shape any particular role set. While our knowledge of this process is rather sketchy[2], a legislator's role conception is most likely shaped by a variety of factors both internal and external to the legislature. It is important to note that a legislator's role set is neither shaped immediately upon entering legislative life nor by any single factor. His social and personality characteristics acquired long before entry into the legislative arena shape his perception of his job. These factors include his age, education, sex, religion, ethnicity, and socioeconomic status, as well as individual personality, attitudes, and previous political experiences. A second major set of influences on role come from the environmental and constituency characteristics of his district: its population size and density, ethnic composition, socioeconomic characteristics, and its political characteristics of party composition, organization, and voter attentiveness. The latter factors are particularly important in shaping representational roles. Although a particular legislator may be well educated, articulate, and characterized by a strong self-conscience pushing him toward a trustee or free agent conception of his job, his constituency may also be of higher socioeconomic status, well organized politically, and characterized by a high level of voter interest—factors which would obviously encourage him to take constituency interests into account. A final set of primary factors influencing one's role concept comes to bear after entry into the legislative system, or in other words, after the legislator is recruited to legislative life. These factors include his legislative experiences and relationships with other decision makers, the formal enactments of the legislative body, and the legal powers and procedural rules which establish basic guidelines for legislative behavior and the enactment of public policy.

One's conception of his role is obviously not the important end product of the legislative system. A legislator's various roles not only shape his behavior and the legislative action, decisions, and services which result from that behavior, but these outputs in turn have a set of important consequences for the political system as a whole and for the legislative system in particular. Legislative outputs shape the distribution of important values in the political system—all of those things which any member of a political community cherishes—as well as the resolution of conflict in the

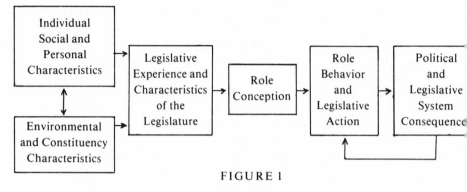

FIGURE 1

A Simple Role Model of the Legislative System

political environment. In addition to these important consequences for the political system, legislative outputs influenced by role behavior shape the legislative system itself— the way legislators communicate with each other; the conflict, tension and group cohesion within the legislature; and the individual's concern, apathy, satisfaction or frustration with legislative life. In other words, the consequences for the political and legislative system relate back to role behavior and legislative action; the system is dynamic and characterized by feedback. This conception of the legislative and political system is summarized in the general model outlined in Figure 1.

Role Conflict

Since a state legislator relates to a variety of interests and people, he obviously takes a variety of roles relevant to his legislative career. However, his role set is much more complex than we have suggested to this point. We have noted above that some political actors may be indifferent to the dimensions of certain roles. It is also possible that from time to time a legislator adopts more than one stance with regard to any particular role; for example, his purposive role may sometimes be ritualist in nature, yet other times he will view himself as a broker or inventor. In addition, there are many instances in which a legislator faces considerable conflict between his roles. Since any single role is based upon a set of expectations, there is understandably some amount of strain that results from attempts to meet expectations that cannot be fully met by either a single person or a social system. Legislators face problems of adjustment to new and difficult situations, and any incumbent of a particular role is subject to a wide range of role strains. Individuals respond differently to such conflicts. Some may be immune to strain, and others may not even recognize its existence. When it is recognized, most public figures attempt some control over the situation, while others may exhibit passive acceptance. While some sources of strain are directly related to the above role typology, there is a more general set of sources for role strain that face state legislators.[3]

Any state legislator may face conflict among his public roles. For example, he frequently has administrative, executive, or procedural roles to play and at the same time he must be a partisan. Indeed, we could imagine various types and networks of role conflicts based upon the categories discussed earlier. There may be strains within each category of roles, such as that between a trustee role and a delegate role, or there may be strains between role categories, for instance, between one's party role and a bureaucratic role. An example of the latter would be a party man who is agency-oriented irrespective of the pleas of the chief executive who is also chief of the legislator's party. The intensity of similar conflicts for a state legislator depends partially on the characteristics of his constituency. Greater conflicts result from more heterogeneous constituencies, and it is therefore likely that senators face more intense conflicts than house members from smaller constituencies.

Although such role conflict is common, there are certain combinations of roles which are less conflict-ridden. Some legislators are able to combine their roles such that minimal strain exists. In a study of four state legislatures[4] it was found that those holding a trustee or free agent representational role are also more likely to have a state oriented areal role. It is also likely that legislators who view their purposive role as that of a broker will also adopt a facilitator interest-group role. Similarly, trustees who vote more by their conscience than constituency demands are also more likely to view their main purpose in the legislature as that of an *inventor* or innovator.

In addition to conflicts among public roles, legislators face strain on the basis of conflicts between private and public roles. An example would be the businessman turned politician who is most used to serving his own ends as a businessman and feels comfortable playing that role, but when he becomes a legislator there is some obvious pressure to represent the public interest. This can be a serious problem because some representatives never lose their previous role orientations acquired during a period before their entry into legislative life.

More general sources of strain result from insecurity of tenure, the ambiguities of political situations, diffused responsibility and limited controls, time and the pressure of demands, and status insecurities. Insecurity of tenure results from a high turnover in public life, a major factor in the lower house of the Oklahoma legislature. Political affairs are competitive, and most thinking suggests that those legislators who must devote more time to security of tenure are more responsive and sensitive to constituency demands. A legislator therefore strives to reduce this strain of insecurity by satisfying constituents, but complete satisfaction never results, since political insecurity is a basic characteristic of any democratic system. The strain resulting from ambiguities in political situations reflects conflicts in public values, and ambiguous laws and constituencies. The adept legislator will attempt to reduce these ambiguities through the use of advisors, public opinion polls, and investigating committees. Since a legislator's role is diffused and often ambiguous no matter how he decides to structure his own role, he often suffers from conflict or strain. He is held responsible by someone for practically everything, and he cannot control many of the outcomes of political situations. One inherent reason for such diffused responsibility and limited controls is the decentralized nature of the American political system and the incremental characteristics of decision making—tasks are often accomplished with the cooperation of many others and on a piecemeal basis. In order to overcome such conflict some state legislators devote their attention to improving legislative machinery to control legislative situations.

Many state legislators, as well as other public officials, suffer from conflict resulting from status insecurity. Legislators frequently work in a situation where there is considerable distrust of politicians and little appreciation for their services. Furthermore, they are unable to measure the degree to which they are respected, and the cynicism of the adult population is often evident. In order to overcome this problem, some legislators leave public life; some form group norms which compensate for their insecurity (that is to say, develop a mutual admiration society where they praise each other in spite of different partisan attachments); some develop a cynical attitude toward the voter; and others may adopt a stoic attitude, claiming that the abuse is petty and unimportant. Others handle such conflicts with humor—in effect, laughing at themselves—but while this may be therapeutic, it is difficult to maintain over a long period of time. Finally, time and the pressure of various demands cause a substantial stress for all legislators. While staff assistants and organizational efficiency may relieve some of these pressures, demands are plentiful and complex, legislative sessions are relatively short, and fifty-hour days are impossible.

Purposive Roles

The most general legislative role orientation derives from one's conception of the basic purpose or function of the legislative body. The central function of the state legislature is law making, and purposive roles adopted by legislators indicate how one orients himself to this fundamental task. We are usually able to isolate four basic, but not mutually exclusive, role orientations dealing with lawmaking. Since formal rules and procedures establish specific boundaries for legislative action, we find that some legislators are primarily concerned with parliamentary ritual and the defense and justification of established procedures (*ritualist*). A second purposive role has historical roots in colonial America and the defense of colonial rights against the Crown and its appointed governors—the *tribune* role in which legislators see themselves as defenders of popular demands and advocates of constituency interests. As legislatures became less reactive and more constructive in the American political system—gaining in power and the ability to govern—a new role orientation became possible. It is the creative role of inventor, the individual who sees his primary lawmaking responsibilities as developing alternatives and solutions to public problems that can be worked out through rational debate and argument. This growth of policy making power in the state legislature and the need for argument, debate, and the resolution of issues placed before the body by various interests and groups throughout the state facilitate a fourth basic purposive role orientation—that of *broker.*

Although most state legislators can be categorized in a single purposive role type, there are times at which an individual may see himself as playing more than one basic role. A study of four American state legislatures[5] suggests that the most frequent combination of purposive role types is the tribune inventor. This individual sees himself both as a defender of popular demands and as an inventor of legislative alternatives and solutions for public problems.

Two recent studies of the Oklahoma House and Senate in the late 1960's attempt to define purposive roles as the legislators perceive them, and to compare the Oklahoma results with a study of four other states.[6] Twenty per cent of the Oklahoma House and 50 per cent of the Oklahoma Senate were sampled and personally interviewed to obtain purposive role orientations through responses to the following questions:

(1)   How would you describe the job of being a state legislator; that is, what are the most important things that you should be doing here?

(2)   What is the main duty or function of a state legislator?

(3)   What approach should a member take to his legislative work?

(4)   The job of a representative is to work for what his constituents want even though this may not always agree with his personal views (agree-disagree).

(5)   A legislator can decide how to vote on most issues by asking himself if the proposed law is right (agree-disagree).

(6)   The job of the legislator is to work out compromises among conflicting interests (agree-disagree).

(7)   The job of the legislator is to arbitrate and integrate conflicting interests within the legislature (agree-disagree).

(8)   The legislature should give the leadership necessary to meet the problems in policy faced by the state (agree-disagree).

TABLE 19.—Purposive Role Orientations in Oklahoma and Four Other States

	Oklahoma		New Jersey	Ohio	California	Tennessee
Purposive Roles	Senate	House				
Ritualist	54.0%	40.0%	70.0%	67.0%	58.0%	72.0%
Broker	38.0	35.0	33.0	48.0	27.0	15.0
Tribune	58.0	40.0	63.0	40.0	55.0	58.0
Inventor	29.0	25.0	49.0	33.0	36.0	30.0

The open-ended questions listed above enabled the legislator to talk freely about how he sees his basic lawmaking job, and the agree-disagree items (derived from actual verbatim responses in studies of other states) provide specific measures related to each role type. Since a legislator may consciously adopt more than one purposive role, the study isolated 30 per cent of the House with multiple purposive roles and 58 per cent of the Senate with various role combinations between the four role types. The categorization of purposive role types in the Oklahoma House and Senate, along with comparable data for four other states (New Jersey, Ohio, California and Tennessee), appears in Table 19.[7]

The table notes the frequent occurrence of a ritualist orientation in Oklahoma, as well as in the four other American states. This frequency of occurrence is certainly understandable in the Oklahoma legislature. Members are often overwhelmed by the routine parliamentary procedure, its consuming impact, and the resultant legislative maneuvering, which sometimes becomes an end in itself rather than a means to an end. Many legislators seem to rationalize their actions by no other purpose than performance of legislative routine. Such an individual sees himself as a cog in the legislative wheel, concerned with the flow of business, bureaucratic organization, and procedures for bill passage. These individuals tend to be more concerned with technical perfection than with the policy content of a bill, with killing certain bills, and with watching every stage in the passage of legislation. The following verbatim comments from several ritualists in the Oklahoma House verify this orientation:

> It's important to keep revising the rules for more efficiency. It's not safe to move too fast. . . . I pay close attention to the constitutional effect of a bill and raise questions. . . . There should be more emphasis on parliamentary procedure. In fact, there should be more legislative procedure talks at schools. I do a lot of this. . . . A good legislator should be a defensive legislator. Bills can be slipped past you. You have your hands full watching this type of thing. . . . The meetings are not formal enough. There is too much clowning around.[8]

Similarly, members of the Oklahoma Senate comment:

> I study the bills well in order to influence keeping out harmful legislation. . . . Our job is to know everything there is to know on every piece of legislation. . . . There are two broad aspects to the job. When the legislature is in session, it is watching the bills introduced by other senators. . . . How we vote is the most important thing.

Supporting evidence from another study of the Oklahoma legislature substantiates the prevalence of ritualist perspectives.[9] Individual legislators in both the House and Senate were asked the extent to which they felt that (1) there is a recognized right and wrong way of getting things done; (2) rules and procedures are useful and ought to be protected against change; and (3) unofficial rules should be defended and protected from change. The attitudes which emerge from responses to these questions are largely ritualist in nature, as shown by the data in Table 20.

Substantial portions of both the House and Senate agree with the above statements. In addition, the Bernick data on which Table 20 is based indicates that when multiple roles exist, a majority of these roles in the Senate include ritualist perspectives, and all multiple roles in the House include the ritualist component.

The *tribune* role orientation was also frequently present in the earlier four-state study, and it was especially prevalent in Oklahoma. The tribune tends to perceive himself as either the defender of popular interests, the discoverer of popular needs, or as the advocate of popular demands. Although these factors may indeed be different, the tribune's primary focus of attention is his popular environment as it influences his relationship to lawmaking. He tends to seek out popular problems, to assess public opinion, and to generally make himself available to the people. But as we shall see in a later chapter, this does not necessarily imply that con-

TABLE 20.—Ritualistic Attitudes in the Oklahoma Legislature

	Strongly Agree	Somewhat Agree	Somewhat Disagree	Strongly Disagree
There is a recognized right and wrong way of getting things done here in the House (Senate).				
House (N = 90)	55.6%	36.7%	7.8%	0.0%
Senate (N = 44)	52.3	29.5	13.6	4.5
I think that the rules and procedures used in the House (Senate) serve a useful purpose and ought to be protected against changes.				
House (N = 90)	27.8	35.6	20.0	16.7
Senate (N = 44)	25.0	52.3	15.9	6.8
The unofficial rules we talked about earlier should be defended and protected from change.				
House (N = 87)	35.6	33.3	17.2	13.8
Senate (N = 44)	36.4	38.6	18.2	6.8

stituency interests will be a primary guiding factor in his legislative voting. Indeed, the tribune may see himself not so much as a mirror of his constituency, but as a guardian of people's interests as he sees them. Therefore, some tribunes take a positive view as spokesmen and advocates for the people, while others take a more negative approach as watchdogs, protecting people from too many laws. His perception of popular wants may be based on actual contacts with constituents, on his perceived needs for constituents, or on an almost unconscious feeling for people's wants resulting from basic similarities of experiences. The following verbatim collection of responses from members of the Oklahoma House is representative of the tribune role:

> It's the civic duty of any capable individual to honestly help the people of their area and state. This leads to better government. The main function of a legislator is to enact a program that will benefit the largest number of people. . . . My main duty concerns all the people of the state. A representative shouldn't be narrow—he deals with the people's welfare. . . . My primary duty during my ten years is to protect the consuming public.

Similarly, several members of the Senate comment:

> I don't know if my constituents expect me to lead—I think they want me to follow. . . . We have an obligation to write a program for all of the people of Oklahoma. . . . Represent the will of the people and try to make sure monies are invested wisely and efficiently, getting the most for their investment.

A much less prevalent role in the Oklahoma legislature is that of *broker*. Although discussions of the broker have played a primary role in studies of American legislatures, this role is not as prevalent as most observers would expect or prefer. It is clear that the Oklahoma legislature functions in the context of various group pressures, constituency interests and executive agency needs; however, it does not follow that most legislators perceive their primary lawmaking function as involving the resolution of such conflicts and pressures. Those that see their role as a broker attempt to coordinate and integrate conflicting interests and demands, and view their major role as that of compromiser. In order to pass good legislation, they find it necessary to grasp an overall picture of pressures and needs by examining all sides of an issue. They see their role as a balancing one with a commitment to hear various perspectives, keep an open mind, and draw relevant conclusions from a variety of viewpoints. The following is a typical medley of broker responses from the Oklahoma House:

> There are many pressures—different pulls such as party and urban-rural conflict. For best representation, we need to strike a balance. . . . If there is a conflict—reconcile. . . . Compromise—that's the name of the game. . . . It's true that the job of the legislator is to work out compromises among conflicting interests. There are hundreds of interested groups who want things to the "nth" degree. . . . Legislation is the product of intelligent compromise.

And Oklahoma senators comment:

> Politics is the art of compromise. . . . The job is judicial—judge all
> the different vested interests that come before us. . . . I must watch
> against a particular segment of the state, try to pass laws for the
> good of the greatest number. . . . The job of the legislator is to work
> out compromises among conflicting interests.

The least prominent of all purposive roles in the Oklahoma
House and Senate is that of *inventor*. Although the textbook
definition of legislative tasks may understandably emphasize the
creative and innovative components of public policy making, the
infrequent occurrence of the inventor role is certainly understandable in today's legislature. Oklahoma society has become increasingly complex and technological, the solutions for public problems
are usually unclear, and legislators are usually without the staff
essential for offering innovative solutions to pressing demands. As
a consequence, the innovative role of most legislative bodies has
decreased in comparison to the powers of the executive branch of
government. While the Oklahoma Legislative Council is an important research arm of the House and Senate, many new proposals
for legislation come from executive agencies and the governor's
program. The small group of legislators who either attempt to fight
this trend or have a serious commitment to creative legislation
perceive themselves as initiators of public policy. They tend to
adopt positive attitudes toward their job—working for something
rather than against things. The inventor sees himself as a
thoughtful, farsighted, imaginative politician who often chooses to
specialize in one or a few areas of public policy. The above viewpoints are evident in comments from members of the Oklahoma
House:

> The legislature should give the leadership in policy. The governor
> doesn't know—his job is to put what we do into effect. . . . It is en-
> joyable to see the results of legislation—like a highway where before
> there were rocks. Also, getting the state to do something different is
> enjoyable. . . . Damn the compromise! A legislator should lead. . . . If
> you have any kind of strong feelings about an issue, you want to be
> where you can do something about it.

A select group of Senators also agree:

> The most important job here in Oklahoma is to look ahead to the
> problems of the state, say five years from now, and plan for solving

them. . . . My job is to approach, introduce, and support legislation that is good. . . . I believe that my job is to lead their thinking on such matters and not to slavishly reflect them. . . . Here you must have some skills in leadership.

In the above model of the legislative system we suggested that, among other factors, individual social and environmental characteristics might shape a legislator's role conception. Although all of the factors posited in the model have never been systematically investigated in any state legislature, the general findings from the four-state study justify such an interpretation, and there is fragmentary and mixed evidence on the role of these factors from studies of the Oklahoma legislature.[10]

It has been found that nearly half of the urban senators in Oklahoma are tribunes, but that urban House members tend to be more ritualistic. Except for the inventor category, rural legislators in both chambers are more evenly distributed among role types. A clearer pattern exists with regard to age and legislative tenure. Younger legislators are more likely to be tribunes, and the older more ritualistic. Also, nearly all inventors in both chambers are under fifty years of age. The most experienced members of the Senate are much more likely to be ritualistic, but role types are more evenly distributed as to tenure in the House. With regard to primary occupational categories, it has been found that lawyers are more ritualistic and concerned for rules and procedures, whereas nearly half of the businessmen view themselves as tribunes. Few clear patterns exist when educational levels are compared to role types, except there is a tendency for nearly all innovators to be college graduates.

It is also understandable that few partisan differences emerge over role conceptions since the gross number of Republicans is so small. Yet there is an interesting partisan trend: House Republicans are more likely to be brokers than House Democrats, and Senate Republicans are more frequently tribunes. Both of these minority party role types probably reflect inherent problems for the minority in Oklahoma, since election and reelection must be achieved in more competitive districts where there is a need for compromising constituency interests and staying closer to the electorate. It may be that minority legislators cannot afford the luxury of being ritualists or inventors. Indeed, all inventors in both chambers are members of the Democratic party.

SATISFACTIONS AND FRUSTRATIONS OF LEGISLATIVE LIFE

In the preceding section we examined the roles taken by Oklahoma legislators as they pursue the primary purposes of policy making. While such orientations tell us how the legislator sees his job, they offer little information about his level of satisfaction and frustration with the complexity of legislative life. We have previously cited the formal perquisites and compensations for being a state legislator, but we have only alluded to the severity of frustrations in the light of complex roles (role conflict and strain). Yet there is a range of benefits and deprivations beyond mere formal aspects of power, remuneration, and pressure. The level of frustration and uncertainty is especially severe for freshmen. It is highlighted here by the comments and recollections of two legislators speaking to a recent presession conference for freshmen:

> Most of you are here following some very intensive campaigning . . . I know that you are feeling a little bit proud to have even a little bit of importance. However, a few years from now, or maybe even a few weeks, you are going to feel a little let down, because many of your constituents are going to have a very difficult time recalling your name, and they're also going to have a difficult time telling you whether or not the legislature is in session.

Another commented:

> The first hazard you have to deal with upon being elected is the hazard of frustration. During my first term in the legislature, the feeling I had was like being a ball in a pinball machine. You pull the plunger back in the pinball machine and you don't know what slot the ball is going to fall in. That's sort of the way you are when you walk in the Capitol. You are like that ball, you don't know who's going to grab you, you don't know what group's going to be there to see you, you don't know where you are going to be next . . . It was so bad my first session that when my wife came into the room I got up and shook hands with her.

Individual legislators, including those mentioned above, are attracted to public life for a variety of reasons. Many run for office with the rewards and power of a legislative career in mind: to serve the people, to influence policy, or even to attract public attention and boost their business, law practice, or primary occupation. We will take a closer look at legislative ambition and involvement later in the chapter. In this section we want to briefly examine the variety and intensity of frustrations and satisfactions tied to the job of a legislator.

While it is apparent that many newcomers have only meager expectations about the frustrations facing them as a legislator, they are quickly inundated by a variety of complicating factors. Although salaries for Oklahoma legislators are certainly not at poverty levels, the remuneration provided is usually substantially short of that derived from private law practices, businesses, or the other occupations which are represented in the Oklahoma House and Senate. As a consequence, many legislators find it necessary to devote at least some time to their primary occupation.

In addition to problems associated with monetary rewards and the suggested role conflicts discussed earlier, a legislator faces a massive tide of legislation—in an average year approximately thirteen hundred bills are introduced for their consideration, and these bills tend to be detailed, long, and complicated. A careful reading of all legislation, even as reported out of committee, may be nearly impossible—especially late in the session. Although Oklahoma legislators do not face the time constraints of a short session meeting every other year, as is the case in some states, the annual Oklahoma sessions have caused a larger number of bills to be introduced, as well as lengthier meetings and more time-consuming interim activities.

These everyday pressures are complicated by constituency demands, phone calls, and contacts, as well as a variety of ceremonial duties, social functions, and public appearances which most legislators find it necessary to perform. While time is consumed with such functions, the pressing and detailed matters of everyday legislative life continue to mount, and a meager system of personal staff assistance includes only secretaries who cannot assume the responsibilities associated with the course of legislation. This should not imply that services are unavailable to legislators (as we shall see in the next chapter), but that the demands of time and expertise are often overwhelming.

TABLE 21.—General Perceptions of Job Satisfaction in the Oklahoma Legislature

	Strongly Agree	Somewhat Agree	Somewhat Disagree	Strongly Disagree
I am well satisfied with my job as a legislator.				
House (N = 90)	52.2%	38.9%	7.8%	1.1%
Senate (N = 43)	48.8	39.5	11.6	0.0
The House (Senate) is composed of the best group of people that I can imagine working with.				
House (N = 89)	24.7	40.4	21.3	13.5
Senate (N = 43)	23.3	46.5	23.3	7.0

Are the rewards and satisfactions of a legislative career sufficient to overcome the mounting frustrations and tensions associated with the job? The answer to this question is neither easy nor simple. It all depends on the individual and the type of balance that is achieved on his personal scale of costs and benefits. While we could expound at some length on the extent to which the desire to influence policy and serve the people outweighs the time-consuming demands of a legislative career, our exposition would be incomplete without making personal inquiries of each Oklahoma legislator. We attempted such a task as part of a large study on the Oklahoma House and Senate in 1972.[11] Legislator's feelings about their satisfactions and frustrations were measured through a series of detailed and lengthy interviews. Among other things, representatives were queried about their general job satisfaction, a variety of frustrations with the legislative process, their feelings of legislative efficacy and their perceptions of power and privilege in both chambers.

Job Satisfaction

The most general indication of satisfaction is found through responses to two basic questions presented in Table 21.

Approximately half of both houses strongly agree that they are well satisfied with their job as a legislator, and some 90 per cent of both chambers failed to disagree with the satisfaction statement. In addition, 65 per cent of the House and 70 per cent of the Senate are pleased with their co-workers and agree that their respective chamber is composed of the best people that they could imagine working with. Although this response is not as high as that associated with general job satisfaction in the previous question, it is probably lower because it directs attention to the type of people they usually worked with in their prelegislative career. Such careers are usually well established by the time one enters the legislature, and it is reasonable to expect that some 30 per cent are more comfortable working with other people, or business associates, who are more likely to share their own specific interests in their own home town.

Frustrations

As we become more specific in our inquiry about problems associated with being a legislator, the strong feeling of general job satisfaction gradually begins to break down. In order to measure attitudes toward specific frustrations with the legislative process, members of both chambers were asked their feelings about workload, their ability to satisfy conflicting demands, their knowledge of expectations from others, their ability to get information, and the extent to which they feel accepted by others in their work group. The responses to these questions appear in Table 22.

Those items associated with feelings about other people in the legislative chambers indicate a high sense of satisfaction. Eighty-nine per cent of the legislative members indicate that they never or

TABLE 22.—Frustrations with the Legislative Process in Oklahoma

	Never	Rarely	Sometimes	Rather Often	Nearly All the Time
Feeling that you have too heavy a work load, too many things to be done.					
House (N = 90)	24.4%	22.2%	31.1%	13.3%	8.9%
Senate (N = 44)	25.0	18.2	25.0	22.7	9.1
Thinking that you'll not be able to satisfy the conflicting demands placed on you as a legislator.					
House (N = 90)	15.6	33.3	32.2	14.4	4.4
Senate (N = 44)	27.3	27.3	27.3	15.9	2.3
Not knowing just what the people you work with expect of you.					
House (N = 90)	36.7	37.8	22.2	2.2	1.1
Senate (N = 44)	50.0	43.2	6.8	0.0	0.0
The fact that you can't get information needed to carry out your job as a lawmaker.					
House (N = 90)	24.4	25.6	26.7	17.8	5.6
Senate (N = 44)	27.3	25.0	34.1	13.6	0.0
Feeling that you may not be liked or accepted by the people you work with.					
House (N = 90)	51.1	37.8	8.9	1.1	1.1
Senate (N = 44)	50.0	38.6	4.5	4.5	2.3

rarely feel a sense of being unliked or unaccepted by others. In addition, 75 per cent of the House and 93 per cent of the Senate rarely or never feel that they do not know what other co-workers expect of them. These figures suggest that the job of a legislator is relatively well defined in Oklahoma, and that members of the Senate have more clearly defined roles as they are shaped by expectations of co-workers. While very few representatives indicate that they are frustrated "rather often" or "nearly all the time" on a variety of items, the substantial satisfied majorities begin to diminish on specifics associated with the legislative process: workload demands, information necessary for the job, and general conflicting demands. As Table 22 indicates, nearly half of the legislators "never" or "rarely" feel that workload, conflicting demands, or information problems are serious; yet from one-fourth to one-third of the representatives freely admit that these factors are "sometimes" a source of frustration. This holds for both houses of the legislature, with few differences between responses from members of the House and Senate. Although most members of the legislature are certainly not so frustrated that they are unable to perform their tasks, many of them acknowledge their frustrations, and those who do may well be underestimating, since it takes some degree of fortitude to admit that a legislative career is not all that it is cracked up to be.

Legislative Efficacy

We have frequently suggested that legislators are exposed to a variety of conflicting demands. Legislative efficacy refers to the feelings and attitudes legislators have about their ability to handle successfully the large number of demands placed on them in their positions as state representatives. This degree of efficacy is measured through four items, two of which relate to legislative proposals and bills, and two of which deal with constituents.[12]

Since the legislative process and the problems associated with resolving public problems have become so complicated, legislators were asked their feelings about the technical and detailed nature of bills and the extent to which they have trouble understanding them. The press of legislative business and the time constraints of the legislative session also create problems for individual legislators, and when this is accompanied by a rather complicated set of rules and procedures, we find that some legislators do not know what they are voting for or against. Responses to items measuring these aspects of legislative efficacy are presented in Table 23.

TABLE 23.—Feelings of Legislative Efficacy

	Strongly Agree	Somewhat Agree	Somewhat Disagree	Strongly Disagree
Many of the bills are so detailed and technical that I have trouble understanding them.				
House (N = 90)	4.4%	41.1%	24.4%	30.0%
Senate (N = 43)	4.7	37.2	32.6	25.6
My district includes so many kinds of people that I often don't know just what the people there want me to do.				
House (N = 90)	2.2	14.4	32.2	51.1
Senate (N = 43)	2.3	18.6	34.9	44.2
There is so little time during a session to study all the bills that sometimes I don't know what I'm voting for or against.				
House (N = 90)	6.7	42.2	24.4	26.7
Senate (N = 44)	13.6	27.3	25.0	34.1
So many groups want so many different things that it is often difficult to know what stands to take.				
House (N = 90)	3.3	38.9	32.2	25.6
Senate (N = 44)	13.6	27.3	31.8	27.3

We find that a substantial portion of both houses—from 41 to 49 per cent—either agree that many bills are so detailed that they have trouble understanding them, or that there is so little time to study the bills that they sometimes do not know what they are voting for or against. Although the differences in response between the House and Senate are nominal, 8 per cent more of the House members (46 per cent) admit that they have trouble understanding bills and that they sometimes do not know what they are voting for (49 per cent). Such findings are obviously bothersome to many readers and common citizens who are unfamiliar with the legislative process, but familiarity with the complications of public policy and the machinations of legislative procedure would probably temper many readers' opinions. While we are writing neither to defend nor sit in critical judgment of Oklahoma legislators, it is difficult for one to come away from these findings with anything but searching questions. We are certain at least that the process of policy making is complicated, and that some individuals must begin to question the institutional arrangements which produce these kinds of feelings on the part of individual lawmakers.

The remaining data in Table 23 are associated with feelings of efficacy relating to constituents. The data suggest that approximately 42 per cent of both the House and Senate are confused about the demands coming from a variety of groups throughout the state; that so many groups want so many different things that it is often difficult for individual legislators to know what stands to take. On the other hand, only 17 per cent of the House and 21 per cent of the Senate agree that their district includes so many different kinds of people that they do not know what constituents want them to do. When we examine a series of more specific attitudes about representation and constituents in Chapter 6, we will see that these findings are understandable since many legislators claim to think like their constituents. Although this may be true, when legislators are queried in terms of groups rather than the general electorate, they obviously sense frustration over conflicting demands.

Perceptions of Power and Privilege

A final area of dissatisfaction with the legislative process relates to the legislative power structure and the distribution of rewards and privileges within each chamber. The need for leadership in legislative bodies is well recognized in order to coordinate the passage of legislation, support political party policy, and effectuate collective action. The formal positions of legislative leadership pro-

TABLE 24.—Perceptions of Power and Privilege in the Oklahoma Legislature

	Strongly Agree	Somewhat Agree	Somewhat Disagree	Strongly Disagree
Some members of the House (Senate) are granted special privileges.				
House (N = 90)	27.8%	35.6%	20.0%	16.7%
Senate (N = 44)	25.0	31.8	27.3	15.9
The House (Senate) is controlled by the action of a few members.				
House (N = 90)	25.6	46.7	16.7	11.1
Senate (N = 43)	16.3	41.9	30.2	11.6
All members of the House (Senate) have about equal power to get things done.				
House (N = 90)	4.4	8.9	30.0	56.7
Senate (N = 44)	6.8	4.5	45.5	43.2
The likelihood of a bill's passage largely depends on who is sponsoring that bill.				
House (N = 90)	20.0	50.0	23.3	6.7
Senate (N = 44)	13.6	54.5	13.6	18.2
I consider myself more influential in the House (Senate) than most other members.				
House (N = 88)	11.4	25.0	37.5	26.1
Senate (N = 42)	9.5	42.9	28.6	19.0

vide directors, gatekeepers, and regulators of activity. The process also necessitates a large amount of committee work to handle specialized needs, and such a necessary structure obviously facilitates certain centers of power within both houses. At the same time, formal leadership and committee positions are not the only source of power and privilege. The complicated nature of public policy, as well as the legislative structure which develops to meet policy needs, places an increasingly high premium on expertise and substantive specialization. While some individual legislators may not achieve formal positions of power, their abilities and level of knowledge in one particular area may considerably boost informal powers. While interpretations of politics that characterize participants in public life as power hungry have come under serious attack from scholars of politics, from time to time legislative leaders emerge with considerable authority to thwart even the will of a majority, and there will always be well established centers of power affiliated with various aspects of the legislative process. Writings on the "inner club" of the U.S. Senate describe this tendency.[13]

Are problems and frustrations associated with power concentration and privilege in the Oklahoma legislature evident in the eyes of a representative? The answer is a very definite yes. The data reported in Table 24 indicate that 87 per cent of the House and 89 per cent of the Senate disagree that members have about equal power to get things done. Seventy-two per cent of the House and 58 per cent of the Senate agree that their respective chamber is controlled by the actions of a few members. In addition, a substantial majority of both houses feel that some members are granted special privileges, and approximately 70 per cent agree that the likelihood of a bill's passage largely depends on who is sponsoring that measure.

Table 24 also indicates some differences between House and Senate members, suggesting that representatives in the lower chamber perceive a more dominant, or closed, power system. The data relevant to an individual legislator's perception of his influence is consistent with this finding. While 52 percent of the Senate members consider themselves more influential than most other members, only 36 per cent of the House agree. These findings suggest that the Senate is characterized by a more equal distribution of power, and that positions of leadership and privilege in the House are more dominant and necessary in the larger chamber, where coordination may be more essential to the legislative process.

CAREER PERSPECTIVES

In addition to a legislator's basic role orientations and level of job satisfaction, his level of ambition and commitment to a legislative career influence job performance. Indeed, the effectiveness of a legislative institution is partially determined by tenure and turnover rates, as well as attitudes about career, willingness to return for more lengthy service, and the actual level of activity and involvement in legislative matters. Each of these factors is also linked to the rate of job dissatisfaction and frustration, which tend to reinforce the part-time nature of legislative careers, to depress one's willingness to return for more than a brief interlude, and to increase the rate of voluntary retirement.

Tenure and Turnover

There appears to be widespread agreement that state legislative turnover is excessive, that it weakens the lawmaking institution, and that it negatively affects performance. In a classic study of legislative turnover in ten states, Hyneman found a rate of 40 per cent and suggested dire consequences for state legislatures, expressing the opinion that three or four sessions are necessary for a lawmaker to learn how to be effective in policy making.[14]

In addition, it is well established that the bulk of turnover activity in state legislatures is voluntary. Hyneman found that less than one-third of all retirements were due to defeats, and Barber's extensive study of Connecticut found that less than one-fourth of the turnover was caused by electoral contests.[15] In their study of four states, Wahlke and his associates found that the percentage of legislators not intending to run again or doubtful about running ranged from 24 per cent in New Jersey to 66 per cent in Tennessee.[16]

Although state legislative turnover rates appear to have subsided slightly from what they were in the 1920's and 1930's, the most recent study of all states found that turnover in senates averaged 24.6 per cent in 1971, and that House rates were somewhat higher at 32.3 per cent.[17] The mean for all states from 1963 to 1971 was 30.4 per cent, and the average rate for House turnover during that period was 36.1 per cent. These rates obviously vary somewhat over time, with peaks during active redistricting and reapportionment years. Although there has been some turnover decrease in recent years, the rate for state legislatures has been consistently higher than that displayed by Congress. In the national legislature, turnover has not exceeded 26 per cent since 1932.[18] Recent data for Oklahoma place it close to the national mean, with a House rate of 31 per cent and a Senate rate of 19 per cent. Although Oklahoma Senate turnover is slightly lower than the average for all states, Oklahoma senatorial elections occur less frequently than in many other states.

The data in Table 25 present an example showing the years of entry and service for members comprising a recent legislature. On the whole, 27 per cent of the total legislature was new in 1973. Although differences between the parties are not glaring, Republicans comprise a third of the Oklahoma legislature, and 40 per cent of the turnover was contributed by them. Although Democrats tend to turnover slightly less often in proportion to their numbers in the legislature, both parties reflect the relatively high turnover rate.

The consequences of rapid turnover are not directly measurable, yet most writers on the subject tend to agree that it weakens legislative performance—and that such performance is more critical than the need for circulating elites in a democracy. A persuasive agrument is made that freshmen come to the legislature with little experience in policy making, and that longer tenure increases skill, expertise, judgment, and the ability to oversee the executive branch.[19] Turnover therefore affects both lawmaking and oversight functions. In addition, if the political parties in a legislature are not very cohesive, the influx of a large number of newcomers is likely to further increase party irresponsibility and individual independence. Therefore, in some legislatures turnover may add to the problems of factionalism. On the other hand, if

TABLE 25—Composition of the 34th Oklahoma Legislature (1973-74) by First Year of Most Recent Continuous Service

Legislature Year	22 49-50	23 51-52	24 53-54	25 55-56	26 57-58	27 59-60	28 61-62	29 63-64	30 65-66	31 67-68	32 69-70	33 71-72	34 73-74	Total
SENATE Democrat	2	2			1	2	2	1	13	3	3	4	5	38
Republican									1	1	2	2	4	10
Totals	2	2			1	2	2	1	14	4	5	6	9	48
HOUSE Democrat			2	1	4	2	3		11	4	10	18	19	74
Republican							2	2	5	2	3	1	12	27
Totals			2	1	4	2	5	2	16	6	13	19	31	101
TOTAL Democrat	2	2	2	1	5	4	5	1	24	7	13	22	24	112
Republican							2	2	6	3	5	3	16	37
Totals	2	2	2	1	5	4	7	3	30	10	18	25	40	149

political parties are well organized and powerful within the lawmaking body, an influx of new members actually may strengthen party control and organization, increasing conformity to policy preferences of the party and its leaders. In Oklahoma, these effects are likely to influence both parties in different ways: greater cohesion among the Republican minority members suggests that party control may not be weakened by disproportionately high turnover rates among Republicans; but from time to time Democratic turnover may exacerbate tendencies toward factionalism within the majority party.

The potential consequences of high turnover rates in American state legislatures point attention to the importance of isolating the factors which heighten those rates. In a recent study of all states,[20] three influential factors were cited for analysis: characteristics of the overall political system, attributes of the electoral system, and characteristics of the lawmaking body. Political system factors do determine turnover rates. For instance, partisan competition and party integration tend to reduce turnover. But such characteristics are less influential than electoral and legislative variables.

Among electoral factors, the number of elections and the frequency of reapportionment tend to stimulate turnover. Although some findings tend to support conventional wisdom, an examination of legislative factors suggests that longer legislative sessions serve to reduce turnover—indicating that work may have appeal to legislators and that it may stimulate a sense of professionalization. The size of legislative institutions was also negatively related to turnover, since larger bodies offer more leadership power and committee specialization. Of all factors, however, financial compensation is the single most important—a consistent finding in discussions of the inadequacies of state legislatures.

Yet the cause of turnover is not monolithic. Increased rates result from an interplay of various political, electoral, and legislative forces. As Rosenthal suggests, "If the legislative institution is feeble, if the perquisites of office are few, and if the frustrations are intense, members are not likely to remain very long."[21] With such causal factors in mind, the future is encouraging for state legislatures; for compensation is continually increasing, fewer drastic reapportionments have occurred in recent years or are likely in the immediate future, and legislative careers appear increasingly attractive.

Political Ambition

Turnover reflects various structural characteristics of the electoral and legislative system. However, legislator's attitudes, frustrations, and career perspectives are more fundamental indicators of the nature of legislative institutions. Knowledge of the underlying and more enduring qualities cannot be extracted from aggregate indicators of turnover—such inquiries must be made of legislators directly. High turnover rates make such inquiries imperative, since they suggest that lawmaking is an avocation for many, and that serious devotion to the tasks of legislative life is a characteristic of a minority of legislators.

Notions of ambition are frequently used in popular parlance as an explanation for politicians' behavior. Although it has received less attention than such influential factors as social background, personality, role and constituency influence, ambition is receiving increased attention in political science research.[22] This new interest in career or ambition theory reflects the contention that individuals differ in their desire to maintain current positions or seek other office, that such ambitions are measurable, and that differences are subsequently reflected in behavior.[23] In order to distinguish levels of desire, Schlesinger suggests a three-fold typology in his study of opportunity structure and career patterns of major political leaders: (1) *discrete ambitions*—reflecting the desire to hold office for a specific period, subsequently followed by withdrawal; (2) *static ambitions*—the desire to make a long-term career of a particular office; and (3)*progressive ambitions*—the desire to hold other political office.[24] These three categories offer some guidance in assessing the ambition and motivational qualities of Oklahoma legislators.

The data presented earlier in Table 25 indicate that 27 per cent of Oklahoma legislators were first-termers in 1973-74. Although a turnover rate of one-third or less is common in recent years for various legislative sessions in Oklahoma, the proportion of individuals with

TABLE 26.—Career Attitudes and Perceptions of Oklahoma Legislators

As of today, is it likely that you would be willing to serve three or more terms in future legislatures?

	Willing	Depends	Not Willing
House (N = 90)	64.4%	11.1%	24.4%
Senate (N = 43)	30.2	30.2	39.5

Have you ever considered seeking election or appointment to some other full-time public office in the future? Would you say you have considered this . . .

	A Great Deal	Some	A Little	Not at All
House (N = 90)	17.8%	26.7%	7.8%	47.8%
Senate (N = 43)	20.9	18.6	16.3	44.2

If you were to choose to run for re-election to your seat in the legislature, what are the chances that you'll be reelected?

	Certainly Win	Probably Win	Either Way	Probably Defeated	Certainly Defeated
House (N = 88)	42.0%	54.5%	3.4%	0.0%	0.0%
Senate (N = 42)	50.0	42.9	7.1	0.0	0.0

If the opportunity arose, would you be interested in becoming a party leader in the legislature? (nonleaders only)

	Definitely	Probably	Undecided	Probably Not	Definitely Not
House (N = 80)	28.7%	13.7%	8.7%	20.0%	28.7%
Senate (N = 36)	36.1	22.2	8.3	8.3	25.0

If the opportunity arose, would you be interested in remaining as a party leader in the legislature? (leaders only)

	Definitely	Probably	Undecided	Probably Not	Definitely Not
House (N = 10)	72.7%	9.1%	0.0%	9.1	9.1%
Senate (N = 6)	66.7	33.3	0.0	0.0	0.0

apparently *discrete ambitions* is substantially larger. Using the 34th Legislature as an example, 43 per cent of the total members served less than three terms. From another perspective, 69 per cent of the Senate and 52 per cent of the House had served three or more terms by 1973. Since such measures can only be rough indicators of ambition, especially since they reflect a host of factors influencing turnover, we explicitly asked legislators if they would be willing to serve three or more terms in future legislatures. The data reflecting this attitudinal dimension of ambition are shown in Table 26.

They indicate that 64 per cent of the House and 30 per cent of the Senate are willing to serve three or more terms. These intentions differ slightly from past historical fact as mentioned above, suggesting that the institution may be changing or that electoral defeat has interfered.

The differences between tenure and intentions are not substantial when the legislature as a whole is considered. With both houses combined, 53 per cent of the lawmakers indicated that they would return, and in fact, over time for the 34th Legislature, 57 per cent served three or more terms. On the whole, by both intention and historical fact, approximately 45 per cent of the Oklahoma legislature holds only "discrete" ambitions. In other words, about 45 per cent of the legislature is made up of first or second termers who appear to have no intention of staying longer. For the latter, defeat is apparently not an issue. The first figure, in fact, reflects some defeats for ambitious legislators, but the attitudinal data is probably more reflective of basic sentiments. This interpretation is supported by data in Table 26 indicating that no one thinks they will be defeated if they run again, despite low ambition for almost half of the legislature. This proportion of lawmakers with low legislative career ambitions appears to be somewhat higher in Oklahoma in comparison with two other states studied in a similar manner: 18 per cent of the Michigan House had no intention of staying,[25] and 35 per cent of the Connecticut legislature did not intend to serve three or more terms.[26]

In addition to discrete ambitions, data in Table 26 indicate that 47 per cent of the Oklahoma legislature has less than progressive ambitions, that is to say, no intention at all of seeking other elected or appointed office. The percentages for the House and Senate are very similar, and on the whole the figures for Oklahoma are slightly higher than those in other states where similar inquiries have been made. In fact, a study in Michigan indicates that 40 per cent of the House had no intention of seeking other office,[27] and combined data from Wahlke's four-state study indicate the same rate.[28] Although nearly half of the Oklahoma legislature exhibits no progressive ambitions, the fact that 53 per cent express at least some desire to hold other public office supports Schlesinger's contention that state legislatures serve as an important stage in political recruitment to higher office.[29] In Oklahoma, 19 per cent of the entire lawmaking body admits to considering future office "a great deal," with about equal divisions between the chambers.

An in-depth study of progressive legislative ambitions by Soule[30] developed a profile of progressively ambitious state legislators which can be reasonably inferred to the Oklahoma situation. Soule's research indicates that progressive ambitions are associated with an early interest in politics (from childhood or adolescence), stemming largely from the individual's family. Higher educational attainment is also most prevalent among those with a desire to seek other office. A personality profile suggests that politically ambitious legislators do not need understanding, support, benevolence or conformity—but that they do have a need for power, authority, and leadership over others. Soule's profile, therefore, corresponds to Lasswell's famous contention that politicians displace private needs in the public drive for power; that power motives fulfill a variety of needs.[31] At least this appears to be the case for ambitious legislators. It is also interesting that legislators with progressive ambitions are most likely to view representation in "trustee" role terms, emphasizing the legislator as a free agent, and to define the area of representation (areal role) as *beyond* his own immediate district. Although there is a blend of ambitions among Oklahoma legislators, a substantial proportion view their service as momentary or discrete.

A different dimension of ambition considers desires internal to the lawmaking body, that is, ambition for leadership. The data in Table 26 indicate that 44 per cent of the nonleaders in the Oklahoma legislature would "definitely not" be interested in becoming party leaders. Senators appear to be more internally ambitious since 58 per cent of the nonleaders indicate an interest in such positions, while only 42 per cent of the House appear to be motivated to seek party leadership. From several perspectives, these figures are actually quite high—especially given the low amount of external ambition, the fact that only a few people actually emerge as leaders to contend for office, and the fact that few positions are available. Once the competition for leadership is over and positions are finalized, nearly all party leaders want to hold on to their office and the powers associated with it (Table 26). Since a few leaders are not definite in this desire, we have witnessed several voluntary resignations from top leadership positions in recent years.

Legislative Activity and Involvement

To this point we have examined legislative satisfactions, frustrations, actual legislative turnover, and several dimensions of political ambition to conclude that substantial minorities in both houses are frustrated with specific aspects of the legislative process, have little intention of making legislative life a career or of seeking higher office—or of even staying more than a term or two. As Wahlke, et al. suggest:

For most state legislators the political career is only a part-time occupation. Politics being a sideline the decision to run for legislative office is not a "big decision" comparable to choosing a nonpolitical occupation or profession. Under certain favorable circumstances it may turn out to have been an important career step as when it leads to a full-time political or governmental position. But for most, the state legislature is likely to be a terminal point of their political career.[32]

For many, legislating seems to be very much a secondary activity, an avocation or a part-time or temporary job—perhaps one to supplement and revitalize a legal career, and for a few, to move on to other (higher) public office.

In order to measure aspects of the problem of commitment to legislative activity, we made further inquiries about involvement, the results of which appear in Table 27.

Although a few legislators are willing to admit that other interests are more absorbing, or that they are not really very involved in their job as a legislator, such an admission is very difficult to elicit, and would perhaps even be prejudicial or damning. However, when the same issue is phrased in less personal terms, the

TABLE 27.—Legislative Activity and Involvement in Oklahoma

	Strongly Agree	Somewhat Agree	Somewhat Disagree	Strongly Disagree
I am not really very involved in my job as a legislator; my other interests and activities are more absorbing.				
House (N = 90)	2.2%	5.6%	23.3%	68.9%
Senate (N = 44)	4.5	2.3	18.2	75.0
I am usually not very active in discussion and debate on the floor of the chamber.				
House (N = 90)	14.4	38.9	22.2	24.4
Senate (N = 44)	13.6	29.5	43.2	13.6
I am usually not very active in discussion and debate in committee meetings.				
House (N = 90)	2.2	24.4	31.1	42.2
Senate (N = 44)	2.3	11.4	45.5	40.9

We hear some talk these days about the need for the position of state legislator to become a full-time job (like other professionals). Are you in favor of such a trend?

	Definitely in Favor	Tend to Favor	Neutral	Tend to Disfavor	Definitely Disfavor
House (N = 89)	31.5	11.2	1.1	23.6	32.6
Senate (N = 43)	14.0	11.6	2.3	23.3	48.8

findings support the avocational and volunteeristic aspects of legislative life in Oklahoma. We inquired whether they felt the position of state legislator should become a full-time job, as in other professions, to which 61 per cent of the legislature expressed disapproval. Indeed, over half of the House (56 per cent) and almost three-quarters (72 per cent) of the Senate did not favor such a trend. Only 32 per cent of the House and 14 per cent of the Senate definitely favored full-time status for state legislators.

As a more specific internal measure of involvement in legislative tasks, lawmakers were asked about their debate and discussion activity, both on the floor and in committee meetings. The scenes of activity are quite distinct, since most of the day-to-day work of the legislature occurs in smaller committees, where interaction is usually high, where formal rules and procedures are relaxed, where votes are usually not recorded, and where the level of visibility is generally lower. All of these factors tend to encourage committee participation and debate and discussion activity at higher levels than on the floor. This tendency is substantiated by the data in Table 27, indicating that only 27 per cent of the House and 14 per cent of the Senate agreed that they were not very active in committee debate and discussion. On the other hand, 53 per cent of the Senate agreed that they were not active on the floor; in fact, one half of the entire legislature claims to be not very active in floor debate and discussion—a fact additionally supported by casual visual inspection of the lawmaking body on days other than those when the most controversial legislation is being considered.

One larger and more important consequence of ambition makes the above considerations crucial to several fundamental aspects of the political system. The tie between ambition and the political system is a vital one. It rests with a concept inherent to all democratic theory: accountability. Although some may speak disparagingly of "ambitious" men striving for power, imposing their own inadequacies on the public, self-interested and ego-driven, some desire either to retain office or to move on to higher public office is necessary for accountability. A democratic system assumes a supply of individuals desiring public office and intent on holding on to it, and, most important, responding to voter preferences and public policy needs partly in response to ambition. As Schlesinger suggests:

A political system unable to kindle ambitions is as much in danger of breaking down as one unable to restrain ambitions. Representative government, above all, depends upon a supply of men so driven; the desire for election and, more important, for re-election becomes the electorate's restraint upon its public officials. No more irresponsible government is imaginable than one of high-minded men unconcerned for their political futures.[33]

When low ambition is coupled with a tendency for state legislative electorates to be small, for incumbents to have significant electoral advantage, and for a high rate of voluntary retirement from office, the impact on accountability is potentially ominous. The result is the norm of volunteerism pervading public life when office holders respond in terms of citizen duty with little sensitivity to voter preferences. While this norm appears to be most prevalent at the local level,[34] state legislatures suffer from many of its ramifications, and its impact upon accountability in Oklahoma is surely not benign.

STYLES OF ADAPTATION

This chapter began with an examination of legislative roles. We now conclude it with a different perspective on roles: one emphasizing styles of adaptation to legislative life. This role perspective incorporates concepts of political ambition and of legislative activity in order to define basic orientation and adaptation to the legislative process. Barber suggests that four fundamental roles are defined by two basic dimensions of ambition and activity discussed above: willingness to return and level of debate and discussion activity.[35] Although Barber's classic study of Connecticut measured activity in terms of the actual number of bills introduced, the extensiveness of comments made in committees, and the number of lines spoken on the floor, our analysis of Oklahoma relies on legislator's perceptions of activity. It recognizes that the level of activity as viewed by individuals is probably most important for his conceptualization of role, at least as important as more objective measures of involvement. The measures employed in the Oklahoma study reflect a personal and individual dimension, plus an institutional component relevant to the office. Furthermore, the activity element is a reflection of personality, and willingness to

TABLE 28.—Styles of Adaptation to a Legislative Career

A. Connecticut

		Activity	
		High	Low
Willingness to Return	High	"Lawmakers" 34%	"Spectators" 31%
	Low	"Advertisers" 17%	"Reluctants" 18%

(N = 96)

B. Oklahoma—Floor Activity

		Floor Activity	
		High	Low
Willingness to Return	High	31%	35%
	Low	18%	16%

(N = 107)

C. Oklahoma—Committee Activity

		Committee Activity	
		High	Low
Willingness to Return	High	50%	15%
	Low	28%	7%

(N = 110)

D. Oklahoma—Floor and Committee Activity Aggregated

		Activity	
		High	Low
Willingness to Return	High	"Lawmakers" 40%	"Spectators" 25%
	Low	"Advertisers" 23%	"Reluctants" 12%

(N = 217)

return reflects attitudes toward the group and the level of attraction to the office. Together they indicate behavior in the group and attitudes about the collectivity as a whole. Since these concepts and the resultant measures comprise a manageable replication of the famous Connecticut study, part A, Table 28 presents the distribution of role types from Barber's analysis.[36]

The data for Connecticut indicate that the variables of "willingness to return" and "legislative activity" are somewhat related, yet they appear to operate relatively independently of one another in that they are distributed across the cells of the typology. Although we have employed two measures of activity in Oklahoma, there is a better distribution on the measure of floor activity (since few claim to be inactive in committees) and it is probably a better reflection of individual motivation and leadership. When the floor measure is employed, the data for Oklahoma offer a nearly perfect fit with Barber's data on Connecticut. Part B of Table 28 indicates that there are nearly identical percentages of the more active and less active expressing a willingness to return (willingness to serve three or more future terms).

The deviant cases in the off-diagonal cells are more interesting: the 35 per cent who are not active, yet willing to return and the 18 per cent who are not planning to return but are active in floor debate and discussion. For such deviant cases, Barber inquires and suggests the following:

Why would a low participant be willing to return in the future? Perhaps because his legislative experience provides rewards for him other than those involved in taking an active part. Why would a higher participant be unwilling to return? Perhaps because his relatively intense activity is undertaken for certain limited transient purposes which can be achieved in a session or two.[37]

More skewed findings result when committee activity is used as a criterion. By this definition, half of the legislators are both active and willing to return. But even this is a striking figure. By no measure is more than half of the legislature sufficiently dedicated to a legislative career to engage actively in discussion and want to stay for three or more terms.

Probably the most accurate typology for Oklahoma would take both types of activity into account. In order to do this without wrestling with empirical inconsistencies between types of activity, and without deciding which type is most important, we have aggregated the responses in parts B and C of Table 28 to appear in part D. What is important about these categories is not only that which is suggested by activity and ambition, but also by a host of other characteristics Barber found associated with each cell, as reflected in the following role terminology.[38]

The lawmaker is typically high in activity and willingness to return, and pays serious attention to legislative tasks of a substantive nature; is interested in full-time elective office; concentrates on decisions and strategies; makes significant contributions, yet may be impatient with formalities; emphasizes individuality, rationality, and the performance of legislative tasks; and is generally issue-oriented. About 40 per cent of the Oklahoma legislature appears to fall in this category, with a slightly higher proportion in the House. One-third or less of the Senate falls in this lawmaker category.

The reluctant is the other extreme of the lawmaker, characterized by discrete ambition favoring a limited tenure and by low legislative activity. According to the Connecticut study, he is most likely to be doing a civic duty under protest, to be not conflict-oriented, to be confused by the decision making process, to feel inadequate and useless, to be likely to withdraw, and to be generally provincial in background, with limited education. He is a classic norm-follower. About 12 per cent of the Oklahoma Legislature fit this category.

The advertiser does not want to stay very long, but is high in legislative activity. He appears to be on exhibit, making contacts for his primary occupation, often feeling exploited and powerless, and concentrating on his own suffering. His intense involvement often makes him indifferent to substantive legislative work; he is generally anxious and has a short political future. In terms of activity and willingness to return, more Oklahoma senators (up to more than half) fit this role than any other, and substantially more legislators in the Senate than in the House, where less than one-fifth can be considered advertisers. Twenty-three per cent of the Oklahoma legislature play the advertiser role.

The spectator is low in activity but high in willingness to return. He enjoys legislative life, watches carefully, likes to be entertained, is easily influenced by others, and is personally inadequate. The spectator is only slightly involved in legislative tasks, he socializes superficially, and is generally noncombative. A few more of these individuals are found in the Oklahoma House than in the Senate. They constitute 25 per cent of the legislature.

Although the above typology implies a "model type" to which few people fit perfectly, these four roles are generally reflective of styles in the state legislature. Our purpose is not to proclaim one style better than another, but to exhibit the mix of styles in a single lawmaking institution in one state. On the basis of the data, we find that one quarter of Oklahoma legislators are primarily there to advertise or promote another career, another fourth are primarily spectators, a few are reluctants in the entire electoral process, and a few more than a third are consciously lawmakers of the civics-text variety.

We could speculate at some length on which role is best, yet a variety of styles seem to enhance the effectiveness of a lawmaking body.[39] It is difficult to imagine the level of conflict in a legislature heavily dominated by lawmaker types. Similarly, spectators raise morale, and reluctants add order, and advertisers may add to rational conflict. The mix exists empirically, and it may be healthy. There is no right combination of styles. The attempt to arrive at a formula begs a more central question inherent in democratic theory: Should the notion of popular representation and the idea that a lawmaking body should mirror the inadequacies, prejudices, and irrationalities of the common people predominate over a more elitist version of democracy stressing rational decisions, efficiency, and effectiveness? This tension in democratic theory is obviously reflected in legislative composition in Oklahoma and in the styles of adaptation to legislative life.

CHAPTER 3

Enacting Public Policy

From the point of view of Oklahoma's constitution, its elected representatives, and their constituents, the development of public policy is the keystone of the legislative process. This chapter and a subsequent one address the enactment of public policy from this perspective. As in the previous chapters, a distinction is made between the formal-legal components of legislative activity and those reflecting individual behavior. The latter draws attention to individual decision making and the mix of factors shaping roll call votes, while the former focuses on the institutional components necessary for legislation. The present chapter examines these institutional components as parts of a larger information processing system. All legislation is produced from a mix of information sources ranging from the demands of constituents to more technical and legal inputs. The primary components of public policy enactment include: (1) the mechanisms for information input to policy and the development of legislation, (2) the formal procedures for the passage of legislation, (3) the range and types of possible legislative measures, and (4) the committee system which serves as a focal point for information and the resolution of conflict. All of these components are addressed in sequence below.

INFORMATION INPUTS AND THE DEVELOPMENT OF LEGISLATION

Since the various rules and procedures, as well as the sources of information and constituency demands, are numerous and complex, there is rarely a single source to guide the legislator in the development and passage of public policy. The process of initiating a legislative measure entails considerable research, discussion, and cooperation among lawmakers and other officials of state government. While a few legislative measures may be so specific and clearcut as to confine discussion to the ranks of lawmakers, it is usually necessary to rely on assistance from a variety of "outside" sources.

Most legislative products require extra-legislative expertise for the early stages of bill formation. Cooperation between legislative and nonlegislative bodies is a key component which insures the production of technically correct legislation. The development of bills cannot operate in a legal vacuum; they stand among other laws and constitutional provisions. Such extra-legislative sources as the attorney general's office, various state agencies, and the Oklahoma Department of Libraries serve as key information sources in this process.

The business of gathering necessary information and discussing it among colleagues, however, is not itself sufficient for good public policy. The actual process of research, both legal and substantive, as well as the technical aspects of drafting legislation are necessary functions. While some of these research sources go beyond the legislative branch of state government, the key component is the Oklahoma Legislative Council.

The Oklahoma Legislative Council

The legislative council movement in America began as an attempt to develop the abilities of state legislatures in the early twentieth century.[1] The states were faced with increasingly complex problems, and the result was the development of legislative reference services and the use of interim committees to provide continuity in legislation. In the period between 1907 and 1917, over thirty legislative reference services were established, most often within understaffed and inadequate state libraries. On the basis of a successful and enduring legislative council experiment in Kansas in 1933, the Oklahoma legislature developed a council to cope with the massive pressures of legislation and the need for efficiency and information. The development of the Council began in 1935 as the state was in the throes of a depression. One observer describes the events surrounding Council formation as follows:

Oklahoma City and Tulsa banks had refused to cash state warrants; 150,000 people were looking to the state for relief from poverty; an open break between Governor Marland and Speaker Phillips of the House of Representatives was imminent because of the Governor's financial recovery programs; bills were clogging the legislative committee sessions and the legislature's calendar; time, effort, and money were being wasted;

and one special interest group was wasting additional time and money on a proposal to regulate the size of a loaf of bread.[2]

In this atmosphere a bill to establish a council was introduced in the House in 1935 and subsequently defeated. Opposition largely focused on doubts of constitutionality and professional jealousy of legislative prerogatives. Yet by 1939 a group of legislators was successful in passing legislation to establish the Council—which was not finally activated until 1947, when a necessary appropriation was made. The interim period between 1939 and 1947 was also chacterized by continuing debate over the constitutionality of the council proposal.[3]

The Legislative Council is organized as part of the legislative body in order to facilitate assistance to individual legislators as well as to the entire legislature. Its basic duties and functions include an interim study program; the provision of legal, research, and fiscal services to the legislature; and the publication of reports useful to the legislator in specific policy areas. The statutory definition of Council duties includes: (1) collecting information about government and the state; (2) examining the effects of enacted statutes; (3) dealing with important issues of public policy; and (4) preparing bills. Although every member of the legislature is also a member of the Legislative Council, the Council statute provides for an Executive Committee to plan and oversee activities. In addition, the Council consists of a permanent professional staff employed by the legislature and charged with the duty of administering the daily work routine. These activities are overseen by the Executive Committee, which consists of fifteen members (plus the leadership) from each house, who have primary responsibility for naming standing and special committees of the Council, developing the agenda for interim studies, and generally carrying out the duties of the Council. Chairmanship of the Executive Committee alternates between the president pro tempore of the Senate and the speaker of the House. In addition, the secretary of the Senate is also secretary of the Legislative Council, but these duties are mostly of a perfunctory nature. Clearly the bulk of the research activity rests with the permanent council staff.[4]

To more effectively direct the actual workings of the Council, its total membership is divided into a number of committees and subcommittees. Each committee has a designated substantive area of interest or expertise, such as reapportionment, constitutional revision, highways, rehabilitation, or agriculture. The primary purpose of these standing committees is to act as a reference point for questions and items of public interest coming from citizens, interest groups, and from within the legislative ranks, If there is a need, for example, to evaluate the state's rehabilitation programs, an inquiry will be referred to the appropriate standing committee or subcommittee of the Council. These committees should not be confused with the regular standing committees of the House and Senate. Rather they are standing committees of the Council, which is itself a permanent interim committee of the legislature. Rather than relying totally on the state welfare department and its agencies for such an inquiry, a committee and its research staff proceeds to gather relevant information. While cooperation with the various branches of state government is still vital, the Council involvement shifts the emphasis from nonlegislative sources to a permanent legislative body. Thus, information on Oklahoma's mental, penal, eleemosynary, and veterans' services is gathered by the members of the Council committee, its staff, and the Council's research department—in essence by the legislature itself.

On the basis of intensive study and research within a particular substantive area, the Council produces a number of recommendations which can serve as new inputs to the legislative arena. These proposals are factually based and more likely to produce public policy firmly grounded upon reliable information. In this way, a fact-finding body (the Council) produces the initial components of policy for an entire legislature, which can subsequently evaluate the needs of the state and its citizens. Yet future action on Council recommendations is completely dependent upon the legislature itself. Indeed, only a portion of recommendations are eventually considered by the legislature and enacted into law.

The Council functions on a continuing basis as a permanent interim committee of the legislature. Yet while the chambers are in session, most lawmakers find their time confined to regular standing committees, to floor activities, or to other duties associated with lawmaking. To meet the various demands for legislation and research, the various standing committees of the Council meet regularly between the legislative sessions, during the interim. During this period, the duties range from collecting data and information to recommending different courses for legislative action. Most of the work is directed toward the upcoming session; thus the interim duties are especially intense.

In order to perform effectively the above duties, both during the session and the interim, the Council is organized into three divisions with the following responsibilities:

I. Division of Research and Reference Services
    A.   General and specialized legislative research
    B.   Legislative reference and information
    C.   Committee staffing during legislative sessions and interim periods
II. Division of Legal Services
    A.   Bill drafting
    B.   Statutory and code revision
    C.   Bill analysis
    D.   Legal counseling
    E.   Audit of attorney general opinions and court decisions
    F.   Review of administrative rules and regulations
    G.   Analysis and review of the operation of statutory provisions
    H.   Committee staffing during legislative sessions and interim periods
III. Division of Fiscal Services
    A.   Budget review and fiscal analysis
    B.   Post audit
    C.   Fiscal note drafting
    D.   Committee staffing during legislative sessions and interim periods[5]

While all legislative recommendations must be introduced by a legislator before they become laws (that is, the Council does not make law), as a legal branch of the Oklahoma legislature the Council has a variety of more specific powers: to administer oaths, to issue subpoenas, and to compel attendance of witnesses at meetings and the production of papers, records, documents, and testimony. Although some of these powers are rarely used, in the event a person fails to comply with a Council request, he may be indicted and tried before a district court on the basis of a request from any Council member. With these broad powers the Council has an important political tool—the threat of legal action—and with this implied threat the Council can effectively gather all necessary information.

The products of Legislative Council activity are varied. The Council and its staff often go beyond the performance of formal duties to provide legislators with several important services. These services may not be required formally by statute, but they are pursued for the benefit of all legislators. The majority of work conducted by the Council and its standing committees results in the production of summary conclusions and reports. These summaries contain a gist of Council committee activities and reflect the results of considerable research and investigation. Such special reports are not regularly issued, but instead reflect a specific legislative interest (versus a general statement of regular legislative business). The majority of such reports are compiled by the Council membership and its staff, yet there is considerable flexibility in enlisting the services of nonlegislative sources. The governor, for example, may appoint individuals to work with the Council's committee and staff; a procedure that was followed in recent efforts to revise several articles of the Oklahoma constitution. The governor's appointees therefore served in an advisory capacity in a study of constitutional change. If a particular study warrants it, supplemental money is sometimes obtained from state and federal sources, and assistance may be contributed by members of the Oklahoma congressional delegation. In 1971, for example, the Legislative Council Committee on Interstate Cooperation met with the Oklahoma congressional delegation to develop new channels of communication between members of Congress and Oklahoma legislators. In rare instances the Council may also defer an inquiry and employ a consultant who has the time and subject-matter expertise necessary to a particular area of inquiry. When a consultant is used, the final report compiled by the expert is made available to the Council committee which actually hired the outside professional help. An example of this type of special report was the analysis of the teacher's retirement system in Oklahoma by a Houston consulting firm in the late 1960's. While these various special reports vary widely in form of presentation, organization, and length, the results are uniformly directed toward providing legislators with an extensive and correct evaluation of measures under investigation. Senior legislators often find the reports of substantial benefit to their lawmaking duties, and freshmen legislators see them as invaluable aids in the research aspect of lawmaking.

In addition to special reports focusing on a specific subject, the Council also publishes a variety of other materials of benefit to legislators. These publications include:

1. *Memoranda.* A memorandum may summarize laws pertaining to a specific issue, project directives, or background information. They are usually short and concise summaries issued to a committee or subcommittee by the Research and Reference Services division of the Council.

2. *Comparative Reports.* The Council periodically publishes comparative data on legislative sessions, usually pertaining to the number of measures introduced, passed, or vetoed during a session. Such reports compare legislative sessions and various measures over time.

3. *Summary Reports and Digests.* The various Council recommendations submitted to a legislative session are compiled, summarized, and printed for all legislators. In addition, the Council publishes a summary digest of laws enacted during each legislative session, organized by subject and bill number, and providing the gist of each measure.

4. *Outlines and Manuals.* Whenever possible the Council publishes various guides or explanatory works, most often compiled by the Research and Reference Services division in order to aid the legislator in the performance of his duties. In addition, the Council's Legal Services division prepares a bill-drafting manual, which outlines the various steps in bill formulation and discusses legislative authority, legislative terms, and the style and form of a bill. In the past, the Council has also published a more general legislative manual which provides a description of the technical aspects of the legislative process. It may from time to time produce various outlines or brief synopses of proposed bills or code modifications.

5. *Regular Reports.* In addition to summaries of laws enacted, the Council publishes a volume of highlights of each legislative session and summary material on state referenda.

Over the years the Legislative Council has become a vital component of the lawmaking process. It is a mechanism for extending cooperation and providing for research needs, and a general source of information necessary for each legislator. Since the entire organization of the Council, from its membership to the professional research staff, is a basic component of the legislative process, Council activities cannot be passed over in any examination of the legislative process. The Council idea insures that a legislator is—at least in concept—never very far away from the problems of the state and his constituency. It is always difficult to translate emerging concerns and demands into effective action in the legislature, and to this end the Council is indispensable. The legislator who takes advantage of these services and perceives a constructive role for the Council is most likely to produce good legislation, effectively represent his constituency, and meet the needs of the state.

In summary, some type of internal professional staff arrangement is necessary in the legislative process, and the primary arrangement for such staff in Oklahoma—as in most other states—is through the use of a legislative council. Previous research has shown that the availability of staff increases the capacity of the legislature to be independent of the executive branch and less susceptible to other outside influences, and encourages more independent judgment by legislators vis-a-vis the governor, bureaucracy, and lobbyists.[6] Yet these important consequences of staff availability should not overshadow or negate the effectiveness of extra-legislative assistance. While the Council is a primary source of expertise, other individuals and agencies play an important role in the development of Oklahoma legislation. More specifically, these sources include the Oklahoma Department of Libraries, the office of the attorney general, and various state agencies whose primary responsibility is the implementation of public policy.

Oklahoma Department of Libraries

The Oklahoma legislator may use the services provided by the Legislative Reference Division of the Oklahoma Department of Libraries. The basic function of the Reference Division is to supply information on any subject upon request, be it for legislation, speeches, personal interests, or constituents. The Reference Division will also provide information to the general public on matters pertaining to the legislature. While it does not undertake research, its holdings are broad in substance and well indexed to facilitate speedy and accurate retrieval of information. Some of the most frequently used holdings include the following: a subject index to all introduced and enacted legislation; a card file on the status of all legislation introduced; U.S. Government Printing Office publications relating to congressional bills (such as *Congressional Record, Congressional Quarterly, Congressional Clearing House, Congressional Index,* and *Congressional Monitor*); a vertical file of reports and studies from other states, periodical articles, reports of Oklahoma state agencies, and other miscellaneous items of legislative interest; and a comprehensive subject file of Oklahoma bibliographical and newspaper clippings.

In addition to maintaining regular holdings, the Legislative Reference Division also publishes the *Oklahoma Gazette* on the first and fifteenth day of each month. Legislators find the *Gazette* a useful item, since it contains notices of all meetings to consider the adoption of rules and regulations, as well as a listing of all emergency and regularly adopted rules and regulations of state agencies. The division also compiles a number of informative publications which can be used by the legislator, such as directories of state agencies, biographies of governors, and biographical data on members of the legislature. The division maintains a copy of telephone directories of all towns and cities in Oklahoma and a number of directories of cities and towns in other states. A wide range of reference and legal material is maintained, including such items as *U.S. Reports, U.S. Lawyer's Edition, Code of Federal Regulations, Supreme Court Reporter,* and *Federal Reporter.* General information and specific subject periodicals are also available to the legislator, and in the event a resource is not available within the Division, it can be requested on inter-library loan from another library. The inter-library loan service involves all libraries in Oklahoma and most libraries in other states.

Attorney General's Office

The attorney general's office may from time to time perform a variety of legal research for the individual legislator, as well as other state officials. By law, the attorney general's legal staff must answer the legal questions of any state officer, board, commission, or department, as well as any district attorney or state legislator.[7] Requests from individual legislators usually take one of two forms: a request for a formal, legal opinion regarding a point of law, or a request for an informal judgment concerning a legal question, usually pertaining to a legislative matter under consideration.

If a legislator needs a formal opinion from the attorney general, his office suggests the following guidelines to facilitate cooperation between the two branches of government. The legislator should be specific in his request so as to facilitate a precise answer. The request for an opinion must be made in writing and should contain the facts as the legislator knows them in addition to an enumeration of the statutes involved. The opinion request should be within the legislator's official area of concern. Technically, the attorney general or an assistant attorney general cannot issue opinions regarding questions outside the area of responsibility of the legislator. Since this is a vague and often misunderstood point of law, complicated by very broad and inclusive powers on the part of an individual legislator, lawmakers are often advised to avoid opinion requests beyond subjects relevant to their legislation.

Once the attorney general receives a written request, his office follows a standard procedure to dispose of the question. First, the request is assigned to an assistant attorney general who has expertise in the subject area (for instance, education, consumer affairs, or water resources). Secondly, after one or several assistant attorneys general receive the opinion request, a suggested opinion is prepared. This suggested opinion reflects the legal viewpoints of an assistant attorney general and does not necessarily reflect the ideas of the entire staff. Thirdly, the suggested opinion is given to the attorney general, who examines it and places it on a conference agenda. Fourth, a suggested opinion is considered in detail by the full staff in a staff opinion conference. In the conference each opinion is discussed, evaluated, and sometimes researched again until a majority of the attorneys can reach agreement. Finally, a written opinion, clearly favored by the staff, is issued by the attorney general. This final product is quite important in Oklahoma politics, since an opinion handed down by the attorney general has the effect of law until it is overturned by a court of jurisdiction or the Oklahoma Supreme Court.

If a legislator requires something less than a formal legal opinion, the attorney general may write a memorandum of law giving his opinion as a lawyer on the subject under inquiry. These informal responses to legal requests, however, do not have the force of law of an attorney general's opinion, but rather reflect the legal opinion of a lawyer in response to more informal questions. While such responses have no legal force in Oklahoma, they are usually viewed by legislators as competent legal evaluations concerning a point of law.

Cooperation between the legislature and the attorney general's office is well established in Oklahoma. In order to facilitate this cooperation and provide more systematic information, the attorney general's office publishes several opinion reports. Each month the office issues and makes available to all legislators a digest of attorney general's opinions handed down in the previous month. At the end of each legislative session a book of opinions is published giving the full text of all decisions handed down during the previous session. A complete copy of specific opinions may also be sent to any individual legislator upon request. While the Oklahoma legislature is primarily composed of attorneys, the complexity of legislation and legal matters places the attorney general's office at a key point in the lawmaking process.

Other State Agencies

While the only state agencies which have the statutory duty to provide services to the legislature are the Legislative Council, the Legislative Reference Division of the Oklahoma Department of Libraries, and the attorney general's office, all executive departments show a willingness to provide limited services to the legislature upon request. These services are often in the form of crucial information necessary for legislation. For example, the Tax Commission and Budget Office often work closely with related legislative committees to provide a level of expertise which may be lacking in the committee or on the Council. In other areas, the Oklahoma Department of Highways may be called upon by legislators to assist in research on highway construction or to provide maps and drafting services necessary to complete the redistricting of Oklahoma legislative districts. Other state agencies aid the legislature in such duties as bill drafting, advice, and manpower. In order to obtain such services, the Legislative Council or a member of the Council staff usually contacts the appropriate source. The result is often close cooperation between the legislature and various state agencies which is very necessary to provide information inputs to the development of legislation.

THE COURSE OF LEGISLATION

While all of the above services are invaluable aids to legislators, they are oriented toward the development of legislation prior to the actual introduction of a bill on the floor of the House or Senate. Once the necessary information is obtained, and the staff research and drafting process is completed, a bill enters a course of legislation with numerous and complex rules, procedures, and legal hurdles. In the Oklahoma legislature, as in most state legislatures, the process of passing a bill entails considerable research, debate, discussion, and cooperation among both House and Senate members. Seldom does one member of the legislature work alone—the passage of bills and resolutions is clearly a team effort.

The freshman legislator will seldom be able to rely upon "outside" experience to aid him in the bill passage process, even though he may be equipped with sufficient information and facts to develop legislation. For the most part, the stages of bill passage are unique to the legislative arena. Furthermore, the expression of legislative intent requires a tedious exactness of language that is often seen as cumbersome and unclear. It is a process where the game of politics is very important, but also where expertise and knowledge are invaluable aids. The veteran legislator, largely through trial and error, has learned the roads and inroads of bill passage, but the freshman must start from the beginning, as he often has very little experience to rely upon.

The following passages and Figure 2 outline the stages of bill passage.It is not intended to be complete, as each bill has its own character, and subsequent debate in committee hearings must deal with each piece of legislation separately. Nevertheless, the general rules apply to most formal legislative activity. The reader wishing greater detail may refer to the study guides on House and Senate rules found in the Appendix.

A bill must have a starting place; it must be introduced before the entire membership of either the Senate or House. There are two ways a Senator may introduce a bill before his colleagues. He may stand and address the presiding officer and, after he has obtained recognition, publicly notify the presiding officer of his intent to introduce a bill or resolution. Another method of introducing bills in the Senate is for a senator to deposit the bill(s) desired for introduction into a basket which is found on the Senate secretary's desk. The reading clerk will then read all bills contained in the basket when the order of business for the introduction of bills has been reached. The reading clerk reads the title of each bill and numbers the bills consecutively in the order they were read. With few exceptions the process is much the same in the House. In both branches of the legislature all bills contain the name or names of members presenting the proposed legislation as well as a caption or title which states the subject matter of the item to be considered. After introduction a bill proceeds to the "first reading." This is done by title only, and the bill is placed on the calendar under "Bills on Second Reading."

The next stage of the bill-passing process is the "second reading" on the next legislative day following the first reading. Again the bill is read by title only, and no discussion may ensue unless "ordered by the House." Such discussion is limited to the reading of the contents of the bill without any reference to its faults or merits. Under House rules no amendments or debates are allowed on bills or resolutions during the second reading. This rule also applies to the first reading. Once a bill has had a first and second reading, it must proceed to committee in the same form or language as introduced.

After the second reading, a bill is referred to committee, where committee hearings are held, and a subsequent report of the committee is given. Each bill is referred to the committee which is best able to discuss the bill in its original form. The committee hearings are held for the purpose of discussion and possible changes. If a committee refuses to consider a bill, it will "die" unless a two-thirds vote of the membership is achieved for a discharge. The committee may freely amend a measure, and it has authority to introduce bills on its own initiative. After a formal report is finalized

FIGURE 2

Course of a Bill Through the Oklahoma Legislature

HOUSE

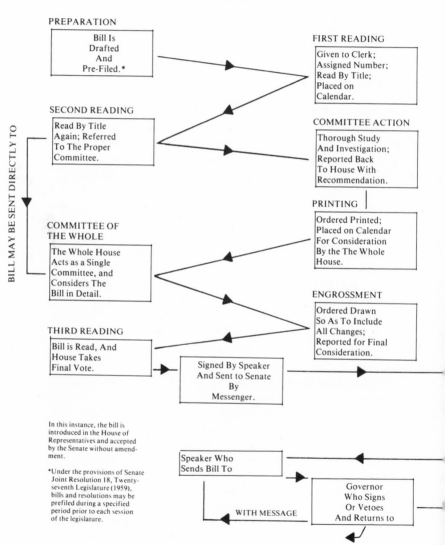

PREPARATION

Bill Is Drafted And Pre-Filed.*

FIRST READING

Given to Clerk; Assigned Number; Read By Title; Placed on Calendar.

SECOND READING

Read By Title Again; Referred To The Proper Committee.

COMMITTEE ACTION

Thorough Study And Investigation; Reported Back To House With Recommendation.

PRINTING

Ordered Printed; Placed on Calendar For Consideration By the The Whole House.

COMMITTEE OF THE WHOLE

The Whole House Acts as a Single Committee, and Considers The Bill in Detail.

ENGROSSMENT

Ordered Drawn So As To Include All Changes; Reported for Final Consideration.

THIRD READING

Bill is Read, And House Takes Final Vote.

Signed By Speaker And Sent to Senate By Messenger.

BILL MAY BE SENT DIRECTLY TO

In this instance, the bill is introduced in the House of Representatives and accepted by the Senate without amendment.

*Under the provisions of Senate Joint Resolution 18, Twenty-seventh Legislature (1959), bills and resolutions may be prefiled during a specified period prior to each session of the legislature.

Speaker Who Sends Bill To

Governor Who Signs Or Vetoes And Returns to

WITH MESSAGE

SENATE

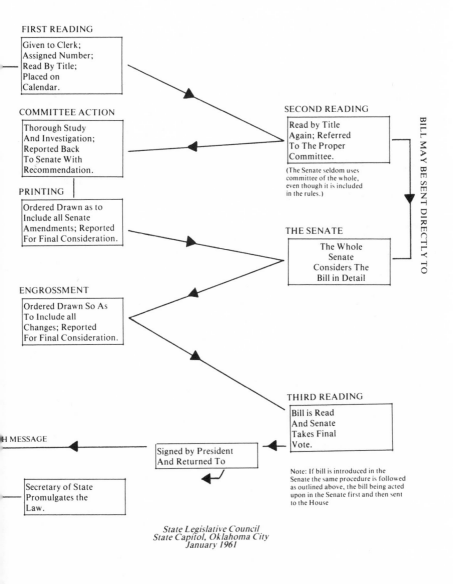

FIRST READING

Given to Clerk;
Assigned Number;
Read By Title;
Placed on
Calendar.

COMMITTEE ACTION

Thorough Study
And Investigation;
Reported Back
To Senate With
Recommendation.

PRINTING

Ordered Drawn as to
Include all Senate
Amendments; Reported
For Final Consideration.

ENGROSSMENT

Ordered Drawn So As
To Include all
Changes; Reported
For Final Consideration.

SECOND READING

Read by Title
Again; Referred
To The Proper
Committee.

(The Senate seldom uses
committee of the whole,
even though it is included
in the rules.)

THE SENATE

The Whole
Senate
Considers The
Bill in Detail

BILL MAY BE SENT DIRECTLY TO

THIRD READING

Bill is Read
And Senate
Takes Final
Vote.

Note: If bill is introduced in the
Senate the same procedure is followed
as outlined above, the bill being acted
upon in the Senate first and then sent
to the House

Signed by President
And Returned To

H MESSAGE

Secretary of State
Promulgates the
Law.

State Legislative Council
State Capitol, Oklahoma City
January 1961

(with minority reports possible), the committee recommends one of five basic motions: "do pass," "do pass as amended," " committee substitute do pass," "without recommendation," or " do not pass."

Following the committee report, the bill is printed and placed on the calendar and, at the proper time, referred to the Committee of the Whole, where the bill is reviewed and reported upon. Resolving into the Committee of the Whole is common in the House, but rarely used in the Senate. While the bill is before the Committee of the Whole, the legislator(s) who introduced the bill may be allowed a reasonable length of time in which to explain the bill. This discussion is limited to exposition of the bill and not its merits. The next step is the debate and amendments (if any) by the whole House. The length of debate and amendment suggestions depend primarily upon the nature and scope of the bill under consideration.

After the bill is engrossed in its final form, it receives a third reading and vote on final passage. No amendments can be made at the third reading unless unanimous consent is obtained. If the bill fails to pass, it may be referred to committee for further study and alteration, or the bill may receive no further consideration at all. If the latter occurs, the bill is "killed," and its progress through the bill passing stages ends. If the bill is referred back to committee, items not acceptable to the majority of the chamber may be altered in hopes of amending the bill so it is acceptable to the body as a whole. If the bill passes the House (or Senate) in its original or amended state, it is sent to the Senate (or House) for consideration.

Once the bill reaches the other house, the stages are much the same as those in the originating house. At first reading, the bill is only presented by title. After the second reading, the bill is sent to a committee, where committee hearings are held and a subsequent report of committee given. The bill is then placed in the Committee of the Whole. Following the review by the Committee of the Whole, the bill receives the third reading and vote on final passage. If the bill fails to pass, it may be sent back to committee for further consideration, or it may receive no further attention.

If the bill passes both houses in identical form, it is "enrolled" and sent to the governor. However, since few bills pass the House and Senate in identical form, the originating house must vote on the bill a second time containing changes initiated by the other chamber. If the first house accepts the amendments by the second house and passes the bill, it is "enrolled" and sent to the governor for signing. Yet at times the amendments made in the second house are not acceptable to the members of the first, and the bill must pass through several more stages before it is passed or rejected.

If the house of origin rejects the changes in the bill, it may be sent to a conference committee. Conference committees are composed of members from both houses, and the primary purpose of these committees is to iron out the differences between the two chambers. Such discussions can involve lengthy and hot debate in attempts to reach conclusions which will be acceptable to both houses. If and when the conference committee reaches the necessary agreements, a report of the conference committee is sent to each house.

When the report of the conference committee is received, each house votes to accept or reject the changes. If both houses accept the changes, the bill is "enrolled" and sent to the governor. Once a bill reaches the governor he may follow four steps. First, the governor may veto the bill, at which time it is returned to the house of origin with an explanation. A vetoed bill can be repassed in each house by a two-thirds vote of the elected membership, or by a three-fourths vote if an emergency clause is attached. Second, the governor may simply fail to sign the bill. If this occurs the bill will automatically become law five days after being received by the governor. Third, the governor may sign the bill as received, and it becomes law. Finally, he may pocket veto the bill by refusing to act within fifteen days after adjournment.

A procedural option which may occur at final vote concerns the immediate necessity of the bill under consideration. Two-thirds of the membership may place an emergency clause on the bill placing it in effect immediately. Otherwise, the bill becomes law ninety days after adjournment. If the governor vetoes an emergency, a three-fourths majority is required to override the veto. In recent sessions, a majority of bills have been declared emergencies.

TYPES OF LEGISLATIVE MEASURES

Although bills represent the primary form of legislative activity, each legislative session considers a variety of legislative products. In Oklahoma there are four fundamental types of products which in some form or another represent public policy. Each product may originate in either the House or the Senate, yet they vary in their intent, scope, and degree of authoritativeness. The primary product is a *bill* or proposed law. It represents the heart of legislation and may be introduced in either the House or the Senate, to be subsequently passed by each house and signed into law by the governor. A bill typically reflects a mixture of ideas from individual legislators, interested constituents, interest groups, and the various agencies of the executive branch.

A second legislative measure which can become public policy is the *joint resolution*. It is similar to a bill and must be approved jointly by both legislative chambers and the governor. If a joint resolution is approved by both houses and properly signed, it has the same effect as a law. A joint resolution, however, may have a less permanent character than a bill, and it may be enacted for the primary purpose of regulating and/or defining short-term policies. For example, a joint resolution may be enacted to direct the secretary of state to submit proposed constitutional amendments to a vote of the people. (It is unnecessary for the governor to sign a joint resolution when it involves submitting a legislative or constitutional question to the citizens.)

A third legislative product which is considered from time to time is the *concurrent resolution*. It is a special measure promoted from an interest in a specific subject by one or more members of each chamber. Since these interests are often similar, the concurrent resolution is jointly authored by members of the House and the Senate.

Finally, there is a residual category of legislative products which are introduced and voted upon, yet which do not become public policy as do other legislative products. They can take several forms and often express the feelings of one chamber. One type is the *citation*—a resolution approved by one chamber to congratulate a person or group of persons. As an example, the House of Representatives passed a citation commending several University of Oklahoma students for their assistance in the 1970 House reapportionment plan. Another type is the *memorial*—a resolution approved by one chamber generally upon the death of a prominent Oklahoman. Both the citation and the memorial are resolutions which indicate some laudatory feelings toward deserving individuals or groups who have performed service to the state or who have been successful in their individual endeavors. These resolutions serve to inform the people of Oklahoma that their state government recognizes deserving citizens; they therefore have a public relations tone aimed toward enhancing the citizen's view of the legislature. A final type of resolution is the *simple resolution* adopted by only one chamber. These measures do not have the force of law and are often adopted when making or amending existing rules and procedures. Such simple resolutions are matters of policy which affect the internal workings of one chamber. However, most serve to declare the "sense" of one house on some matter or to memorialize Congress.

Like other policy making bodies, the Oklahoma legislature is not characterized by a constant volume of activity from year to year. Indeed, the past eighteen years of legislative activity were characterized by an ebb and flow of legislation reflecting several underlying patterns. Throughout the entire eighteen years (fourteen sessions) from 1959 through 1976, there was a massive total of over 19,000 legislative products considered. In recent years, however, these products include bills carried over from the immediately preceding session and therefore represent some duplication.

Table 29 presents the figures for total legislation introduced in either bill or resolution form for the contemporary period. In general, more legislative activity originates in the House than in the Senate, and the trends for both chambers reflect the change from a single session every two years to annual sessions beginning in 1967. Indeed, the amount of legislation considered by the entire legislature peaks at over 1,700 bills and resolutions in 1965, and subsequently declines with the introduction of annual sessions. The availability of annual sessions obviously reduces the amount of legislation for each session, but in subsequent years the amount of activity per session has again increased to over 1,600 bills and resolutions in 1974 and 1976. In effect, each annual session now appears to be considering about the same number of bills and resolutions as were considered during a session when the legislature met only in odd-numbered years.

Part of this increase, however, is inflated by the possibility of carrying over legislation from a previous session. On the average, approximately forty-five per cent of all legislation in the first

TABLE 29.—Frequency of Legislative Measures (Bills and Resolutions) Introduced in the Oklahoma House and Senate: 1959-1976

Year	Chamber	Number Introduced	Number and Per Cent Carried over from Previous Session*	Total
1959	House	635		635
	Senate	508		508
	Total	1143		1143
1961	House	970		970
	Senate	603		603
	Total	1573		1573
1963	House	800		800
	Senate	521		521
	Total	1321		1321
1965	House	935		935
	Senate	771		771
	Total	1706		1706
1967	House	633		633
	Senate	579		579
	Total	1212		1212
1968	House	564	208 (33%)	772
	Senate	446	238 (41%)	704
	Total	1030	446 (37%)	1476
1969	House	613		613
	Senate	492		492
	Total	1105		1105

1970	House	418	297 (48%)	715
	Senate	392	213 (43%)	605
	Total	810	510 (46%)	1320
1971	House	660		660
	Senate	539		539
	Total	1199		1199
1972	House	388	313 (47%)	701
	Senate	369	210 (39%)	579
	Total	757	523 (44%)	1280
1973	House	629		629
	Senate	585		585
	Total	1214		1214
1974	House	544	325 (52%)	869
	Senate	525	260 (44%)	785
	Total	1069	585 (48%)	1654
1975	House	718		718
	Senate	609		609
	Total	1327		1327
1976	House	468	413 (58%)	881
	Senate	417	313 (51%)	730
	Total	885	726 (55%)	1611

*When the legislature converted to annual sessions after 1965, House and Senate rules were changed to permit bills still in committee (except for those in conference committee) at the time of adjournment of the first session to be carried over for consideration by the second session.

**TABLE 30.—Percentage of Bills Considered by the
Oklahoma House and Senate Relative to the
Total Number of Legislative Products: 1959-1976**

Year	House	Senate
1959	70%	71%
1961	78	73
1963	72	69
1965	67	66
1967	73	77
1968	76	76
1969	80	78
1970	81	77
1971	77	68
1972	83	77
1973	74	66
1974	76	74
1975	87	79
1976	89	82
Mean	77.4	73.8

legislative session is carried over to the second legislative session to be reconsidered. Additionally, as the frequency of legislation has increased in recent years, there is a tendency for a slightly increasing proportion of bills to be carried over to the second session. While this increased amount of legislative activity is potentially alarming, given the time constraints and individual competencies of legislators, it has not approached crisis proportions, since most recent sessions have completed business well within the ninety legislative days imposed by the constitution. The last ten sessions since 1967 have completed work in an average of seventy-five days. Nevertheless, the 35th legislature completed work only two days shy of the total 180 allowed, and it should be remembered that such "days" may be misleading since they are not coterminous with calendar days and refer instead to days when the legislature is officially in session. In other words, weekends and various recess days are not considered, even though legislators are typically at work during those periods.

Most of the legislative activity described above involves bills considered by the Oklahoma House and Senate. Table 30 presents the percentages of bills considered by each chamber relative to the total number of legislative products (which includes resolutions) from 1959 through 1976. It shows that the proportion of activity devoted to bill consideration has remained relatively constant in both houses vis-a-vis other possible categories of legislative products, with the exception of the most recent legislature. Although the House is characterized by a slightly greater proportion of activity devoted to bills, on the average, bills represent three-quarters of the legislative products examined by the entire legislature.

The above data are further reinforced by Tables 31 and 32, which present the relative proportion of legislative products devoted to joint resolutions, concurrent resolutions, and single-chamber resolutions. On the whole, these resolutions have been relatively stable in their proportion of total products over the years, with joint resolutions forming the smallest category for both House and Senate. On the average, about six per cent of legislative products are joint resolutions, eight per cent are concurrent resolutions, and another ten per cent are simple resolutions. The total resolutions therefore reflect approximately one-fourth of all legislative activity. However, there is an indication that more recent sessions have seen a larger per cent of bills introduced, and that the proportion of concurrent and simple resolutions has declined.

While the above figures refer to the consideration of various legislative products, there is a vast difference between the quantity of bills introduced and the number finally adopted or enacted by each chamber from 1959 through 1976. On the average over the years, less than four in ten bills introduced in either house are finally enacted (Table 33). Furthermore, the enactment rate for bills in the House is somewhat lower than in the Senate, and this is especially true for the most recent years. This indicates that while the volume of bills introduced in the House has generally increased in proportion to those introduced in the Senate, an even smaller number are being enacted. In the two most recent carry-over sessions, for example, the House passed less than one-fifth of the bills considered. Furthermore, the likelihood of eventually passing carry-over bills is

**TABLE 31.—Percentage of Resolutions Considered by the
Oklahoma House Relative to the
Total Number of Legislative Products: 1959-1976**

Year	Joint Resolutions		Concurrent Resolutions		House Resolutions	
1959	7%	(45)	9%	(58)	14%	(88)
1961	5	(48)	7	(70)	10	(100)
1963	7	(55)	10	(78)	12	(93)
1965	6	(59)	8	(73)	19	(179)
1967	5	(31)	7	(47)	14	(90)
1968	6	(45)	6	(49)	12	(91)
1969	6	(37)	6	(34)	9	(54)
1970	8	(55)	7	(47)	5	(34)
1971	4	(29)	8	(56)	10	(65)
1972	5	(32)	7	(46)	6	(44)
1973	4	(23)	10	(63)	13	(80)
1974	4	(38)	8	(66)	12	(104)
1975	4	(32)	4	(32)	4	(32)
1976	6	(52)	4	(31)	2	(17)
Mean	5.5%		7.2%		10.1%	

quite slim. Since 1971, for example, less than seven per cent of those carried over have been enacted by the legislature. Thus the citizen and the legislator—especially the House member—should realize that the odds of a bill being enacted are considerably less than even.

The success of any bill requires not only support from the majority of each chamber, but the final approval of the governor as well. Indeed, the governor may veto any bill or joint resolution passed by the legislature. While the veto is not officially a "legislative measure," but rather an executive prerogative, it must be considered in the context of our discussion of such measures. Technically, there are several types of action which may be taken by the state's chief executive. The governor may approve a bill by signing it into law within a period of five days of receipt of the legislation (Sundays excepted). If the governor approves the bill it

TABLE 32.—Percentage of Resolutions Considered by the
Oklahoma Senate Relative to the
Total Number of Legislative Products: 1959-1976

Year	Joint Resolutions		Concurrent Resolutions		Senate Resolutions	
1959	8%	(39)	6%	(32)	15%	(77)
1961	7	(41)	9	(56)	11	(65)
1963	7	(34)	12	(63)	13	(67)
1965	6	(50)	12	(91)	16	(123)
1967	8	(44)	6	(33)	10	(59)
1968	8	(57)	8	(56)	8	(58)
1969	5	(26)	8	(39)	9	(42)
1970	7	(44)	9	(56)	6	(37)
1971	7	(40)	13	(68)	12	(67)
1972	6	(34)	10	(57)	7	(40)
1973	6	(36)	15	(89)	13	(74)
1974	6	(49)	10	(78)	10	(80)
1975	7	(40)	8	(47)	6	(39)
1976	7	(54)	6	(42)	5	(37)
Mean	6.8%		9.4%		10.1%	

becomes Oklahoma law, and it is filed with the secretary of state and subsequently officially printed in the Oklahoma session laws. Yet the governor may take another action which results in a bill becoming law—he may let the bill rest for a period of five days, thus allowing it to become law without his signature. The reasons for this type of executive action are varied and are highly dependent upon the particular measure under consideration. Sometimes a governor personally opposes a bill yet is reasonably sure that his veto will be overriden by the legislature. He therefore permits it to become law without his personal stamp of approval. Although the legislature's initial intent is successful, the governor has shown his disapproval symbolically by letting it become law without his signature.

As suggested previously, the governor may also *veto* legislation.

**TABLE 33.—Percentage of Bills Enacted by the Oklahoma House
and Senate Relative to the
Total Number of Bills Considered: 1959-1976**

Year	House	Senate
1959	40% (176)	38% (136)
1961	48 (358)	41 (179)
1963	40 (229)	40 (143)
1965	47 (294)	47 (238)
1967	41 (190)	47 (209)
1968	35 (204)	40 (211)
1969	41 (200)	40 (152)
1970	30 (174)	35 (164)
1971	37 (190)	45 (163)
1972	21 (124)	29 (128)
1973	31 (142)	35 (136)
1974	18 (121)	33 (189)
1975	33 (205)	34 (166)
1976	19 (148)	24 (146)
Mean	34.4%	37.7%

Any bill can be rejected by simply returning it to the house in which it originated. Such action must take place within five days after receiving a bill and is accompanied by a veto message setting forth the specific reasons for rejection. Once the originating chamber receives the bill, it has several options. It may be rewritten so as to accommodate the wishes of the governor, thereby insuring its subsequent enactment. Quite often, however, the suggestions of the governor with regard to the vetoed bill will not be acceptable to the members in the originating house or, for that matter, in the other chamber. Such a situation often results in a complex and difficult political battle, with a group of legislators squarely facing the governor on the issue. Since there are various political risks involved in such a conflict, the importance, sensitivity, and urgency of the bill are taken into account by the legislature. If success is to be achieved by either party, however, the result is usually some form of compromise. Of course, this is only one form of final compromise following a series of previous compromises between individual legislators and between the two chambers. As one representative reminded us recently, compromise is "as much a part of your life as the clothes you wear." If compromise is impossible, or conflict extremely severe, the originating house has the final choice of scrapping the bill, either permanently or until a later session. The avoidance of conflict is often the overriding consideration.

Another option open to the goveror is the *item veto*. Unlike the president of the United States, who must accept or reject a bill in its entirety, the governor of Oklahoma may veto certain parts of bills, yet this power is limited to appropriations measures. Such bills finally become law except for those items specifically vetoed by the governor. If the item veto is not acceptable to the legislature, it may be overridden by an extraordinary majority of both houses (two-thirds, or three-fourths if an emergency).

A final action which may be taken by the governor is termed the *pocket veto*. This prerogative is employed near the end of a legislative session and refers to the governor's refusal to sign a bill within fifteen days after adjournment. In other words, if the governor receives a bill several days prior to legislative adjournment, and he wishes to "kill" the bill without formally vetoing it, he simply fails to act on it within a fifteen-day period. This action effectively vetoes a bill without the governor actually having to return it to the originating house. The only appeal is to start over again in the following year.

The above actions are indicative of several important powers which reside with the office of the governor. The governor's primary influence, however, is in the development of legislation—which if carefully pursued, avoids the veto problem. Indeed, few governors have placed substantial reliance on veto powers, and this is especially true for the most recent period. Since 1959, consistently less than two per cent of all bills considered were actually vetoed by a governor, and in the most recent period since 1971, a Democratic governor working with a Democratic legislature vetoed less than one per cent of all bills introduced.

Therefore, when a governor chooses selectively to veto an item, it is likely to reflect his strong personal sentiment. The most obvious reason for an executive veto is that the governor simply does not approve of the proposed law. Although this appears to be a simple matter on the surface, it must be remembered that the disapproval of a bill has many facets. For example, disapproval by the governor may focus on the financing necessary to implement a proposed law. When the governor meets with both houses during the first week of each new session, he outlines his proposed state budget, which has been carefully developed with the help of other executive agencies and various legislators. Since one of the governor's primary inputs to the legislative process is reflected in his budget message, potential conflicts are most likely to arise from this source. Yet not all bills that are vetoed are necessarily appropriations measures. Under special conditions public opinion, or the expression of interest group attitudes toward a bill, may become sufficiently intense and visible so as to encourage the governor to exercise this veto prerogative. In such instances, a governor is likely to draw on his perception of public opinion as a rationale for the veto.

Finally, partisan considerations may also enter the veto equation. While such effects are most likely to occur during times when the legislature and governor are from two opposing political parties, an examination of the veto patterns for the 1962-1970 period, when Oklahoma had two Republican governors, suggests that visible partisan considerations may not translate into veto behavior. During this eight-year period there is little evidence to suggest that a legislature controlled by the Democrats had any particular veto problems with Republican governors. On the other hand, these veto statistics fail to represent an important partisan consideration—that some legislative measures are simply not introduced or passed if the probability of a veto is high.

THE COMMITTEE SYSTEM

The final component of public policy enactment is a key subsystem of the legislative process: the standing committees. In the Oklahoma legislature, as in many other states, the committee system is an integral part of legislating. Each lawmaker finds himself working in the committee system, and whatever the committee, the work performed has important consequences shaping the legislation that eventually becomes law.

Legislative committees in the fifty states vary somewhat in power and influence, and on the whole, standing committees are rarely as powerful and as independent as those in Congress. Committees in the various state legislatures tend to be more numerous than in Congress, and more decisive action is likely to take place on the floor of the legislature. Furthermore, state legislative committees are less likely to strangle legislation as so frequently occurs in Washington.[8] A variety of factors, including lack of staff, time limits on sessions, high legislative turnover, and a larger number of standing committees partially account for the weaker state legislative committee systems throughout the nation.[9] Indeed, Malcolm Jewell suggests that state legislative standing committees "usually are but pale shadows of their congressional counterparts"[10] largely because legislatures meet for very limited time periods, thereby limiting the examination of specific legislative measures. Their effectiveness tends to be further constrained by a tendency for important legislation to be introduced late in each session.

The dilution of power in legislative standing committees may also be traced to the number of committees within the system. An excessive number often results in split sources of power, thus reducing the effectiveness of the committee system. In recent years some state legislatures have recognized the organizational problems associated with large numbers of standing committees and have reduced them. By 1965, the median number of senate and house standing committees in the fifty states was twenty,[11] but at that time in Oklahoma each chamber had thirty-six standing committees. As we shall see shortly, the number of committees in the Oklahoma legislature was subsequently reduced, only to be followed by a later and considerable expansion.

In addition to the number of committees, their size and rate of membership turnover determine the individual legislator's ability to develop subject expertise. Comparisons between the states and Congress suggest that in most state legislatures the majority of committee members rarely serve as long as congressional committee members.[12] In order to acquire specialization, the members and the chairman must serve long enough to become familiar with the subject matter addressed by the committee. The acquisition of knowledge takes time as well as intense involvement in specialized areas of legislative concern. When the legislative turnover rate is high, or when committee members are constantly shifted from committee to committee, it is difficult for them to develop an area of specialization. Although these actions tend to weaken the effectiveness of the entire committee system, it is also possible that an excessive multiplication of committees and excessive specialization results in the avoidance of general concerns and overall effects. That is, excessive specialization may lead to fragmentation, which becomes a serious stumbling block in the policy making process.

In Oklahoma it is not uncommon to find legislators shifted in their committee assignments. The seniority system does not function with the same degree of rigor as in Congressional legislative committees, and sometimes these assignments are more often based upon political favoritism which can be translated readily into support for the legislative leadership. The House leadership in Oklahoma has virtually unlimited power in filling standing committee seats. The Senate leadership's appointment power is broad, but in actual practice the president pro tempore has more constraints on his power to make appointments. In the state Senate, standing committee members are actually elected by the Senate, yet the party of the president pro tempore has a dominant say in the matter. The Senate presiding officer also has the power to appoint members to temporary and special committees. Such power and influence exercised by Oklahoma's legislative leadership has often resulted in a lack of continuity in committee membership from session to session. The end product may well be a committee composed of loyal supporters of the leadership and achieved at some expense to the development of specialization and competency.

Not all of the above weaknesses attributed to state legislative committee systems are necessarily present in Oklahoma. It has been suggested, for example, that committees exercise more influence in one-party states where the governor does not exert strong leadership,[13] yet this is also apparently dependent upon how members receive their assignments.[14] On the whole, Oklahoma tends to deviate slightly from the norm set by other states. Legislative power in Oklahoma tends to be less centralized, thereby enabling committees to operate more independently than in highly centralized states.[15]

Recent evidence for Oklahoma also suggests that there are important differences between the House and Senate. As part of the Bureau of Government Research Oklahoma Legislative Study in 1972, lawmakers were asked whether legislative committees or legislative leadership were more important in the process in their respective chambers. Fifty-two per cent of the senators indicated that legislative committees or subcommittees were more important, and only twenty-four per cent suggested legislative leadership, with the remaining undecided. But in the House, the evidence is reversed: forty-seven per cent chose legislative leadership as more important, while only twenty-six per cent indicated that committees played the key role in the legislative process. While legislative leaders in both houses are powerful, the differences undoubtedly reflect the more powerful position of the House speaker in comparison to the president pro tempore, and the fact that the Senate is characterized by smaller and less centralized pockets of influence. The relative power of Senate committees also reflects their smaller size, whereas the House system tends to be more unwieldy.

Committee Functions

The committee system is a multipurpose component of the entire legislative process, and like most complicated systems it performs a variety of duties. The basic function of Oklahoma legislative committees is to allow detailed study of pending legislation. Bills and resolutions may be studied and evaluated in other ways, for instance, by individual legislators or the body as a whole, but in the committees pending bills receive the most detailed and critical scrutiny.

One legislator suggested to us that the purpose of committees was to "screen (by killing or passing), correct, and legalize (by putting in constitutional form) bills introduced by legislators." This task is accomplished by a relatively small group of lawmakers, many of whom have substantive interest and expertise in certain policy areas. Aside from allowing the committee members the opportunity to evaluate the merits of bills, there is an important activity which benefits the entire evaluation process: the public hearing. During committee deliberations there is a public hearing which gives the general public, lobbyists, and interest groups the opportunity to indicate the pros and cons of a bill under consideration. The public hearings allow the committee members an extended examination of the details of a bill, and enable the citizenry to get involved in the legislative process.

Some committee hearings in Oklahoma have been held behind closed doors, and committees have had discretionary power to decide whether a public hearing will be held at all. However, recent "sunshine" rule changes have served to open the committee process to greater public scrutiny. Upon written request of a member, House committees must hold a hearing on a bill or resolution, public notice must be given, and hearings must be held within three days of the request. In addition, all committee votes must be in open, public meetings. In the Senate, public hearings may be required by majority vote of the committee, and upon request of any committee member, public votes are recorded. In addition, no committee may meet on a bill or resolution until the chairman has notified all members, and no action can be taken to report a bill or resolution without a quorum present.

A second function of the committee is closely related to the first—to siphon out legislation. Many bills are authored and introduced, and not all bills are of equal importance or value. The committees attempt to separate the good legislation from the bad. Committee members generally feel that if a bill cannot get through a committee, it cannot pass the entire body. Thus, in screening bills the members of the committee act as pre-evaluators of the merits of a bill. The capacity to determine the merits is an important and powerful one, but as a small group the committee represents a microcosm of the entire legislative body, and the elimination of legislation that for various reasons would not be acceptable to the body as a whole saves a great deal of time for each lawmaker. Every legislative day is filled with activity and the duties of bill passing. Because the committee limits the number of bills which are placed on the calendar, more time can be devoted to the task of passing legislation which by committee standards is good enough to be considered by the chamber as a whole.

Thirdly, the committee is a pool of legislative policy expertise.

Members are generally experts on the subject addressed by the committee, perhaps even more so than the original author(s) of a given bill. The author of a bill is often not an expert in the subject area of his proposed legislation; a fact which does not diminish the capabilities of a legislator, as it is virtually impossible for everyone to be an expert on all legislative areas. The committee is created to have expertise in a given area, and this pool of expertise can evaluate the merits and faults of a bill more adequately than any individual can. Furthermore, since amendments may be made in the committee, the expertise of each committee member is a valuable aid in evaluating a bill so that it will cover only those areas which can legally be initiated. The committee may also expand or reduce the focus of a bill or insert or delete phrases that would benefit its passage.

A fourth and somewhat subtle function of the committee system involves killing legislation at the request of the author. At some time during a legislator's career he may be asked to author a bill at the request of certain constituents. Often such legislation is basically of interest to small groups within a legislator's district and does not benefit his entire constituency or the state. A lawmaker may be obliged to author this type of bill, but he sometimes realizes that it should not be passed when other factors are taken into account. At this stage the author(s) can rely upon the committee to kill the bill before it can be debated on the floor. By permitting the committee to stop the bill, the legislator can remain in good faith with the constituents who lobbied for it.

Number of Committees

In any complex organization there is a tendency to create large numbers of secondary or tertiary units to facilitate specialization, discrimination, and the flow of information. Standing committees have such a function in the legislature, but to be effective the number of committees must be limited in order to minimize wasted time and duplication of specialization. In the Oklahoma legislature there has been a tendency to create rather large numbers of stan-

TABLE 34.—Number of Standing Committees in the Oklahoma House and Senate: 1959-1976

Year	House	Senate
1959	38	33
1961	39	34
1963	39	36
1965	36	36
1967-68	35	12
1969-70	15	15
1971-72	32	29
1973-74	34	29
1975-76	34	24

ding committees, considerably higher than the national average. Table 34 presents data on the number of standing committees in the Oklahoma House and Senate from 1959 through 1976.

There have only been two instances throughout the entire period when the total number of committees was below the national median of twenty in 1965. These instances include the Senate in 1967-68 and both houses of the legislature in 1969-70. While there was an attempt during these latter years to reduce the number of committees (accompanied by a formal subcommittee structure), it did not become a trend as the Oklahoma legislature quickly returned to an excessive number of standing committees shortly thereafter. The large reduction in the number of standing committees in the Senate in 1967 was accomplished by the Senate leadership: the president pro tempore reduced the number of standing committees in an attempt to develop greater efficiency in the committee system. This overture on the part of the Senate was subsequently followed by the House leadership, so that in 1969-70 both the Senate and House had fifteen parallel standing committees. In 1971, the House leadership pushed for a return to the original committee system, and the Senate leadership followed these initiatives to expand committees.

TABLE 35.— Range in Size of Oklahoma House and Senate Standing Committees: 1959-1976

Year	House	Senate
1959	2-30	3-26
1961	2-31	3-20
1963	4-32	3-24
1965	3-32	3-28
1967-68	3-30	2-20
1969-70	10-28	7-18
1971-72	4-29	3-21
1973-74	2-28	1-18
1975-76	2-26	3-14

It should be remembered that legislative leaders often maintain and secure political support through committee appointments. When the number of committees in a chamber is decreased, it often reduces the flexibility of the leadership and places constraints on their bases of support. It is also not uncommon for legislative leaders to create new committees in an attempt to secure the loyalty of a legislator or to repay lawmakers for past support. Although it is difficult to ascertain the extent of this activity in the Oklahoma legislature, the practice has been a common one in the legislative process.

Table 34 also indicates that the House normally has more standing committees than the Senate. Since there are no formal requirements that both chambers have an equal number of committees, each body's leadership must decide on the total number. Since there are twice as many House members as there are state senators, the House speaker has greater flexibility than the president pro tempore in the number of committees he can fill, as well as the number of legislators he can appoint to serve on any single committee. Future action on the number of committees in the Oklahoma legislature is uncertain and highly dependent upon chamber leadership. Obviously, any attempt to reduce the number of committees will have to be a cooperative effort between both chambers, since unparallel committee systems are likely to make the legislative process more unwieldy.

Committee Assignments

The appointment of a legislator to a standing committee is not simply a matter of political favoritism. Individual preferences are considered in making committee assignments, and it is usual practice for the speaker of the House and president pro tempore of the Senate to send out committee preference forms prior to the beginning of a regular session. In the House, the speaker will try to place each member on one major committee, such as appropriations, revenue and taxation, judiciary, or roads and highways. In addition to placing each member on at least one major committee, the speaker also attempts to assign each member to a committee he prefers. The logic behind this procedure is two-fold: first, such attempts provide for better rapport between the members and the speaker; and secondly, it is felt that if a member is on a preferred committee, he will be more active and attentive, since he is interested in the committee subject area. Aside from the general powers of the speaker with regard to committee assignments, the maximum number of standing committees each member may serve on, as well as the maximum number of members on any single committee, is regulated by House rules. In recent legislative sessions the maximum number of committees any one House member may serve on has been limited to four, and the maximum number of members who can be appointed to any single committee is limited to thirty. Although these limits are usually adhered to, "stretching" the House rules is not an uncommon occurrence.

In the Senate, the president pro tempore possesses much the same power as the speaker of the House. The only important difference is a technical one in that the president pro tempore makes committee recommendations which are in turn followed by the Rules Committee, which he appoints. Recent Senate rules place the maximum number of committees any one senator may serve on at four. However, there are several minor Senate standing committees where an appointment does not count toward the maximum. Given the above exclusions, it is possible for a Senator to stay within the rules and serve on a total of five committees.

The actual number of committee assignments varies somewhat from session to session, but on the average, legislators in both chambers serve on four to six committees. In the 1973-74 legislature, for example, the average number of committees for House members was 4.2, and the average for Senators was 4.6. The range of committee appointments for senators was from three to five. However, only one state senator served on three committees, whereas over twenty senators served on at least five. The range in the House is from one to five appointments per member. However, two House members served on only one committee, while over twenty members were appointed to five.

The size of the various standing committees in the House and Senate has also varied over time and by chamber. Table 35 presents the ranges in the size of standing committees in both chambers from 1959 through 1976. The low end of the ranges indicate fewer appointments to smaller and less important legislative committees, such as Senate or House administration, and engrossed and enrolled bills. Each chamber also tends to have at least one excessively large committee. On the whole, however, such important committees as appropriations and judiciary tend to have a large number of appointees. The trend in the minimum size of House and Senate committees also reflects the evidence presented in Table 34 about the number of standing committees. For example, when the legislature substantially reduced the number of committees in both houses in 1969-70, the minimum size of committees increased to seven in the Senate and ten in the House. However, the data also indicate that the size of the largest committees does not necessarily increase with a reduction in the number of standing committees. The data in Table 35 also indicate larger committees in the House over time, reflecting that chamber's magnitude.

Since the appointment process in both the House and Senate takes into account individual preferences of lawmakers, it is reasonable to expect that most members are satisfied with committee assignments. As part of the Oklahoma Legislative Study in 1972, we asked lawmakers how satisfied they were with committee assignments, and the data indicate parallel feelings in both houses: sixty-two per cent of the Senate respondents and fifty-seven per cent of the House members indicated that they were "very satisfied" with committee appointments, while another thirty-five per cent of both chambers were "satisfied." Indeed, only two to four per cent of either chamber were "dissatisfied" or "very dissatisfied." With this high level of committee appointment satisfaction, any further moves to decrease the number of committees is unlikely to be acceptable. Furthermore, some have suggested that the proliferation of committees in state legislatures enables most members to appear impressive.[16]

Appointment of Committee Chairmen

Just as committee assignments are determined by the president pro tempore and speaker for their respective houses, the appointment of committee chairmen also rests in their hands. Although there is no formal rule which promotes the most senior member to chair a committee, the president pro tempore and speaker use length of service as an important criterion. Each house leader realizes the importance of assigning competent and knowledgeable legislators to chair committees, and it is felt that length of legislative service is correlated with legislative expertise. An experienced legislator has acquired a great deal of knowledge about subject matter, as well as knowing how to get things done.

Another, but much more political consideration in assigning chairmanships is the support the president pro tempore and speaker receive from the members. Since the committee chairmen must work very closely with their respective house leaders, past support is an important criterion. It is assumed that if the chamber leaders and committee chairmen can work together in a harmonious manner, the relationship will approach that of a "team effort".

As in any series of decisions, a mistake can be made, and the appointment of committee chairmen is no exception. The most noted mistake is the appointment of a legislator to chair a committee when he has insufficient expertise to function as a viable and effective chairman. This situation may occur when a chairmanship opening is created, and another legislator desires the position because of his tenure and/or past support given to the president pro tempore or speaker. Such events are not commonplace, but they do occur.

Standing committees also have vice chairmen, but they are without power unless it is given to them by the committee chairman or exercised in the absence of the chairman.

Powers and Duties of Chairmen

The primary power of the committee chairman relates to setting the agenda of business. The importance of this power rests in the chairman's capacity to call up or refuse to consider bills. In the past, if a particular piece of legislation was perceived to be inadequate by the chairman he could simply refuse to consider it. One rare procedure was available to force the chairman to consider a bill: a petition could be circulated in the committee asking that the bill be heard and discussed by the committee as a whole. Such a petition could be initiated and circulated by anyone: citizens, legislators, or the author of the bill. A petition of this type carried no legal force, but when used, it allowed the committee system to be more democratic in practice and in certain instances curtailed the power of committee chairmen.

But with recent rule changes mentioned earlier, there are fewer opportunities for domination by a chairman. Furthermore, Senate rules now provide that the author of a bill shall be notified of the committee's consideration and be given an opportunity to be heard. House rules entitle a bill or resolution to a vote upon the author's written request. It is generally agreed that the chairmen of committees need the power to determine the agenda, and that chairmen are much more than figureheads—more than simple arbiters of parliamentary procedure—yet they are not omnipotent.

A primary duty of the committee chairman is to decide what legislation will be heard and at what time it will be heard. If, for example, public sentiment is against a bill, and the chairman favors it, he will bring the bill up quickly (that is, place it on the agenda so it will be considered early in the committee process). However, if the chairman favors a particular piece of legislation, and there is no public sentiment for the bill, he may prefer to wait until public interest in the bill has developed before considering it. As was explained by one former committee chairman, "why bring up a bill on legalized horse racing?" According to this legislator, such a bill is doomed from the start, and so the committee chairman kills it before it gets to the floor. However, such instances are less likely to occur with newly imposed constraints on a chairman's power.

A second and somewhat implied duty of the committee chairman is that he be the most informed and knowledgeable member of the committee. The committee chairman should have, and usually does possess, the most expertise in the area of the committee he chairs. By possessing the greatest amount of subject expertise, the chairman can function better as a leader and subsequently provide more direction to the committee.

Thirdly, the chairman has the duty of presiding over the committee meetings. In his leadership role he ensures the meeting is conducted in a fair and equitable manner. Performance of these duties augments the speed and accuracy by which bills are discussed and evaluated.

Fourth, the committee chairman has the duty to be "tough." As one legislator told us, he must be "tough enough and strong enough" to say, for instance, when a bill will not be considered for discussion. This is a subtle duty, but an important one: a weak chairman can become an ineffective chairman, and the committee is a place of action requiring quick and decisive behavior.

Finally, the chairman has several technical duties related to his job. He must keep track of all committee business (here the chairman's duties are augmented by the aid of a committee secretary). One important order of business is to trace and monitor all amendments and to keep such amendments in proper order. Closely allied to this technical duty of recording all amendments is the element of "timing." The chairman is aware that amendments may pass or fail depending upon who is present.

Committee Procedure

The first order of business in a committee meeting is for the chairman to call the meeting to order. Next, the roll is called, and the committee refers to the agenda. Preceding the actual meeting, the chairman develops an agenda, which is followed throughout the proceedings. In special circumstances the agenda may be altered, but generally the meeting proceeds along the specified lines.

Once a bill is called up for consideration, the committee members will hear an explanation of the bill from the author. This is an expository practice and is not for the purpose of argumentation. During this time any member of the committee may ask questions of the author. These questions are limited to the gathering of information, to answer such questions as, "What will the bill do?" or "Why do you think this bill is necessary?" The questions perform two functions: first, they allow the committee members to gather information concerning the nature and intent of the bill; and secondly, such questions give the author an opportunity to defend his bill. Since committee meetings by their structure and purpose do not allow for positive argumentation from the author, the second point is in fact a "stretching of the rules."

In committee meetings the author of a bill does not debate the bill unless the author is a member of the committee. Therefore, he must secure some member of the committee to support and debate the bill. Debate may occur in committee prior to and after amendments are completed, or when the bill is accepted without amendments. A debate usually occurs prior to the "do pass" motion. Once all the amendments have been completed, or if none are made, any member of the committee suggests a motion, which must receive a second. If there is no second on a "do pass" motion, the bill is killed. If the motion is seconded, debate follows concerning the amended bill. Prior to the actual debate the chairman will inform the members, "You have heard the motion—any debate?" The ensuing debate, if any, is rather informal, and according to the rules the member making the motion is entitled to be the last pro speaker.

There are five types of committee reports, each having its own importance. (1) The *do pass recommendation* from a committee sends the bill to the Committee of the Whole, where the bill is placed on the calendar for a floor vote. If the committee has added amendments, it might recommend *do pass as amended*. (2) The *do not pass* recommendation is rare. Once this recommendation has been made, the bill is subject to a floor vote—but the floor will usually not vote upon a bill receiving a *do not pass* from committee. (3) Another rare committee report is where the committee votes on the bill, but votes *without* giving a *recommendation*. In this case there is no strong feeling one way or the other among the committee members, but they feel the House or Senate body should vote on the bill. (4) The *report progress* measure keeps the bill in committee and off the floor. Such a recommendation is usually used to kill a bill in committee. (5) The *committee substitute do pass* alters the bill as received in some manner. In the House a bill may be rewritten, but must deal with the same subject as the original. The Senate committees may initiate what is called a "shucked bill," where the subject itself is changed. The House rules forbid the creation of "shucked bills."

Interim and Special Committees

In addition to the regular standing committees, either house may appoint special or select committees. This is done when problem areas fall outside usual committee jurisdiction, or when one of the houses decides to conduct an investigation. The conference committee is a type of special committee; it is actually two committees appointed by the presiding officers of each house to resolve differences in bills. The two houses may also appoint joint committees (standing or special). For the Oklahoma committee system those committees empowered to meet during the sessions do not have the power to meet during the intervals unless they are specifically authorized. Interim committees are special creatures of the Legislative Council.

Committee Jurisdiction

Committee jurisdiction is determined by the speaker of the house or the president pro tempore of the Senate. Each leader has the power to assign all bills to committees. In the actual assigning of bills the president pro tempore and speaker need not assign a bill to the "proper committee." This is a means of killing a bill in committee. An example of this procedure as it applies to the House is when the Speaker assigns a bill to the Ways and Means Committee.

This committee tends to be a catch-all committee for unfavorable bills and is sometimes referred to as the "no way and no means" committee. Technically, the only jurisdiction a committee has rests with the five committee reports it can recommend.

THE COMPONENTS OF POLICY ENACTMENT

The above discussion has enumerated four key components of the policy enactment process in the Oklahoma legislature. They include a variety of political actors and formal procedures governing their action: information inputs from within the legislature (largely the Legislative Council) and those from such extralegislative state agencies as the Oklahoma Department of Libraries and the attorney general's office; formal procedures and "course rules," which guide the passage of legislation; rules prescribing the range and types of legislative measures possible; and the committee system which enables detailed scrutiny of policy proposals. Since all of these components relate to more formal aspects of legislating, the next chapter will examine less formal factors influencing roll call voting.

CHAPTER 4

Legislative Behavior and Roll Call Voting

Roll call votes are the most important outputs of legislative activity. They have clear policy significance, and offer a variety of information about the individual legislator as he is forced to choose formally between competing demands from constituents, pressure groups, his party leadership, colleagues, and his own conscience. A legislators' public role is revealed by his voting behavior. Yet an analysis of roll call votes does not necessarily tell us the causes of decisions simply because they are recorded and capable of easy measurement.

As suggested in the previous chapter, the enactment of public policy is a complex process, from which roll call votes are only one recorded output. While they may represent the most significant decisions, they are not necessarily the most decisive—a variety of actions throughout the policy making process shape ultimate outcomes. Furthermore, as indicated in Chapter 2, a knowledge of legislators' private roles may contribute significantly to our understanding of legislative behavior, yet their precise influence on roll call voting may be difficult to measure. Figure 1 in Chapter 2 presents a general role model of legislative activity showing individual personal characteristics, environmental and constituency characteristics, and legislative experiences and chamber characteristics, as they influence the role conceptions that are the basis for a variety of legislative actions. This chapter's focus on roll call voting must be read in light of these previous discussions of role, the various stages of the policy enactment process, and subsequent discussions of specific norms and relationships with interest groups and constituents. When a familiarity with roll call analysis is added to knowledge of the other subjects of this book, it should enable the reader to judge the complex array of influences on legislative decisions and the relative importance of different and conflicting cues on individual legislators in Oklahoma.

Roll call votes are more likely to tell us how legislators vote the way they do than to offer precise information about why legislators make specific choices. An answer to the why question obviously requires an examination of a variety of factors discussed throughout the book. As Jewell states:

A legislator who votes for the Governor's bill to expand the state park program may do so because he belongs to the Governor's party, because he serves on the committee that studied and recommended the bill, because his constituents hope to get a park in their district, or perhaps because he likes to spend his vacations camping and appreciates the need for state parks.[1]

With such reservations in mind, including warnings about the noncontroversial nature of many roll call votes in American legislatures, the following pages describe a variety of influences on voting that are measurable and frequently treated in analyses of state legislatures and the U.S. Congress. Our discussion is guided by a general model of roll call voting which highlights the importance of forces internal to the legislature, the pressures from outside the chambers, and their complex interactions. The following model suggests that both internal and external forces operate on a legislator's individual conscience and judgment to shape subsequent policy decisions in roll call votes.[2]

Research on state roll call voting will be analyzed in terms of the above model, and inferences will be made to Oklahoma on the basis of findings in other states as well as specific roll call research on the Sooner state.

INTERNAL FORCES ON DECISIONS

A variety of factors, largely internal to the legislature, influence subsequent decisions made by individual lawmakers. This range of influences includes political party forces, cues from colleagues, and a vast array of individual characteristics and legislative rules and procedures. While individual characteristics such as personality traits, experience, and socioeconomic standing, as well as legislative procedures, undoubtedly have an influence on roll call voting in particular circumstances, they tend to have no systematic or uniform impact that is generalizable to a wide range of cases. Socioeconomic characteristics, for example, are highly skewed in the legislature, and there is little variation between members. Furthermore, tenure and experience are not likely to determine individual roll call votes, nor are rules and procedures, which tend to

FIGURE 3

A Model of Influences on Roll Call Voting

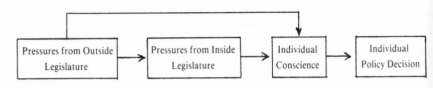

be rather uniform across a variety of issue areas. For these and other reasons, the bulk of research on internal forces shaping roll call voting has focused on the influences of party and of cues from colleagues resulting from legislative interaction.

Party Influences

Of all internal and external forces associated with legislative decision making, political party influences are generally viewed as most important, especially in comparison with regional interests, the personal characteristics of legislators, or urban-rural differences. Yet the isolation of party influences poses a variety of problems in legislative analysis, especially among less competitive states such as Oklahoma.

In the United States a "responsible party" model rarely operates, and in many areas it is virtually nonexistent. Party impacts on voting not only presuppose some level of competition between the two major political parties, but requires that state parties develop relatively consistent and different policy positions in matters of interest to the state, and that such differences are perceived by the electorate. Since these conditions are rarely found, party conflict in the states is difficult to analyze, especially with the presence of many unanimous or near unanimous votes in state legislatures. Partisan differences and the resultant partisan conflict exist in the American states, yet when they occur, the differences occur largely by issue areas.

When party is found to be significant, it may be a surrogate for other factors. For example, Democrats and Republicans may come from very different constituencies, have different personal backgrounds and different views, or the differences between Democrats and Republicans within the legislature may reflect more informal friendship groups indirectly tied to party. That is, partisan differences may simply be a reflection of differences among constituents and legislators. Some of these differences may be traced in several of the fifty states (for instance, in New York with its division between upstate conservatives and Republicans on the one hand and downstate, big city liberals on the other), yet such clear demographic distinctions are a luxury in analysis.

The above is not to gainsay important regional differences in Oklahoma. Still, demographic cleavages are not as clear as in many other states. In Oklahoma, the political parties tend to have rather diverse constituences, less programmatic emphases, and legislators tend to be elected more on the basis of personal ability and experience than on clear partisan stands. The complexity of party influences is further compounded in less competitive states like Oklahoma by the presence of relatively weak state and local party organizations. In such states, party has less impact on the nomination and recruitment process, and legislators tend to be less sensitive to pressures from party leaders or the governor.[3]

An analysis of twenty-six state Senates[4] found that more partisan behavior is present in the highly industrialized states of the Middle West, the mid-Atlantic, and the lower New England regions where high proportions of the population are of foreign stock, where the Democratic party has firm strength in urban centers (especially among ethnic groups, nonwhites and non-Protestants), and where the Republican party draws its strengths from very different and contrasting constituencies that tend to be more suburban, rural, and small-town in character. Less industrial states such as Oklahoma are less likely to have clear-cut class conflicts, ethnic divisions, or strong labor unions. Indeed, a comprehensive analysis of a sister state, Missouri, found only weak urban-rural alignments, few fundamental socioeconomic conflicts, and a pattern of weak ideology.[5] While party influences have been found to be predominant in other state legislatures, the warnings above are particularly relevant for Oklahoma and for neighboring mountain and western states where political machines and the "immigrant ethnic'' are practically nonexistent, and where individualism looks disparagingly on partisan politics.

The absence of high partisan competition and clear-cut distinctions between the political parties in Oklahoma's legislature need not imply that other forces cannot be isolated. The absence of party as a key variable leaves room for the influence of factional or regional cleavages, influences from the governor, and some residual party influences depending upon the area of roll call voting under examination. While the role of the governor may be important, studies in other states suggest that such factions that develop around gubernatorial programs have relatively short duration and are likely to vary according to the style and character of individual governors. This is particularly true in such uncompetitive states as Louisiana, Texas, and Kentucky.[6]

The influence of party may also vary by substantive areas. Even in weakly competitive states, bills of interest to the political parties, such as matters of legislative organization, are likely to be characterized by partisan influences. Votes associated with the governor's or the political party's program, such as matters of taxation and appropriation, will show mild party influence. Health and welfare issues are less clearly defined by party differences.[7]

Furthermore, regional differences, as discussed above, may operate in lieu of the party, although such differences are not likely to be predominant in Oklahoma—a fact which prevents the addition of much-needed clarity in analyses of roll call votes in Oklahoma. Any attempts to estimate precisely the contending influences of party and region in Oklahoma are dampened by the fact that major urban-rural or regional factions are most likely to occur in highly industrialized states—which are also states where the parties tend to be more competitive. Therefore, both party and regional influences on roll call voting may be too interrelated and relatively weak to isolate in the Oklahoma legislature, though an attempt to do so is made later in this chapter.

Cue Taking From Colleagues

Another conception of internal forces on roll call voting suggests that individual decisions are largely the result of cues taken from legislative colleagues. In a study of the U.S. Congress, Matthews and Stimson[8] suggest a rational framework where roll call votes are seen as a means to achieve individual legislator's own goals. The achievement of such goals, however, is dependent upon collecting and processing information, the absence of which can be a major impediment to success. It is suggested that legislators therefore work to reduce information costs by relying on the most obvious and cheap sources of information: their colleagues in the legislature. Such a model is most likely to operate on complex issues about which individual legislators know very little. As a "rational" way to handle the problem, they rely mainly on cues from the committee chaimen, the party majority, or the chamber majority (and possibly the governor). Most of these cues are therefore party-related.

Although the cue taking model is a relatively new emphasis in analyses of roll call voting, a more generalized form of the cue concept has been tested in one state legislature—Michigan. Porter[9] analyzed interaction among legislators considered to be experts, their less expert colleagues, lobbyists and administrators. By viewing the legislature as an information processing system, he concluded that legislative experts serve as a major source of information and voting cues for colleagues, but that such interaction varies by policy areas under consideration. While such a model has yet to be applied to the Oklahoma legislature, it has considerable appeal and is likely to provide more information about details of the legislative process and subsequent roll call voting.

EXTERNAL FORCES ON ROLL CALL VOTING

In a democratic system a variety of outside forces, especially those associated with constituents, are likely to play a key roll in legislative decisions. The role a lawmaker assumes toward his constituents will obviously shape his legislative performance—a factor which will be discussed in greater detail in Chapter 6. There has been considerable interest in different conceptions of representation in the United States, especially in the difference between legislators who view themselves as delegates and those who view themselves as trustees of the people emphasizing their individual judgments on legislation. Although this difference will be examined in greater detail later, it should be remembered that the role of trustee or free agent vis-a-vis constituents is not necessarily an "unrepresentative" role, since individual attitudes, party, and constituency interests often coincide. That is, a legislator may prefer to exercise his own judgment and vote his own conscience rather than serve more specific interests of his constituency, yet the two may in reality be the same, since the legislator shares his constituent's perspectives.

Constituency Influences

While constituency influences often play a secondary role to party,[10] district characteristics (such as levels of industrialization and racial, ethnic, and religious composition) have been found to be of considerable importance in roll call voting,[11] even though such influences obviously vary from state to state.[12] Constituency characteristics have been found to be particularly important in Pennsylvania.[13] The level of partisan competition and the homogeneity of constituencies plays a key role in Ohio roll call voting.[14] Yet, the impact of constituency forces is mediated by longer terms of office and larger districts.[15] Indeed, legislators with longer terms, those from larger districts and from districts which are atypical of their party are more likely to deviate from party positions.[16] If party issues are generally not salient, legislators will tend to follow constituency cues.[17] Furthermore, a study of one state—Idaho—found that such external forces as constituents, interest groups, and the governor were more significant in roll call voting than internal forces such as party and interpersonal relationships.[18]

The Environment of the Legislative System

The external environment in which legislative systems operate has often been cited as a general influence on roll call voting.[19] The dominant attitudes and values in a state political culture obviously shape legislative output, yet such conceptualizations have rarely been specifically structured and analyzed. Indeed, concrete findings fail to extend beyond the general conclusion that legislative performance depends upon public support, which is most likely located among higher strata of a state's society and among the most informed and active members of the electorate. Characteristics of the electoral system are also likely to influence internal legislative decisions, yet such studies analyzing roll call voting have been limited to those on reapportionment. Some have suggested that malapportionment makes little difference in policy choice in the legislature,[20] and that there is little change in those legislatures having undergone reapportionment change.[21] On the other hand, some studies have found that reapportionment does affect factionalism[22] and party conflict[23] within the legislature, as well as legislative outputs.[24]

Interest Groups

While we will investigate legislator's orientations toward interest groups in Chapter 6, such organized external pressures often play a key role in legislative decision making. These influences, however, are difficult to measure, and various research findings have been contradictory. For example, it has been suggested that the strength of interest groups and party influence on roll call voting varies inversely—the conclusion of a study on California business influences during that state's nonpartisan era.[25] Yet a major study of the fifty states indicates that pressure groups and partisan conflict occur together,[26] but their respective roles are highly dependent upon the particular policy issues under consideration.[27]

Gubernatorial Influence

The role of the governor in the legislative process is a much under-researched area in American politics, yet as we shall see shortly, one of considerable interest to scholars of decision making in Oklahoma. Generally, governors' powers to influence legislation have increased, especially in industrialized and urban states, and are still increasing with the adoption of longer terms in office, more control of the budget, considerable appointment powers, and important programmatic interests. In many states, the governor is indeed the chief legislator. Yet such gubernatorial leadership seems often overrated when the check-and-balance system evident in state government is taken into account, and when legislators are asked about gubernatorial influence.[28] In a national survey Francis found that on issues seen as most important by legislators, only 45 per cent of the respondents saw the governor as pressing hard for legislation.[29] That is, governors tend to be selective in their involvement and in their use of formal and informal powers.

THE MIX OF INTERNAL AND EXTERNAL FORCES

Much of the above suggests that internal and external forces have an interrelated influence on legislative roll call voting. Although such interrelationships are difficult to isolate among a wide array of contending influences, several studies have adopted rather complex models in their attempts to order such forces and their impact on voting. As discussed below, a classic study on Oklahoma by Patterson found that the impact of specific forces varies widely by policy areas, and equally complex analyses of the U.S. Congress reached similar conclusions.[30] Clausen, for example, found that party was a key factor in the government management domain, that constituency influences were predominant in the area of civil liberties, that both influences interacted to explain roll call voting on social welfare and agricultural assistance measures, and that constituency and presidential influences were most likely to operate on votes dealing with international affairs.[31] A study by Miller and Stokes supports such distinctions, indicating that legislators abide more by the wishes of their constituency in matters of civil rights, whereas in matters of foreign policy they are more likely to act as free agents.[32] Kingdon found that constituency influences and cues from fellow congressmen were the most important influences on individual decisions, especially in comparison to the role of party leaders, the administration, legislative staff, and interest groups.[33] He found that most congressmen abide by the wishes of a significant supportive group of constituents, although these are likely to be elites among his electoral coalition. His basic model of "consensus decision-making" suggests that legislators vote to reflect a consensus among trusted sources, which are largely fellow members and particular groups of constituents.

INFLUENCES ON ROLL CALL VOTING IN OKLAHOMA

Specific research on roll call voting in the Oklahoma legislature—as in other states—has never been able to treat simultaneously the multitude of potential decision influences discussed above. Nevertheless, there has been a rich and rapid development of findings by a number of scholars in the field. The base from which most findings have developed was established in a seminal and now classic article on the Oklahoma House by Samuel Patterson.[34] Since party influences on legislative roll call voting have been found to be a dominant force throughout the American states, Patterson's inquiry was shaped largely by the absence of party divisions in the Oklahoma legislature. Indeed, roll call voting in one-party legislatures was largely avoided in previous research, and Oklahoma was an obvious place to begin to look for explanations beyond party. Given the relative absence of partisan conflict in Oklahoma, Patterson's research also made a lasting contribution to our appreciation of the complexity of roll call voting. His basic finding was that in the absence of partisan cues, legislators are likely to respond to different pressures in different areas. In other words, there is no consistent or pervasive influence on roll call voting; instead, those influences vary by policy areas under consideration.

In order to examine nonparty influences, Patterson analyzed a variety of factors for their influence on several substantive dimensions of roll call voting. These factors included the level of partisan competition within legislative districts, urban and rural cleavages, and income levels in legislative districts. While each of the above are constituency influences, their specific impact varied by substantive areas of legislative decision. It was found that the level of partisan competition in legislative districts is most relevant for legislation dealing with campaign regulation (legislators from competitive areas are more supportive of such regulation); and that income levels in legislative districts are most influential with regard to public school measures. While urban and rural district differences were observed across several roll call dimensions, such cleavages were neither consistent nor pervasive. Furthermore, Patterson found a tendency for the extremely metropolitan and rural legislators to form coalitions against urban and semirural legislators when voting on tax matters. Finally, Patterson suggested that the role of the governor is related to voting on a variety of substantive dimensions, since votes on the governor's program were related to scale scores in other substantive areas. Support for the governor's program came primarily from legislative leaders, freshmen, and legislators from competitive districts.

Patterson's research is widely cited for the diversity of impacts on roll call voting, and it has stimulated subsequent research in Oklahoma for two primary reasons: since his examination of the Oklahoma House in 1959, Oklahoma has witnessed substantial reapportionment changes that could affect roll call voting; and secondly, for the first time in history two Republican governors were elected, while Democrats remained dominant in both houses of the legislature. These two factors directly stimulated research on changing party influences and on the role of the governor, as well as research on the effects of changing urban and rural coalitions resulting from reapportionment.

Partisan Factors and the Role of the Governor

In an important piece of unpublished research, Bernick and Hebert[35] analyzed eighty-six roll call votes which exhibited conflict in the second session of the 33rd Legislature (Oklahoma House, 1970) to investigate the hypothesis that control of the governorship by the minority party increases the importance of partisanship as a factor which structures legislative voting under one-party dominant conditions. Their research is influenced by the demonstrated importance of partisanship in structuring roll call voting in two-party legislatures,[36] the repeated confirmation of the role of party during the last ten years,[37] and the hesitancy of researchers to examine one-party states.[38] They have replicated Patterson's investigation with an eye toward isolating the impact of growing Republican strengths, especially in terms of the governorship. Their analysis of votes on which at least 10 per cent of the members voting cast votes against the majority confirms the hypothesis that control of the governorship by the minority party increases the importance of partisanship as a variable structuring legislative decision making.

The authors employ two summary statistics which give an indication of the impact of party on voting, including an index of cohesion and an index of party likeness. The first is a measure of voting cohesion within the party (the absolute difference between the percentage of the total party voting yea and the percentage of the total party voting nay), and the second is a measure of similarity between the two major political parties (the percentage of yea votes cast by one party subtracted from the percentage of yea votes cast by the other, subtracted from 100). In calculating a mean index of cohesion for all roll call votes, they found that the Republicans were somewhat more cohesive than the Democrats in 1970 (63.1 and 52.9 respectively). On 36 per cent of the roll calls the Republicans had a cohesion score higher than 80, whereas the Democrats achieved that level on only 11 per cent of the roll calls. The impact of party was therefore more pronounced in the minority party than in the majority party. Results from the measures of party likeness indicate that the Oklahoma legislature must still be considered among those wherein party is of relatively little importance. The mean index of party likeness was 74, indicating a relatively high degree of similarity in the voting of members of the two parties.

While the above conclusions are based upon summary measures utilizing all 86 roll call votes, they conceal other important information that emerges when different policy areas are examined. In order to replicate Patterson, roll calls were divided into various substantative categories, and subjected to Guttman scale analysis to test for their level of unidimensionality and interrelatedness. As expected, they found that the content areas on which controversial legislation focused have changed since 1959, and that the categories diverged somewhat from Patterson's original classification.

Table 36[39] shows that a voting dimension generally indentifiable with labor legislation has persisted in Oklahoma, yet new dimensions have emerged on various issues including racial integration, judicial reform, and general government reform. They comment on this as follows:[40]

The decade of the 1960's saw the judiciary become the center of a controversy which culminated in the impeachment of one justice and the sudden resignation of two other justices of the Oklahoma Supreme Court. We also found a scalable content area which we designated government reform. This included votes on bills having to do with investment of idle funds, a reapportionment commission, provision of voting booths, and modifications in the boundaries and responsibilities of an improvement and zoning district. . . . The last of our five scales was found in a content

TABLE 36.—Universe of Content and Scale Analysis Results for 1970 Oklahoma House of Representatives and 1959 Oklahoma House of Representatives[1]

1959 Universe of Content	Number of Roll Calls	Results of Analysis[2]	1970 Universe of Content	Number of Roll Calls	Results of Analysis
Appropriations	11	Scale; c.r. = .95	Law and Order	7	Not scalable
Business Regulation	10	Not scalable	Judicial Reform	6	Scale; c.r. = .94
Campaigns & Elections	7	Scale; c.r. = .94	Local Government Affairs	10	Not scalable
Conservation	6	Not scalable	Schools	12	Not scalable
County Affairs	6	Not scalable	Conservation	4	Scale; c.r. = .92
Crimes & Punishment	6	Not scalable	Fiscal Matters	5	Not scalable
Labor and Welfare	10	Scale; c.r. = .95	Government Affairs	6	Scale; c.r. = .90
Public Morals	9	Scale; c.r. = .95	Labor	4	Scale; c.r. = .99
Regulation of the Professions	8	Not scalable	Racial Integration	4	Scale; c.r. = .98
Schools	8	Scale; c.r. = .93	Professions & Budget	17	Not scalable
State Officials & Employees	9	Not scalable	Miscellaneous	11	Not scalable
Taxation	10	Scale; c.r. = .94			
Transportation	17	Not scalable			
Governor's Program	7	Scale; c.r. = .95			
Miscellaneous	3	Not scalable			
Total	127		Total	86	

[1] Source of 1959 data: Samuel Patterson, "Dimensions of Voting Behavior in a One-Party State Legislature," *Public Opinion Quarterly*, Vol. 26 (Summer, 1962), p.191.

[2] c.r. = Coefficient of Reproducibility; a value of .90 or above is necessary to meet Guttman Criteria for a unidimensional scale.

TABLE 37.—Relationship Between Party and Five 1970 Roll Call Scales*

Scale	Tau Values
1. Judicial Reform	—.575
2. Conservation	.031
3. Labor	.477
4. Government Reform	—.132
5. Racial Integration	.281

*Positive relationship indicating a "pro" position on the scale is associated with Democratic party membership.

area which was among those Patterson considered, but which he found not to scale, namely conservation. Again, developments during the past decade afford a reasonable explanation. The attention which environmental issues have received has no doubt contributed to the structuring of legislative voting sufficiently to result in a scalable dimension.

When Patterson found a low relationship (correlation) among his various roll call dimensions, he suggested that interrelationships between various policy areas are more likely in a legislature where party is relevant than in one where party is not available as a reference group for members. If his conclusion is correct, and if party has become more important in the Oklahoma legislature, Bernick and Hebert suggest that dimensions are more likely to be interrelated in 1970. Their findings substantiate this hypothesis: whereas Patterson found only 14 per cent of his correlation coefficients to be above .20, 40 per cent were above that level in 1970. The various dimensions of voting in 1970 were therefore less independent than were those in the 1959 session.

In order to estimate more precisely the impact of partisanship on roll call voting, Bernick and Hebert computed a set of correlation coefficients (tau) between party and each of the dimensions. Their findings presented in Table 37[41] suggest that judicial reform exhibits the strongest relationship with party (a negative relationship indicating that the Republicans are more favorably disposed to judicial reform than are the Democrats). A similar finding holds for the governmental reform scale. The strongest relationship, however, is that between labor voting and party, with Democrats taking the prolabor position. The Democrats also support racial integration to a greater extent than the Republicans. However, conservation is found to be unrelated to party.

Since the primary characteristic of policy making in Oklahoma that changed between the Patterson study and the one by Bernick and Hebert was the shift in control of the governor's office, they suggest that its impact was a primary influence on their more recent findings. Although Republicans also increased their control of the House from 7.5 to 22.3 per cent during the same period, the Democrats nevertheless retained substantial majority control of the chamber, having enough votes to win even when a two-thirds majority was required. While they cannot dismiss completely the growth in the size of the minority party as an influential factor, the primary change responsible for ten-year differences is attributed to the governorship.

In order to isolate more precisely the impact of a Republican governor, indices of party likeness and cohesion are examined in the context of the governor's program. Using the index of party likeness, Bernick and Hebert select those votes on which the parties differed most sharply and find that 12 of the 86 votes had an index below 50. When those twelve votes are scrutinized, they find that six involved clear gubernatorial action: one was part of the governor's program, while the other five were on bills vetoed by the governor. It is likely, then, that the governor played an important role in bringing about these votes which divided the parties. When the index of cohesion is examined for these six votes that were important for the governor, several interesting findings emerge. Bernick and Hebert comment as follows:

The Democrats (who were in a position to embarrass the Governor) had an Index of Cohesion score of 89.1. What makes these scores so interesting is the fact that over the entire 86 votes, the Republicans had an average Index of Cohesion Score of 63.1 while that of the Democrats was considerably lower, 52.9. On the bill that was introduced as a part of the Governor's program, his party's members had a cohesion index of 100 while the dominant party had a score of only 13. All of these scores suggest that the existence of a Governor of the party opposite to the majority of the House had an important effect on the voting behavior of legislators from both parties.[42]

Bernick and Hebert conclude that while party is still not a dominant point of reference in the Oklahoma House, it took on considerable importance in certain issue areas and on certain controversial votes directly involving the minority party governor (Dewey Bartlett).

The above research documents the importance of gubernatorial influences, yet subsequent findings suggest that partisan conflict is not necessarily greater when a minority party governor is in power. Contrary to his expectation, Bernick[43] found that in Oklahoma, as in Vermont, greater partisan conflict developed in the legislature when the governor was a member of the dominant legislative party. This conclusion was reached through an analysis of state Senate roll call votes in 1967 (Republican governorship) compared with roll call voting in 1971 (Democratic governorship). There was partisan conflict in Oklahoma in 1967 with a Republican governor and a Democratic Senate, but it was not sufficiently intensive to be classified as highly partisan. Yet the subsequent 1971 legislative session which exhibited partisan congruence between the governor's office and the legislature showed lower party likeness scores than in 1967. Bernick attributes these greater party differences to similarity in voting among Republicans in the absence of solidarity among the Democrats. He comments as follows:

The Democrats were faced with the problems of trying to cooperate with a Democratic Governor, but this meant supporting two highly controversial pieces of legislation that the Governor wanted enacted. The Governor had as his major piece of legislation an oil and gas tax, a revision in the state income tax (to insure that everyone in Oklahoma paid his "fair share") and the elimination of the sales tax on food and prescription drugs. While he did not achieve the latter the first two were accomplished. Governor Hall attributed his success to the leadership of the Legislature reacting to a Democratic Governor after a long period of Republican governors. Queried about its effects, Governor Hall said, "Yes, I think there was a reaction. The Democrats trying much harder to get along with the Governor than if I had succeeded a Democratic Governor."[44]

Bernick also found that there was little or no increase in party cohesion elicited in the majority party by the governor coming from the opposite party. While these findings add some confusion to what we would normally expect, they point to the importance of the substantive components of a governor's program, which are apparently more important than the existence of partisan differences between the governorship and the legislature.

Non-Party Influences on Party Support

While the previous study by Bernick and Hebert deals only with party-related and gubernatorial impacts on legislative roll call voting, an analysis by Bernick of the same 86 roll call votes in the 1970 House sheds some light on the nonparty factors.[45] Although the analysis deals exclusively with party support (as a measure of the percentage of times a legislator votes with the majority of his party), it is based on a systematic examination of roll call votes, albeit without regard to issue areas.

The Bernick analysis treats such factors as residency, electoral margins, legislative experience, and legislative leadership position as potential influences on party support. Residency is considered in terms of rural and urban differences, reflecting the hypothesis that legislators from the two types of districts will vote in conflicting ways because of the demographic composition of constituencies. He suggests that conflict results from the different needs and interests of legislators, expecting that rural lawmakers will vote on conservation matters differently than urban legislators, and that rural legislators will tend to vote differently on urban renewal than on conservation legislation. Another source of controversy may arise between urban and rural districts in the struggle for legislative power resulting from malapportionment. Urban legislators have felt victimized in the past by the small number of seats they have held in proportion to the large number of people they represent. Meanwhile, rural legislators have steadfastly held on to their disproportionate share of American legislatures. Inconsistent findings exist for this factor, with some researchers finding little cleavage on an urban-rural dimension,[46] where others have found cleavages to bear directly on the character of party conflict in state legislatures.[47]

The margin of victory in a legislative district has also been hypothesized as an influence on voting.[48] It has been suggested that legislators from districts with a close electoral margin will reflect their constituency views more closely than legislators from safe seats with wide electoral margins. The major contention of this

**TABLE 38.—Effect of Office Holding on Legislative
Party Support Scores**

Party Support Score	Democrats		Republicans	
	Percentage Office Holders	Percentage Non-Office-Holding Legislators	Percentage Office Holders	Percentage Non-Office-Holding Legislators
High	54.8	19.6	50.0	69.0
Low	45.2	80.4	50.0	31.0
Total	100.0	100.0	100.0	100.0
	(N = 31)	(N = 46)	(N = 6)	(N = 16)

Tau = .336   Tau = .—174

theory is that competitive districts are more "middle of the road" politically between contending parties, thus resulting in more moderate legislative voting. Furthermore, a legislator from a competitive district is more likely to be deviant (less supportive) of his party.[49]

Other factors of importance include the experience of legislators and the degree to which they hold leadership positions. Bernick suggests that a more experienced legislator is more likely to be supportive of his party—he has more to lose if he upsets his position in the party and is more likely to be socialized to his party's legislative perspective. Furthermore, legislators tend to be rewarded by colleagues for their performance and loyalty by being elected to a leadership position. Holding an office is important because it enhances a legislator in the eyes of his fellow members and in the eyes of his constituents. Since legislators who follow norms are often rewarded with a position, there may be a relationship between party support and office holding in the legislature.

While the above suggestions were supported by other states, Bernick finds little to support their influence in the Oklahoma House. His findings are cast only in terms of party support, yet they are indicative of legislative influences in the absence of an overwhelming impact of party. When party support scores are examined for Republicans and Democrats according to whether a legislator holds office or not, Bernick finds substantial differences for Democrats only.

**TABLE 39.—Effects of Residency, Experience, and Competition
on Legislative Party Support**

Factor	Tau Values		
	Democrats	Republicans	All Legislators
Residency[a]	—.064[d]	.039[d]	—.066[d]
Competition[b]	—.011[e]	—.182[e]	.006[e]
Experience[c]	+ .231[e]	—.231[e]	—.116[e]

[a]Residency is dichotomized as urban vs. rural (urban legislators represent districts with 1 or more cities of 10,000 or over or within an SMSA; rural legislators are from districts with no cities over 9,999).

[b]Three categories were established for this variable:
   (1) Noncompetitive: no electoral opposition to the legislator from 1962 to 1968;
   (2) Semicompetitive: all vote totals for the legislator greater than 60 per cent, but opposition existed to his election;
   (3) Competitive: the legislator received less than 60 per cent of the votes in any one of the three elections from 1962 to 1968.

[c]Legislative experience has been divided into four categories by years: (1) 0-2; (2) 3-4; (3) 5-10; and (4) 11-32.

[d]Values are results of using Tau b for an equal number of rows and columns.

[e]Values are results of using Tau c for an unequal number of rows and columns.

As Table 38 indicates,[50] 54.8 percent of the Democratic office holders scored high in terms of party support, and 45.2 per cent scored low. The major difference, however, appears when comparisons are made with non-office-holding legislators. Eighty per cent of the nonleadership legislators fell in a deviant category among the Democrats, while only 45 per cent of those in leadership positions had low support scores. In other words, of the so-called Democratic deviants, 73 per cent were nonoffice holders, while 27 per cent were in leadership positions (House or party officer, committee chairmanship or vice-chairmanship). While it appears that a formal position in the legislature shapes the extent to which the dominant Democratic Party legislators support their party, the converse appears to be the case for Republicans. Regardless of holding office, Republicans are expected to follow their party leadership. Office holding is apparently an important determinant of party support for Democrats, but it has little importance for the minority party.

When other factors are examined for their impact on party support scores, weak and mixed findings result. As Table 39 indicates,[51] the correlations (tau) for residency, competition, and experience are generally quite low. When partisan differences are controlled, length of legislative tenure appears to be influential as a voting reference, yet there are opposite effects for Republicans and Democrats. As an explanation, Bernick suggests that newly elected Republicans voted into office during an upsurge of their party are more likely to adopt that party as a reference, whereas party may be irrelevant generally until a certain level of institutionalization is achieved within the legislative body and electoral system.[52] In addition, a small negative relationship (-.182) for Republicans offers only weak support for the hypothesis that legislators in competitive districts are more likely to be mavericks than those from districts which are considered safe. Place of residency (urban versus rural) also has little impact on level of party support, and this holds for both Democrats and Republicans. However, better measures of residency and roll call voting are necessary if we are to unravel urban-rural cleavages. Such an analysis would require attention to finer distinctions between types of districts, as well as differences between legislative policy areas in terms of specific roll call votes. A more direct examination of this impact is presented below.

Constituency Influences in Oklahoma

Research on constituency influences on roll call voting in the Oklahoma legislature is underdeveloped in comparison with research on party influences. While financial constraints have largely prohibited a matching of constituent opinions with specific legislator's roll call decisions, there have been efforts to infer such influences by examining the relationships between aggregate constituency characteristics and subsequent votes.

The most developed area in this regard is the analysis of urban and rural impacts on legislative decision making. In Patterson's study of the 1959 Oklahoma House he found no persistent organized factional combinations within the majority party and only few important urban-rural differences.[53] An exception was his finding

**TABLE 40.—Summary of Mean Relationships Between Urban-Rural
Cleavages and Roll Call Categories and Proportion
of Curvilinear Relationships in the 1970 Oklahoma House**

Roll Call Category	$\bar{x}$ Gamma Coefficient	Percentage of Curvilinear Relationships*	Number of Roll Calls
County Affairs/Local Government	.56	0	4
Taxation	.46	20	5
Appropriations	.39	20	5
Schools	.29	42	12
Agriculture	.27	0	3
Crimes/Punishment/ Judiciary	.23	38	13
Transportation/Highways	.18	67	3
Regulation of Professions/ Business Relations	.13	22	9

*The relationship between the urban-rural dimension and roll call voting was considered curvilinear if the percentage yea or nay for both the extreme urban-rural categories (metropolitan and rural) represented the largest or smallest percentages of all four categories.

about urban-rural cleavages on issues of public morals (beer sales, horse racing, regulating marriages of underage persons), where metropolitan legislators voted considerably more liberal or permissive than small town or rural members. This early study, of course, was prior to reapportionment when urban members were badly outnumbered. Since that time legislative alignments perhaps have shifted sufficiently so that more votes in the House might now be based on urban-rural cleavages.

In order to examine this type of district impact, Morgan and Kirkpatrick[54] analyzed a total of fifty-eight roll call votes involving substantive issues (including appropriations) that resulted in an opposition vote of at least 10 per cent in the 1970 Oklahoma House. Members of the House were also assigned to one of four urban-rural categories based on the nature of their legislative district: (1)

metropolitan (part of an SMSA urbanized area), (2) urban (district with a city of 10,000 or over, yet not in the previous category), (3) semirural (district with a city of 5,000 to 9,999 inhabitants), and (4) rural (district with no city of 5,000 population). The search for urban-rural differences between the fifty-eight roll calls was undertaken by examining a series of contingency tables with yeas and nays on each issue compared to the four-fold urban-rural typology. The gamma correlation coefficient was used as a measure of association (with a range from + 1 to -1), with a higher gamma value indicating a greater degree of association between roll call voting and urban-rural cleavages.

The mean gamma coefficients by various substantive categories of roll calls are presented in Table 40.[55] The ordering of these categories indicates that urban-rural voting differences are most distinguishable on issues of local government. These roll calls generally involve local control and related matters that are apparently sensitive to urban-rural differences among Oklahoma House members. Voting on taxation and appropriation measures is less related to regional differences, yet the mean gamma correlations are higher than those found in other substantive categories. Although Patterson concluded that public morals issues were most sensitive to variations in urban-rural voting, a category of this type did not develop for the universe of 1970 roll calls.

Over the years there has been a tendency for rural and metropolitan areas to converge politically, as, for example, in their greater degree of support for statewide Republican candidates. Also, we observed earlier that among such urban-rural categories Republican party membership was more prominent among legislators from the metropolitan and rural areas. Thus, we might anticipate that on some issues a metropolitan-rural voting coalition would emerge among House members. One way of testing the existence of such a voting pattern is to observe those roll calls for which the percentage of "yes" votes was largest or smallest among metropolitan and rural legislators. A metropolitan-rural coalition would be said to exist, then, if the percentage of "yes" votes on a particular bill was higher or lower for metropolitan and rural House members than for members in the middle two categories. Thus, any measure for which such a curvilinear effect develops is considered to be an example of metropolitan-rural convergences.

Table 40 also presents the percentage of roll calls in each category that was curvilinear. Such relationships are more likely to appear on roll call votes where the urban-rural variables fail to discriminate (i.e., those votes with lower gamma values). If voting alignments are not closely related to the four-fold urban-rural classification of House members, then a metropolitan-rural coalition is more likely to appear. Thus, school issues and those relating to prosecution and transportation are more frequently characterized by metropolitan/rural vote combinations.

These findings suggest that while urban-rural divisions are not uniform and therefore not generally ascribable to roll call voting in the Oklahoma House, there are important variations according to policy areas. Cleavage along this dimension is most likely to occur in such issue areas as city and county government, taxation and appropriation measures. Also, metropolitan and rural legislators tend to form voting combinations in selected issue areas, especially on measures dealing with highways and transportation, schools, and criminal justice. Subsequent research has also confirmed the tendency for rural and metropolitan legislators to vote differently on a number of issues, especially those most controversial in the legislative setting. Furthermore, it appears that block voting among Democrats has increased since reapportionment, as has their success with important legislative measures.[56]

A comprehensive analysis of the impact of district characteristics (other than urban-rural cleavages) on various types of legislative policy decisions is nonexistent for Oklahoma, yet recent research has focused on one issue area where constituency characteristics may indeed be important: taxation and finance. Voting on taxation proposals is more likely to reflect constituents' social and economic characteristics especially when the proposals are so controversial as to break down partisan ties. Furthermore, it is generally evident that there is a link between the socioeconomic and political environment in legislative districts and the type of tax measures passed by state legislators.[57] In order to test for possible demographic effects on tax measures, Bernick analyzed twenty key roll call votes associated with two major pieces of Governor David Hall's tax "reform" program in 1971: oil and gas tax, and income tax reform.[58] An index of party likeness on these roll calls suggested that the two political parties were dissimilar and thus to be considered important references for voting. An index of party cohesion was used to test the solidarity of the individual parties, suggesting that the majority party was less cohesive than the minority party. In addition to the key role of party, Bernick also found that five socioeconomic district characteristics displayed some predictive power, especially on votes dealing with oil and gas tax changes. On the latter, both educational level in legislative districts and the percentage of constituents below poverty levels had a substantial independent effect upon legislative roll call voting. While the district's characteristics often played a secondary role in comparison with the power of party influences, the findings suggest that socioeconomic characteristics can be important under special legislative circumstances.

While the secondary and transient role of constituency characteristics in legislative roll call voting may be unsuspected by the casual reader, our previous commentary, as well as subsequent discussions in later chapters, indicates that the role of "delegate" is neither predominant nor pervasive in the Oklahoma legislature. In other words, we should not expect a direct tie between constituency characteristics and roll call voting, especially when many legislators prefer to act as "free agents" and do not feel bound to constituency pressures. Further evidence of the weak transmission from constituency opinion to roll call voting is evident in research on prohibition and liquor-related items in the Oklahoma legislature. A recent study by Morrison[59] compared legislators' voting records on these items with the preferences of their constituents as evidenced through statewide referenda votes on similar measures. None of the liquor-related issues demonstrated a substantial relationship between the legislators and their constituents. Morrison suggests that the legislator's vote is not necessarily a good predictor of constituency votes and that additional outside factors influence district voting. Also, prediction of one vote from another may be extremely difficult with divergent personalities involved. He suggests that Oklahoma legislators may have neither the knowledge nor the interest necessary to understand constituents, and that this is more likely in an issue area, such as liquor-prohibition, where emotional factors may not lend themselves to a rational evaluation of the linkage between the represented and the representative. Certainly, the issue of the linkage between elected representatives and constituents is a more complex one and likely to vary by issue area, as does the impact of urban-rural cleavages and party.

Legislators' Political Beliefs

In addition to constituency opinions, an area of legislative research most in need of exploration is the impact of legislator's political beliefs on voting. While party may often be a useful explanatory device for roll call voting, party impacts often hide more fundamental differences among legislators about politics and the role of government. If Oklahoma political parties were truly responsible, characterized by clear and important policy differences among members and elected representatives, it would not be necessary to search for more fundamental differences in political attitudes. Since this is not the case, the search for underlying political beliefs and their impact on roll call voting is a concern of some significance. Such research on political beliefs requires considerably more effort than mere utilization roll call votes and partisan identifications. Therefore, research on the subject in Oklahoma has been limited to members of the Oklahoma County House delegation.

The author (in conjunction with David R. Morgan and William Lyons) has analyzed a vast array of roll call votes for Oklahoma County legislators across six fundamental dimensions. Votes on these dimensions were then correlated with operational and abstract political beliefs, individuals' characteristics (age and party), and self-proclaimed ideology on a liberal-conservative continuum. Among this entire set of variables, those associated with individual characteristics of party, self-identified ideology, or age tended to contribute least to the statistical explanation of variance in roll call voting. Basic political beliefs, especially abstractions about individual initiative, government involvement, and business regulations, were found to be most prominent and salient in their impact. Furthermore, the salience of factors in an explanatory model of roll call voting heavily depends on the underlying dimension of policy under examination.

Although the impact of specific beliefs varies by roll call dimensions, knowing a legislator's basic political predispositions is almost always more important than knowing party in predicting roll call voting. While party is neither monolithic nor uniform in its impact on legislative voting, there are obviously strong ties between basic political attitudes and partisan attachments. That is, party itself tends to be the best predictor of attitudes, and without taking attitudes into account, party is the best predictor of roll call voting. Specifically, when political attitudes are omitted from the model, the average variance in roll call voting explained by party, age, and self-identified ideology is fifteen per cent, whereas the addition of basic attitudes to the model increases the average explained variance to forty per cent. When attitudes are known and included in a model of voting, they are more important than other factors. There is also evidence that they underlie party; that is, party is a central integrative force around which other beliefs cohere.

Until further comprehensive research on roll call voting in Oklahoma appears, we must live with the above sets of sometimes confusing and inconsistent findings. Unlike many other states, Oklahoma defies a simplistic partisan interpretation of roll call voting. At the same time it appears that its urban-rural cleavages are not sufficiently developed so as to serve as a uniform force on voting. If we have any lesson to learn from the above, it suggests that, in the absence of clear partisan forces, the impact of gubernatorial influence, constituency factors, and individual legislative attitudes varies widely by the type of issues being considered by legislators. Only further research—conducted over time—treating a host of influences simultaneously will be able to isolate more precisely the "whys" of legislative decision making.

CHAPTER 5

Informal Rules of the Game: Legislative Norms

The Oklahoma legislature is characterized by formal rules and procedures, as well as more informal roles which legislators adopt depending upon their view of the legislative task. Yet there are basic elements of legislative life which complement formal procedures and underlie roles. We refer to these underlying elements as norms: the base elements from which roles are drawn or from which they are defined. In our previous discussion of legislative roles, we suggested a model with a variety of factors shaping one's role conception or potential. This has been discussed at some length elsewhere:

We might fairly assume that the various persons entering a legislative body, where the behavioral expectations are rather equally applied, will differ significantly in their role potential, and that this difference will account for differences in role interpretation and performance. To continue the legislative example, one's role potential is a composite of the human ecology of his constituency; short-run situational factors, such as the tone and character of his election campaign; the composition of his supporting coalition; his own socioeconomic characteristics and background; and his personality. Taken together, these variables act to restrict a legislator's range of options, and help to determine for him which forms of legislative activity and which issue areas it will be most efficacious for him to engage in.[1]

Although these factors are undoubtedly important in shaping roles, the most direct determinant is the legislator's specific set of beliefs about what is expected of him in his legislative career.

The state legislature is a group of distinct individuals who have come together to perform a set of common functions. As individuals they may have considerable power from independent electoral bases. Some may have influence to thwart the majority will and reduce the speed of the legislative process. Strong personalities may emerge either to shape expectations or to test the outer limits of the normal operating procedures of the legislature. Yet it is nevertheless a group; a set of individuals functioning together. Despite the legislators' individuality, their diversity, and legislative turnover, each chamber coheres as an institution or as a work group, and its norms serve (if only vaguely in some instances) as functional behavioral "oughts." In any group situation people develop somewhat standard expectations about how they and others will or should behave. These behaviors appear in regular patterns based upon common or shared beliefs about how things should be done. All organizations develop their own culture or climate, part of which is dependent upon formal rules, and the remainder of which is dependent largely upon an informal value system or a set of "unwritten rules of the game." As one scholar of the legislative process observes:

The member of the legislature attributes certain meanings to his and other members' behaviors, selects his own courses of action on the basis of certain standards, and sees the legislative environment from a particular perspective. These meanings, standards, and perspectives are not random: individual perspectives are inextricably interwoven with common perspectives, meanings are shared, and standards often emerge through the reciprocal influence of legislative interactions. The beliefs, attitudes, and perceptions of the members of the legislature not only define the boundaries of that system, but largely determine the circumstances within which that system functions, the processes by which it operates, and, in short, the social reality in which the legislature is enveloped. . . . Legislative norms are the carriers of tradition, the constituitive elements of social roles in the legislature, and, for the participants, a part of the daily environment of legislative life.[2]

The concepts of legislative power, roles, and norms are obviously interrelated. Although formal rules and procedures attribute formal power to certain positions in the legislature, power may also be derived from one's reputation or from his level of expertise. The various roles that one plays may include those which accompany a formal position, plus the role that one chooses to play on the basis of his understanding of the legislative process. This understanding is rooted in the sharing of beliefs referred to as norms. The author has referred to these complex interrelationships in an earlier study on norms and roles in the U.S. Senate:

In any system of human action there is an identifiable relationship between role structure and the distribution of influence. Some roles have "officiality," and carry with them the perquisites of organizational power; others evolve as functional elements in a system of behavior aimed at the achievement of institutional objectives; still others are consciously chosen modes of participation, played in a manner to comport with one's psychology, and bounded only by what the system regards as tolerable in the choice of behavioral options. Formal rules and the stated requisites of the institution provide an infrastructure, around which various role performances are interrelated. These formal elements also define hierarchy and division of labor, and accordingly affect the allocation of at least one type of power base position. But a system of human behavior must be viewed in broader perspective—in terms of observed patterns of behavior and influence, as well as the formal structure of roles. It is in that sense that norms are important as providing additional constraint for the system, resulting in the coherence of roles into a meaningful pattern.[3]

While the above interrelationship is probably generalizable to most legislative bodies, observers of the U.S. Senate were the first scholars to begin thinking seriously about the importance of legislative norms. Even casual observers of the Senate quickly discovered what they called an "inner club" of participants who not only shared beliefs, but who exercised a substantial degree of power in the institution. In effect, this relatively large set of individuals established the boundaries for how others in the legislative body were to behave. Ralph Huitt, upon whose work all modern students of the Senate must depend, wrote some time ago that:

Members have generally acepted notions of the way the Senate as a body ought to perform its public business and regulate its internal affairs, and the way members ought to behave toward the Senate and toward each other.[4]

In some of his later work, Huitt described Senate norms as prescribing a range of tolerable behavior within which the individual senator has considerable latitude in developing a role which suits him and which is also regarded as legitimate. In a related work on the Senate, Matthews described the basic set of Senate norms or "folkways" as apprenticeship, legislative work, specialization, courtesy, reciprocity, and institutional patriotism.[5] Close adherence to these norms, according to many writers, characterizes the Senate "insider." These "insiders" have been typically characterized as the most effective senators. Indeed, Matthews found that sanctions existed to enforce norms and that norm violators were less effective in legislative affairs.

In related research on four state legislatures, Wahlke and his associates describe norms as developing ". . . in a systematic way to complement more formal directives in promoting accomplishment of the legislature's recognized primary functions,"[6] and they suggest that "their observance would nonetheless seem to be obtained not primarily through members' fear of . . . punishment but through their general acceptance of the functional utility of the rules (of the game) for enabling the group to do what a legislature is expected to do.''[7] In addition to the Wahlke study, research on the Wisconsin legislature[8] has identified three basic types of norms in a state legislature: those which limit floor speaking, those that deal with a legislator's relationship with lobbyists, and those which support party loyalty. This study by Patterson then focuses on what happens to the deviants: the "talkers, moochers, and party mavericks."

It should be understood by now that these things which we are calling norms have meaning only in a group context. They are those beliefs and expectations about how one should behave which are shared widely—on which there is consensus. Norms are therefore a group property which govern behavior on the part of individual members and pertain to most salient aspects of legislative life, including the business of policy making. As the author has commented earlier:

all groups have a formal role structure which allocates specialized tasks and leadership positions . . . But we know that informal patterns of communication and influence evolve also during the life cycle of a group, and that these often are as important to policy outcomes as are the formal definitions of leader-follower relationships.[9]

But for these norms to have meaning and relevance to public policy and legislative behavior, the legislature must consciously view itself as a group, and individual legislators must perceive a relatively high degree of interaction with other colleagues and surveillance on the part of those who occupy formal leadership positions as well as by other colleagues who are not in leadership positions. That is, while the actual degree of interaction in the legislative body may be important, it is essential that legislators see themselves as interacting with others, that they see others as watching their behavior, and that they see individuals in leadership positions watching their behavior. This is not to imply a "big brother" atmosphere in a legislative chamber; it merely suggests that if norms govern behavior they can only do so if individuals subject to norms see themselves as members of a group and as individuals interacting with others in the group. Indeed, the norms of friendship govern a considerable amount of legislative behavior,

**TABLE 41.—Levels of Legislative Interaction and Observation in the
Oklahoma House and Senate**

	Great Deal	Often, But not A Lot	Not Very Much	Hardly At All
As you think of a typical legislative day, how much would you say you communicated with or interacted with other legislators?				
House (N = 90)	76.7%	18.9%	4.4%	0%
Senate (N = 43)	74.4	20.9	4.7	0

	Strongly Agree	Somewhat Agree	Somewhat Disagree	Strongly Disagree
Other members of the House (Senate) are usually aware of my behavior here in the House (Senate).				
House (N = 89)	50.6	48.3	1.1	0
Senate (N = 44)	54.5	40.9	2.3	2.3
House (Senate) leaders are usually aware of my behavior here in the House (Senate).				
House (N = 90)	51.1	46.7	2.2	0
Senate (N = 44)	56.8	40.9	2.3	0

not so much through formal sanctions or punishments, but through personal ties with other individuals. In his study of the Wisconsin assembly, Patterson[10] found that friendship roles are functional in the legislative group, and that no social group can be maintained if there are not significant interpersonal relationships among its members. Friendship roles are not only important for maintaining the legislative group, but for the resolution of political conflict. This friendship tie and the norms of informal groups may even influence individual decision-making behavior. The basic import of friendship norms is characterized by Patterson as follows:

Individuals who assume the legislative role have diverse backgrounds and diverse social, political, and economic experience, and different reference groups are salient for them. The informal friendship structure of the legislature tends to lessen such differences, to mitigate against the development of potential conflicts, to provide channels of communication and understanding among members who share goals, and to facilitate logrolling.[11]

It follows that one of the first inquiries about the Oklahoma legislature is whether individuals who are members of that body perceive themselves as interacting with others or being watched by others—factors which make norms possible and relevant for behavior. As part of a large research effort on legislative norms in 1972, legislators were asked specific questions about their interaction and their perception of observations in both the House and Senate. The data for these items appear in Table 41.

The first question concerned the individual's perceived level of communication or interaction with other legislators. As the table indicates, three-quarters of all legislators view themselves as interacting or communicating with other legislators a "great deal" in a typical legislative day. Only a small fraction of either chamber claims little interaction. In addition, over half of the members of both houses strongly agree that other members of their respective chamber are usually aware of their behavior, and nearly all of the members of both houses feel that they are being observed at least to some extent. Similarly, individuals in both chambers feel that legislative leaders are usually aware of their performance in the legislature. These high levels of interaction and observance or surveillance by others make it possible for shared beliefs to exist and for norms to be relevant for legislative behavior in Oklahoma.

NORMS IN THE OKLAHOMA LEGISLATURE

Norms may be central to the functioning of a legislative body, yet they do not govern every aspect of legislative life, nor do they necessarily exist as a shared consensus on certain aspects of a legislator's work. Some legislative behavior can be directly explained by formal procedures, such as voting rules, and some focal points of legislative work may engender little feeling from legislators, or their beliefs may be in substantial conflict over some particular aspect. In addition, any legislative body is likely to share

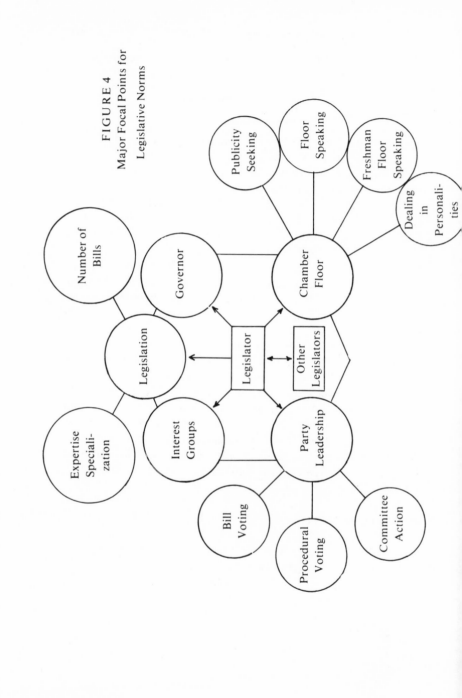

FIGURE 4
Major Focal Points for
Legislative Norms

a set of social norms which are borrowed directly from the American culture and have no unique impact on the legislative process. Although courtesy is an example of a widespread norm that obviously exists in most legislative chambers, it is not specific to legislative life. Yet there is a logical set of major focal points in the legislative process about which individual legislators share beliefs. These reference or focal points are important components in the legislative process and the existence of norms about them shapes a considerable amount of legislative behavior. These focal points are specific items about which norms may exist. While voting is obviously an important component of the legislative process, there are no general norms specifying how an individual should vote. Instead, there may be specific partisan norms which tend to specify how an individual should behave with regard to his political party and that party's leadership, and the extent to which he should support the party on partisan issues.

The major focal points for legislative norms tend to be associated with specific individuals, activities, and pieces of legislation. There are at least five of these major foci in the state legislature: party leadership, interest groups, legislation, the governor, and chamber floor activity. These elements are represented in Figure 4, which depicts the individual legislator interacting with other legislators to develop common or shared beliefs about how one should behave or relate to a variety of key individuals in the legislative process. Each element in the legislator's immediate environment is linked to every other element involved in the process of policy making. These five major focal points are in turn subdivided into eleven areas about which there may be specific prescriptions and proscriptions governing behavior: norms regulating procedural voting, voting on bills, committee action, interest groups, expertise specialization, the number of bills introduced, relations with the governor, publicity seeking on the floor, floor speaking, freshman floor speaking, and dealing in personalities on the chamber floor. For each of these eleven areas there may be a variety of courses of action or choices which govern behavior.

The above areas represent major points of research emphasis in a recent study of the Oklahoma House and Senate by Lelan E. McLemore which was supported and partially funded by the Bureau of Government Research and the H. V. Thornton

Memorial Fund of the University of Oklahoma.[12] In order to measure legislative norms in each of the eleven areas, five possible courses of action or choices were prescribed for each area. These choices delineate a range of five possible behaviors preferred for any single focal point. They typically represent a range of behaviors from one extreme through more moderate choices to another extreme. An example of the five possible behaviors for the focal point relevant to the role of party leadership on bill voting is as follows: (1) a House member who always follows his party's leadership in deciding how to vote on a bill; (2) a House member who usually, but not always, follows his party's leadership in deciding how to vote on a bill; (3) a House member who sometimes follows and sometimes does not follow his party's leadership in deciding how to vote on a bill; (4) a House member who seldom follows his party's leadership in deciding how to vote on a bill; (5) a House member who never follows his party leadership in deciding how to vote on a bill.

Once each of five possible behaviors are taken into account for the eleven major focal points, we have a total set of fifty-five possible behaviors which people may agree with to varying degrees. In order to measure legislator's levels of agreement for each of the fifty-five items, they were asked to judge them or state their preferences on a nine-point scale ranging from "strongly approve" through "indifferent" to "strongly disapprove." Although this procedure enabled a variety of complex manipulations for assessing many aspects of legislative life, our interest will be to delineate any single behavior within each of the eleven sets of five possible behaviors which could be referred to as a norm. By isolating an optimal behavior for each of the eleven areas on the basis of the highest average level of approval, it is possible to satisfy the consensus or "widely shared" component of legislative norms regarding appropriate or right behavior for legislators.[13]

PARTISAN NORMS

The political parties are the fundamental organizing units of the State legislature. Individual legislators are recruited largely through partisan mechanisms. Legislative party caucuses play a major role in the distribution of influence, the assigning of responsibilities, and in the content of legislative proposals. Political parties organize the leadership of a legislature. They serve as a primary influence on roll call voting in many states. In addition, the meaning that a party label has for individual legislators is dependent largely upon norms associated with partisanship in any single legislative body.

Partisanship norms establish a degree of legitimacy to party claims for loyalty and allegiance, and they determine the impact and efficacy of party leadership in bringing about a party vote. Although party allegiances appear to have a greater impact on roll call voting in states where legislative bodies are more competitive or more equally divided along partisan lines, the dominance of one party over another should not imply that partisan norms are absent or ineffective in guiding behavior. In any legislature the political parties are an important part of the decision making environment, whether or not that particular legislature is competitive or one-party dominant. In a one-party dominant legislature like Oklahoma's, the degree of partisanship may be more a product of norms than the level of competition between the parties. Although a variety of constituency characteristics may indeed modify and shape partisan differences in the legislature, the way individual legislators see the role of party probably has more direct bearing on their behavior.

Since the political party is the basic organizing force for each legislative chamber, party leadership can play an especially crucial role in the legislative process. From time to time strong personalities will emerge among the party leadership. However, strength of personality will tend to vary not only from leader to leader, but in response to a variety of conditions shaping the power of the legislative leader.[14] Furthermore, leaders may vary in the extent to which they choose to view party unity as their primary goal.[15] The norms which regulate a legislator's relationship to his party leadership are going to be a crucial factor at any single point in time. Although there is obviously a reciprocal influence between the personality of a leader and the beliefs of members of the legislative chamber, the shared beliefs or norms governing a legislator's relationship to the leadership establish the boundaries within which leaders must act.

This view of legislative parties as organizations directs our attention to norms affecting a legislator's willingness to follow party leadership. Such an analysis should give an indication of the importance of the political party as a reference group in the legislature, the influence of party leadership, and the role of the party in the legislative process. An example of different cases clarifies the meaning of party support:

Where legislators highly value the "party man"—the legislator who always goes along with party leadership—legislators can be expected to choose behavioral alternatives supporting party leadership more often than not. Party leadership would be a significant reference group for the members of the legislature and the high evaluations of those who follow party leadership would serve as a substitute for the open use of power and manipulation by party leadership. Conversely, where legislators highly esteem those who seldom or never follow party leadership, party leadership would be regarded as illegitimate; even attempts to sanction the party maverick would be unlikely to have member approval.[16]

Other possible options exist, however. A large group of legislators may reject both the party man and the party maverick and tend to prefer or accept the individual who only sometimes follows his party's leadership. Such a norm would tend to emphasize a high regard for the independent legislator while rejecting more extreme cases of party support. In addition, it is also possible, but not likely, that norms will be absent from any relationships between a legislator and his party's leader. Some legislators may merely be indifferent towards party leadership, or in some instances a particular legislative body may share no consensus with regard to an approved relationship between the individual and his party's leaders. There may also be instances in which norms relating to an individual's willingness to follow party leadership may vary widely for different stages of the legislative process. Since this may indeed be the case, it is necessary to examine several different areas of party behavior and leadership support: behavior on procedural votes, substantive votes, and in committees.

Procedural Voting

Scholars of the legislative process have been most concerned with the role of party in roll call voting. One of the prerequisites for party to have an impact on voting is a set of norms which promote cohesion or solidarity. A study of the Wisconsin assembly has found that members are expected to follow their party in voting, especially on procedural items and legislation relevant to party platforms.[17] Wahlke and his associates in the four-state study also noted partisan norms and the emphasis on behavior which supports political parties, especially in competitive two-party states.[18]

It is necessary to make some distinctions, however, in the type of roll call voting relevant to party support. Although voting on matters of procedure is closely related to issues surrounding matters of substance, there are important distinctions between procedural and substantive roll calls, and these distinctions are most important for party leadership. Since procedural votes are less visible and sometimes viewed as less important by outsiders, the party leadership may have greater influence in the procedural areas. Procedural matters are especially complex, and they are of little interest to constituents, whereas substantive problems are highly visible and more likely to generate conflict between the legislator and his diverse constituency. Indeed, both a legislator's constituents and his party's leaders are more likely to tolerate defection from the party on substantive matters than on procedural votes. Adherence to party leadership on procedural votes may also serve to reduce conflict within legislative parties generated by disagreement over substantive matters. In effect, norms more supportive of a political party on procedural issues offer the leaders the opportunity for reducing conflict within the legislature.

In order to measure procedural voting norms, the members of the Oklahoma House and Senate were asked the extent to which they approve or disapprove (on a nine-point scale) of five possible behaviors ranging from "always" supporting the party's leadership to "never" supporting the party's leadership on procedural matters.

The optimal procedural voting norm selected on the basis of the highest mean level of approval from all legislators appears in Table 42. Members most approve of the individual who usually but not always follows his party's leadership in deciding how to vote on a procedural matter. This holds for both members of the House and of the Senate. Although this is an optimal procedural voting norm, members also expressed approval for the individual who sometimes

TABLE 42.—Optimal Partisan Norms in the Oklahoma Legislature

Behavior		Mean Level of Approval	
		House	Senate
A House (or Senate) member who . . .			
Procedural Voting	*usually*, but not always follows his party's leadership in deciding how to vote on a procedural matter.	5.7	5.7
Bill Voting	*sometimes* follows and sometimes does not follow his party's leadership in deciding how to vote on a bill	6.4	6.4
Committee Action	*sometimes* follows and sometimes does not follow his party's leadership in determining a course of action in committee.	6.2	6.4

follows his party's leadership in such matters. It should be noted, however, that neither means are high—suggesting that legislators' approval of this item borders on indifference. The other three possible procedural voting options fall outside the range of acceptable behavior. That is, there is disapproval for the legislator who always supports his party leadership, who seldom follows his party leadership, or who never follows the leadership in deciding how to vote on procedural matters.

Substantive Bill Voting

If the difference between procedural voting and substantive bill voting is as substantial as we suggested above, we would expect different norms to operate for the role of party leadership in substantive voting. Table 42 indicates that the optimal norm for bill voting is slightly different than the optimal norm for procedural voting: legislators in both houses strongly approve of individuals who follow and sometimes do not follow the party leadership. Only three per cent of the House and sever per cent of the Senate disapprove of such an individual. Although it was not an optimal norm, legislators also approve (but not as strongly) of the individual who usually follows the party leadership in substantive voting. Again, the extreme cases of the party man and the party maverick generated the greatest disapproval.

Committee Action

Floor voting on matters of procedure and substance, while most visible to the public, is only a part of the universe of important voting that takes place in any legislative chamber. Important votes occur at stages prior to any final vote on the passage of legislation and the most important of these occur in committee. We have suggested earlier that committees are sometimes a formidable hurdle in the passage of legislation and that considerable power rests at that level of the legislative process. We have also noted that in Oklahoma the majority party leadership plays an especially powerful role in the control of committee assignments and personnel. This points to an especially salient role for committee action. In order to measure a partisan norm relevant to behavior in committees, members of both houses were again asked to express their level of approval or disapproval for the extent to which an individual follows party leadership in determining a course of action in committee. The optimal norm presented in Table 42 indicates that legislators in both chambers approve most of the individual who sometimes follows and sometimes does not follow the leadership. Legislators also expressed some approval for the individual who usually follows leadership in guiding his behavior in committee. Both the frequent party man and the party maverick were widely rejected.

In summary, we find that members of both the House and the Senate accept a range of partisan behavior which includes only the legislator who usually supports party leadership and the legislator who sometimes supports the leadership. However, there was greater support for individuals who more frequently follow party leadership on procedural matters than on substantive bills or committee votes. It appears that legislators as a whole prefer members who remain relatively independent of party leadership on matters relevant to the substance of legislative policy—voting on bills and committee behavior. These differences are best captured in an analysis by McLemore:

The fact that members of both houses disapprove of both the party man and the party maverick but tended to be relatively indifferent towards the legislator who usually supports party leadership perhaps reflects the ambiguous character of party politics in the Oklahoma legislature. The vastly outnumbered Republicans have no power as a party, lacking even the ability to enforce party regularity. This was apparent in the comments of a Republican House member: "So I don't go along with the party—what can Republican leadership do to me? They simply don't control anything around here." Conversely, the wide majority enjoyed by the Democrats suggests that numerous party defections would probably not affect partisan outcomes in the legislature.[19]

FLOOR BEHAVIOR NORMS

We now move from a consideration of partisan norms in the Oklahoma legislature to those norms which regulate a variety of tasks encountered almost daily while the legislature is in session. In effect, these tasks pertain to all of the remaining major focal points in Figure 4. The daily activity of the legislature involves a complex set of tasks, including committee meetings, floor sessions, bill drafting, contacts with interest groups, the introduction of bills, and consideration of the governor's program. They all occur in a group or social context and there is reason to expect that basic norms govern all of them. Without such norms, individual legislators would have no way of judging the difference between appropriate and inappropriate ways of conducting the daily business in each chamber.

Studies in other legislative bodies have found support for the existence of such norms related to legislative tasks. In his now classic study of the Senate, Matthews found that U.S. senators are expected to serve an apprenticeship, specialize in some area of substantive expertise, be courteous to others and reciprocate, be loyal to the institution, and be "work horses and not show horses."[20] Similarly, research on state legislatures suggests that rules of the game are "couched in terms directly relevant to specific legislative functions and purposes,"[21] and that impersonality and a proper set of relationships with lobbyists are areas governed by shared beliefs.[22]

One of the basic areas of legislative life apparently governed by shared beliefs delineating behavior that is approved or disapproved is the area of floor activity and publicity seeking. Floor behavior and discussion is obviously one of the most visible aspects of a legislator's work—and that most familiar to the general public—but it would be naive to suggest that the core of legislative work occurs on the floor rather than in committees. Nevertheless, floor debate and activity is a vital element of the legislative process in Oklahoma. Such activity may be devoted to rational argument and debate or to attempts by individuals to seek publicity in the press. Both extremes obviously exist in the Oklahoma House and Senate. More specifically, there are four major areas of floor behavior which are potentially governed by norms: publicity seeking, floor speaking, freshman floor speaking, and the extent to which individuals deal in personalities during debate.

Publicity

State legislators achieve publicity in a variety of ways. They may speak actively on the floor in anticipation of reactions from their colleagues, a few constituents in the galleries, interest groups watching the legislature, and the mass media covering a legislative session. The entire area of floor behavior and publicity seeking poses a serious dilemma for the legislator. If he actively seeks publicity, he may antagonize or alienate his colleagues or gain the reputation of being a "show horse" rather than a "work horse." On the other hand, good publicity increases the individual's chances for reelection and may play a significant role in his ambition for higher political office. Sometimes he may even consciously avoid publicity, especially if his actions are likely to be unpopular with constituents. Similarly, a legislator may give a speech or hold a press con-

TABLE 43—Optimal Floor Behavior Norms in the Oklahoma Legislature

Behavior		Mean Level of Approval	
		House	Senate
A House (or Senate) member who . . .			
Publicity Seeking	*neither seeks nor attempts to avoid* publicity for his actions in the House (Senate)	6.6	6.6
Floor Speaking	speaks on the floor *almost as often* as other members	5.9	6.4
Freshman Floor Speaking	as a freshman speaks on the floor *less often* than most other members	6.2	6.1
Dealing in Personalities	*always avoids* dealing in personalities in his remarks on the floor of the chamber	8.2	8.3

ference aimed at achieving a particular legislative goal, but his colleagues and others may view this primarily as an attempt to gain favorable publicity for other ends. What is crucial, therefore, is not the individual's purpose in floor speaking or seeking publicity, but how his colleagues perceive his reasons for publicity seeking or his motivations for action. The legislator may be caught coming and going on this score, but the important determinant of that rests with the perceptions and attitudes of his colleagues.

In order to measure any general norm relevant to publicity seeking, individual legislators were asked their level of approval for five different behaviors, ranging from a conscious attempt to avoid any publicity to a conscious attempt to seek as much publicity as possible for actions in the House and Senate. The optimal norm in this area is listed in Table 43 with the respective mean levels of approval for both houses.

The data suggest that members of both chambers tend to be somewhat indifferent toward a legislator who always or usually avoids publicity, but they clearly disapprove of the individual who usually or always tries to seek publicity. The optimal norm favors the individual who neither seeks nor avoids publicity for his actions in the chamber. While there is disapproval of the legislator who usually seeks publicity, this disapproval is not intense. Only the individual who always tries to seek publicity is condemned in both chambers. As McLemore suggests in his analysis, "Oklahoma legislators appeared to be indifferent toward publicity seeking and most approved of the legislator who is also indifferent."[23]

Floor Speaking

A more concrete area of floor behavior relates to the frequency of floor speaking. Norms governing such activity have been noted in other state legislatures, including the Wisconsin assembly and the four states treated by Wahlke, *et al.*[24] These studies suggest that frequent talkers violate legislative norms and are viewed as monopolizers of debate or obstructionists. Indeed, these studies have ignored the possibility that individuals who do not speak may also be violating a norm; that is, that the norm may encourage at least a minimal amount of floor-speaking activity. In order to account for a broad range of possible behaviors, legislators were asked their level of approval of five different options ranging from never speaking to speaking much more often than others. The optimal behavior for members of both houses of the Oklahoma legislature was the middle category: speaking on the floor about as often as other members (Table 43). However, there is an indication that legislators tend to be indifferent to the frequency of others' floor speaking, except for the legislator who speaks much more often than others. Although it was not an optimal choice, legislators also approved of an individual who speaks less often than other members. The only behavior which is clearly prohibited in the Oklahoma legislature is that of speaking much more often than other members: only 15 per cent of the House and 12 per cent of the Senate approve of the individual who speaks that frequently. Legislative feelings about this behavior are reflected in the comments of one party leader in the Senate who suggested that "just because you know how to dance, doesn't mean you have to dance every dance," and the comment from a House leader that "the talkers don't accomplish much around here. Nobody likes them."

Freshman Floor Speaking

Is a different standard of acceptable floor speaking evident for freshmen than for the veteran member? Such a question is part of a larger set of issues that have been treated by a variety of legislative scholars, namely those associated with the idea of apprenticeship in the legislature. Studies of both the U.S. Senate and state legislatures[25] suggest that freshmen legislators are expected to serve an apprenticeship period during which they must work harder, speak less often, introduce fewer items of legislation, and show general respect or deference to veteran members with greater seniority.

The most integral aspect of this apprenticeship, and certainly the most visible, is the extent to which a freshman speaks on the floor of each chamber. When this issue was posed to all members of the legislature, their optimal choice was for a freshman who speaks on the floor less often than most other members. There was substantial agreement between members of both houses on this frequency. However, this should not suggest that other degrees of floor speaking activity are necessarily prohibited for freshmen. Indeed, the only behavior outside the range of acceptable behavior for freshmen is speaking more often than most other members. While they most approve of the freshman who speaks less often and most disapprove of one who speaks more often than others, members of the legislature tend to be indifferent towards the freshman who never speaks. In other words, the latter individual tends to draw little attention, either positive or negative. We must therefore conclude that there are different expectations for freshmen compared to other members with regard to floor speaking, but that the range of choices acceptable to other legislators are as wide for the freshman as for the veteran member.

Dealing in Personalities

To this point we have noted norms governing the frequency of floor speaking and publicity seeking without attention to the content of those activities. The specific content of floor speaking obviously varies from issue to issue and from day to day. Nevertheless, there is one underlying dimension of the content of floor speaking which is more general in nature and subject to normative influence: the extent to which individual legislators deal in personalities during their remarks on the floor of each chamber. Other studies of legislatures have found a clear prohibition against dealing in personalities. Indeed, in the Wahlke, *et al.* study of Ohio, New Jersey, California, and Tennessee this proscription was the third most commonly mentioned norm. Although courtesy may be an important component, some readers may wonder why there is a norm in favor of impersonality in the legislative chamber. The argument is a classical one dating from early consideration of fundamental aspects of debate and rational argument. Legislative floor discussion, as well as other means of formal political debate in the United States, is often governed by the belief that issues can only be resolved if their substance is separated from the individuals who are making particular substantive points. Separating personality from substance of debate, however, is often a very difficult task. A norm prohibiting dealing in personalities serves therefore to govern and counteract the tendencies to mesh personalities with critical substantive issues.

Members of both houses of the Oklahoma legislature feel strongly about this issue. The optimal norm favors the total avoidance of personalities while making remarks from the floor of each chamber and the means for both the House and Senate in Table 43 indicate relatively intense feelings on this issue. Although legislators give weak approval to the individual who seldom deals in personalities, they strongly disapprove of all other possibilities. For example, the extreme case of the individual who always deals in personalities is strongly disapproved by 83 per cent of the House members and 92 per cent of the State senators. This prohibition is clearly the strongest norm existing in the Oklahoma state legislature.

LEGISLATIVE SPECIALIZATION

With a complex array of public problems facing each session, observers of the legislature and members alike have often argued that specialization of task is essential for good legislation. Some degree of specialization is recognized through existing committee structure. However, this merely provides a framework within which subject-matter experts operate. The existence of a committee system does not necessarily guarantee that specialization will develop. Although the jurisdiction of some committees may be vaguely defined and quite broad, political scientists have noted that specialization of task is a primary and essential characteristic of contemporary legislatures.[26] In order to examine the extent to which norms supporting specialization have developed in the Oklahoma legislature, two aspects of legislation are explored in the McLemore study: subject matter or expertise specialization, and norms relevant to the number of bills introduced by individual legislators.

Expertise Specialization

A variety of legislative roles may develop reflecting norms about subject-matter expertise and the needs and styles of individual legislators. Specifically, legislators may see themselves as generalists, specialists in one primary area of legislation, or as something in between. The generalist is one who attempts to develop subject-matter expertise in all substantive areas faced in the legislative process. The individual who promotes this conscious role is most likely to be frustrated with the legislative process. There is a variety of forces at work in any legislature which limit the range of concerns that any lawmaker may attend to: a diversity of substantive areas faced in the legislative process, the brevity of legislative sessions, and the relative absence of individual legislative staff. While these factors may hinder the work of a generalist, there are also forces which are conducive to a generalist role: the absence of a firm seniority system which would guarantee regular service on particular committees, a diversity of constituency interests which may prohibit specialization, and a lack of expertise on the part of other legislators which may encourage the individual to broaden his substantive perspective. A second possible role is that of specialist in one primary area of legislation. This is the individual who is either more tied to one particular interest segment in his constituen-

TABLE 44—Optimal Specialization Norms in the Oklahoma Legislature

Behavior		Mean Level of Approval	
		House	Senate
A House (or Senate) member who . . .			
Expertise	tries to be an expert on *only a few* of the subject matter areas dealt with by the House (Senate).	7.1	7.1
Bill Introduction	introduces *about as many* bills as most other members	5.8	5.9

cy or has had considerable experience in only one area of public policy. A third role is the individual who attempts to achieve a balance between the extreme generalist and the extreme specialist by focusing on only a few areas of legislative activity. Of course, there is one other possible role that we have not yet mentioned: the individual who makes no effort at all to develop expertise in any area of legislative work. A study of the Connecticut legislature, for example, found that a large proportion of freshmen had little active interest in the legislative process.[27]

Data from both the Oklahoma House and Senate reported in Table 44 indicate that the optimal specialization norm for subject-matter areas prefers the individual legislator who attempts to be an expert on only a few of those areas dealt with by the House and Senate. House members are also willing to accept the individual who specializes in only a single subject-matter area, but they reject a legislator who does not try to be an expert at all and one who tries to be an expert on most areas or in all areas. Indeed, there is greater disapproval of the individual who tries to develop competence in all matters brought before the House than there is toward the individual who simply makes no effort at developing any subject-matter expertise. While the optimal norm is the same for both House and Senate, members of the latter chamber are willing to tolerate a wider range of behavior—including those who try to be experts in only one, a few, or even most subject-matter areas dealt with by the Senate. Both Houses reject the individual who makes no effort to be an expert as well as the generalist who tries to focus on all subject-matter areas. In effect, both houses lend strong support (as evidenced by the means in Table 44) for the individual who attempts to strike a balance between extreme generalization and extreme specialization to focus on only a few areas of policy.

Number of Bills Introduced

The need to specialize is reflected in some members' feelings that only a limited number of bills should be introduced by an individual each session. The forces in favor of a limited number of bills per legislator are similar to those which force specialization: legislative sessions are relatively brief, individuals have a large number of demands placed on their time, and individuals find it difficult to develop and push a large number of bills. This is especially true for legislation which is likely to develop conflict and controversy among colleagues and the public. As one member of the House commented, "You've got to do your homework and then educate the membership, talking to them one at a time." On the other hand, it is possible for some legislators to take a contrary view. They feel the need to comply with a variety of constituency demands, to gain favorable publicity, or to do the work of a legislative session as they see it: all of these forces encourage the introduction of a larger number of bills each session. There may also be legislators who fail to introduce any bills. Some of these people may have little confidence in their ability to get bills passed or in their ability to draft good legislation. Others may not lack legislative efficacy or expertise, but may firmly believe that no additional legislation is needed. Such a position is evident in the remarks of a senior Democratic House member: "All of these new bills introduced each session are a waste of time. Hell, we need to repeal the laws we've got"

In order to determine the most preferred behavior in the House and Senate each member was asked the extent to which they approved or disapproved of the member who never introduces any bills, who introduces fewer bills than others, and those who introduce about as many, slightly more or a great many more bills than other members. The results indicate that behavior falling within the extremes of introducing many more bills or never introducing legislation are accepted in both houses. Both extremes are rejected. However, legislators disapprove more of the individual who never introduces legislation than the one who introduces many more bills than others. Although the optimal norm for both houses favors the individual who introduces about as many bills as most other members, approval is not high compared to other norm areas (see Table 44). Indeed, members of the legislature are practically indifferent toward the number of bills their colleagues introduce, except for the two extreme behaviors which are obviously disapproved. While the number of bills introduced by each legislator is not subject to strong normative control, the data support the need for selective specialization, and should serve to discourage legislators who fail to introduce bills or who introduce many more than their colleagues.

INTEREST GROUPS AND THE GOVERNOR

Two major focal points for legislative norms complete the set of relationships outlined in Figure 4. These are norms which govern the relationships between legislators and two important "outsiders" in the legislative process: powerful pressure groups and the governor. While individuals in these two focal areas are not members of the legislature and therefore termed "outsiders," they are vitally interested in the work of the legislature; they have a close working arrangement and set of alliances with certain lawmakers; and they are crucial elements in the legislative decision making process. Their impact on the process, however, is guided by norms shared among legislators.

Members in each chamber must at some point decide how they are going to relate to requests from the executive branch and from the public. From time to time the individual legislator must evaluate these "outside" sources and make a decision about his primary loyalties—and he will have to make these decisions over and over again as he faces a variety of appeals from both pressure groups and the governor. Whether or not these groups and the governor will have an impact on the process is largely determined by the extent to which legislators are willing to accept appeals from them. If there were strong normative prohibitions in the legislature against working with professional lobbyists, their voices would not likely be heard. In addition, a governor's impact on legislation—regardless of political party arrangements—is likely to be governed by some basic group norms. Although partisan alignments and the partisanship of the governor obviously influence legislative voting, the degree to which his programs are adopted and the extent to which his influence continues throughout the session is dependent upon some basic agreements between legislators—Republicans and Democrats alike.

Interest Groups

In order to assess the norm for dealing with interest groups, legislators were asked the extent to which they approved or disapproved of those members who are known as spokesmen for interest groups; those who are closely affiliated with interest groups; those who are friendly but not committed; those who have nothing to do with interest groups but do not oppose them; and those who always oppose special interests and their lobbyists. The optimal norm for both the House and the Senate supports the legislator who is friendly with special interest groups and their lobbyists, but who is not committed to such groups (Table 45). In the House, the only other behavior within the acceptable range favors the individual who has nothing to do with special interest groups, but who does not actively oppose them. House members most disapprove of the legislator who is known as the spokesman for lobbyists.

Although the optimal preferred norm is the same for both the House and the Senate, the McLemore study brings evidence to bear which would indicate a closer working relationship between lobbyists and legislators in the Senate chamber. On closer examination, we find that those behaviors supporting a closer relationship between the legislator and interest groups had higher levels of approval in the Senate than in the House. Whereas 80 per cent of the

TABLE 45.—Optimal Norms for Relations with Interest Groups and the Governor

Behavior		Mean Level of Approval	
		House	Senate
A House (or Senate) member who . . .			
Interest Groups	is *friendly* with special interest groups and their lobbyists, but is *not committed* to such groups.	6.4	6.4
Gubernatorial Support	*sometimes* supports and sometimes opposes the programs of the governor regardless of the governor's party affiliation	6.7	7.2

House respondents disapproved of a member who is known as a spokesman for lobbyists, only 56 per cent of those in the Senate disapproved. And on those items suggesting more minimal contact with lobbyists or even opposition to their activities, higher means were found in the House than in the Senate. While both Houses tend to reject extreme positions for dealing with lobbyists, there is evidence to suggest that senators are "likely to maintain less distance between themselves and the lobbyists than are House members."[28]

Gubernatorial Support

Members of both the House and the Senate accept behavior which usually, but not always, supports the programs of the governor, and behavior which sometimes supports the governor regardless of his party affiliation. However, the latter (as shown in Table 45) was the optimal norm and support for the individual who usually, but not always, supports the governor's program tended to border on indifference. The optimal norm was strongly shared by members of both the House and the Senate: only 8 per cent of the House and 2 per cent of those in the Senate indicated disapproval for sometimes supporting and sometimes opposing the governor.

The following other possibilities fell beyond the range of acceptable behavior in both chambers: always supporting the governor; usually, but not always, opposing the governor's programs; and always opposing the governor regardless of his party affiliation. Among these, there is greatest disapproval for the legislator who always opposes the governor's program and less disapproval for those who always support the governor. Since both extremes are rejected on a widespread basis, it would be easy for some to conclude that the governor has no influence in the Oklahoma legislative process. This is certainly not the case. However, there is widespread belief that legislators should be relatively independent of gubernatorial influence, and that the governor's programs should be judged on the basis of their own merits.

This interpretation is supported by the comments of several legislators: "If the governor's programs are good, we support them. If they're bad, we beat the hell out of them . . . . I support good legislation—whether it comes from the governor or not . . . We try to cooperate with the governor when we can. His bills usually get serious consideration, but then his bills usually affect the state more than most of those introduced around here." Perhaps the most important impact of these views is that they do not prohibit gubernatorial influence. As we saw in Chapter 4, the governor's program has substantial impact on partisan voting trends in the legislature. In addition, McLemore suggests:

Indifference toward the member who usually supports the governor's programs—and disapproval of the member who usually opposes these programs—suggests that Oklahoma lawmakers accept the legitimacy of gubernatorial influence in the legislature. What is clearly rejected by members of both chambers are behaviors implying an automatic reaction to gubernatorial programs, Senate and House members condemned both those who always support and those who always oppose the governor's programs.[29]

The above discussion and the data reported in Table 45 support the existence of normative controls in the legislature over relationships with interest groups and the governor. In both areas, the attitudes of fellow legislators tend to support the independent lawmaker—a factor which is supportive of the integrity of the State legislature as a political institution.

AWARENESS OF SHARED BELIEFS

Throughout this chapter we have emphasized that the basic indicator of legislative norms is widespread agreement or consensus on a particular set of behaviors. It was also suggested that in order for norms to be operative, there must be interaction between legislative members and evidence that group processes are at work. Both of these conditions are met in the Oklahoma legislature. Yet for norms to be well developed and to have an impact on legislative behavior, members must not only share beliefs (consensus) about the appropriateness of certain behaviors, they must also perceive other legislators as sharing these beliefs. If such sharing exists, it is a good indication that group processes are at work, that an individual's attitudes are disseminated to other members of the legislature, and that behavior will be in conformity with evaluations. This is another way of saying that norms have both subjective and objective components: on the subjective side, legislators have preferences which reflect their own sense of the appropriateness of certain behaviors, and on the objective side, legislators have perceptions about the preferences of other legislators. Norms are most likely to be well developed and influential for behavior if legislators not only share beliefs, but see other legislators as sharing these same beliefs.

There are two types of evidence relevant to judging the level of subjective and objective similarity. The first is the extent to which individual legislators are consistent in preferring a certain behavior and perceiving that others also prefer that same general behavior. On the whole, members of the Oklahoma legislature are quite consistent in their perceptions and preferences: the average level of congruence across the eleven norm areas for the House is 64 per cent; and for the Senate, on the average 70 per cent of the members are congruent in their perceptions and preferences.[30] Although these figures are relatively high, it suggests that senators are more likely to be congruent in what they prefer and what they see others as preferring. Furthermore, there are slight differences from one behavorial area to another: members of both the House and the Senate (especially the House) tend to be less congruent on those behaviors related to political party. The greatest inconsistency occurs in the procedural voting area: only 45 per cent of the House and 46 per cent of the Senate perceive that others prefer the same behavior as is preferred by the individual legislator. In addition, McLemore reports evidence suggesting that there is a relationship between the level of congruence and seniority: that as legislative tenure increases, there is a greater tendency for norms to be well developed, in the sense that legislators prefer the same behavior as they see others preferring. In the other behavior areas examined earlier there is higher level of agreement between perceptions and preferences: members of both chambers tend to prefer personally the behavioral possibility they believed most preferred by others.

Another type of evidence relating to the congruence between subjective and objective components of norms takes into account those norms which are optimally preferred. When a legislator's optimal preferences are taken into account for those behaviors listed in Tables 42, 43, and 44, we also find a high level of consistency. This suggests that some legislators may prefer the optimal norm and see others as preferring it, while other legislators do not prefer the optimal norm, but see others as preferring it. The latter individual is a consciously styled "maverick" who thinks that other legislators prefer a certain behavior (and in fact they do), but he has another preference. Of course, the more of these people there are in the legislative body, the less well developed the norms. In both chambers of the Oklahoma legislature, this type of individual is in a substantial minority; most legislators in both chambers not only prefer the optimal norm, but see others as preferring it also. The only exception to this pattern is behavior relating to following party leadership when voting on procedural matters: among those who "correctly" see the optimal norm (to usually follow party leadership in deciding how to vote on procedural matters), only 43 per cent in the House prefer the norm, and 42 per cent in the Senate. However, for the remaining ten optimal norms, on the average 77 per cent of the House members and 83 per cent of the senators who perceive that others prefer the optimal norm, also prefer that optimal behavior themselves. The difference between these averages suggests further that norms are slightly better developed in the

Oklahoma Senate than in the House. Most important, this evidence indicates that individual legislators in both chambers clearly have a sense of what their colleagues prefer.

NORM SANCTIONS

A final indicator of the extent to which norms are well developed in any legislative body is the presence or absence of various sanctions to enforce adherence to particular norms. If norms are to be effective in regulating behavior, they must not only be widely shared and widely perceived, but in addition, the group must have means for enforcing adherence to agreed-upon behaviors.

In general, four basic conditions should be met if a sanctioning system is to operate and be effective in preserving legislative norms. First of all, individual legislators must, of course, be aware of norms, and the legislature must have ways to communicate norms to new members. The McLemore study, as well as others dealing with state legislatures, indicates that individuals are aware of unwritten rules of the game.[31] Secondly, members of the legislative chambers must believe or perceive that their own behavior is "monitored" by others. This surveillance of individual legislators may be a function of more specialized individuals in the legislative process (legislative leaders), or it may be performed by virtually all members of the chamber. Thirdly, in order for norms to be enforced there must actually be a set of either positive or negative sanctions which are applicable to behavior. In other words, the violation of a particular norm must "cost" the violator something, or, on the other hand, there must be ways for individuals who conform to norms to achieve some rewards. As we draw from studies of other states and the U.S. Senate, [32] we see that negative sanctions or "punishments" include reprimands, the obstruction of legislation, and general low effectiveness in the legislative process. On the rewards side, it has been found that those conforming to norms are most likely to be more effective, more influential, and members of an "inner club." Finally, a legislative body must have sets of individuals who actually apply these rewards or punishments for adherence or violation of legislative norms. Sometimes this rests with a single individual, such as a legislative leader, or it may rest with all other members of the legislative body who are capable of rewarding with praise or punishing with ostracism.

While at first glance the above conditions appear to be rather abstract or theoretical, they actually occur with associated mechanisms in most legislative bodies. A real-life example for the Oklahoma legislature relevant to an "embarassment" sanction is evidenced in the following description by McLemore:

Before a half filled gallery an elderly Senator rises, announces the first reading of his bill to increase the salaries of election judges, and proceeds to enumerate the benefits of such legislation. After five minutes of rhetoric in the best tradition of rural politicians in the southwest an equally aged Senator rises and calls for a "point of order." A third Senator reminds the first speaker that debate on the first reading of a bill is highly unusual and in this circumstance uncalled for. Still another member rises to suggest that the first speaker has "perhaps forgotten" the procedures of this somber chamber. At this point the enraged and frustrated speaker opens a brief but bitter exchange with his critics. The presiding officer, a first term Senator substituting for the President Pro-Tempore, is unable to settle the dispute arising over the point of order and a page is sent to the Senate Majority Leader asking for assistance. Quickly surmising the situation, the young and ambitious majority leader asks that the entire exchange be stricken from the records. He then asks the first speaker to withdraw his comments and await a later reading of his legislation for debate. Red with anger, the Senator agrees and is seated. Surprisingly, a younger member asks for special privilege and speaks for a few minutes praising the chastised member for his lengthy service to this chamber and to the state. Business then proceeds as usual.

What happened? When asked about these events a Senator who has remained silent during the exchange commented, "That S.O.B. was showboating, wanting to look good for his folks. A few of the members wanted to embarass him. He got what he deserved." Most of those in the gallery that afternoon were election judges from the main speaker's district. His bill, which later died in committee, had no chance whatsoever of passage: budgetary limitations precluded even a token salary increase for election judges (and there was strong sentiment that salaries were already high enough). What happened? A member violated a norm of the "somber chamber," was chastised, and the entire event smoothed over with the kind words of the last speaker.[33]

The above exchange is a good example of general norms and sanctions existing in the Oklahoma legislature, but a closer examination of the four conditions provides us with more concrete information about legislative sanctions.

Norm Awareness

All of the evidence, some of which has already been discussed, suggests that members of the Oklahoma House and Senate are quite aware of existing norms governing behavior. Most of these norms appear to be learned gradually through experience over the years, but the learning process appears to be most crucial for freshmen lawmakers. When a new member begins to perform in the rather complex and unfamiliar environment of the legislature, he begins to adjust to legislative norms. Since the Oklahoma legislature is an institution which people enter and leave, some observers might contend that new members in any particular session are capable of substantially changing the character of norms. This is rarely the cause. As documented in other studies, including a major research effort for the Connecticut Assembly,[34] the existing norms of a legislature have more impact on new members than vice versa. In other words, freshmen tend to be molded by the institution they are entering.

There are several ways by which freshmen can learn these legislative norms. Most members of the Oklahoma House and Senate have expressed the belief that other members made at least "a little" effort to inform them of various unwritten rules of the game, and only 15 per cent of the House and 12 per cent of the Senate claimed that colleagues made no effort at all to tell them about norms. This kind of information is passed along to freshmen largely during the first several months of a new legislative session and from preliminary contacts with colleagues during the presession legislators' conference organized by the Legislative Council and the University of Oklahoma. Yet some freshman legislators become aware of norms through more unpleasant channels. One individual, for example, told us that his first acquaintance with norms came when "they lowered the boom on me." In addition, a Senate party leader relayed the following attempt on his part to inform a norm violater of "proper" behavior:

I'm not a religious nut, but I believe that the Bible gives good counsel on these matters—my church applies them and I try to apply them here in the Senate. First, I personally go by his (the norm violator) office and discuss the matter with him on a one to one basis—he may not know that what he is doing is wrong. If they continue in their ways a group of Senators, including myself, will visit with the member and try to persuade him. If this fails, we are forced to bring the matter before the full membership (of the Senate). And if this fails . . . (hesitation) we wipe him out.[35]

Although individuals may be informed of norms through a variety of mechanisms, there is no evidence to suggest that Oklahoma lawmakers are unaware of these norms. When they were asked to identify the "unwritten rules" of their chamber, only two House members failed to identify a norm, and only one senator claimed to know of no norms in the Senate. In total, 57 per cent of the House were able to name three or more norms, and 61 per cent of the Senators were capable of doing so. These data suggest that lawmakers recognize that there is something more to the legislature than formal rules, and that any efforts to enforce norms are likely to be seen as legitimate by lawmakers. This is further supported by our previously cited finding that a large majority of both the House and the Senate felt that there was a right and wrong way of getting things done in each chamber.

Norm Monitoring

If norms are to operate effectively, individual lawmakers must believe that their behavior is being monitored or watched by others. The amount of surveillance is likely to vary from one norm area to another, and the individuals who do the "monitoring" are also likely to vary. As an example, when a lawmaker personally attacks a colleague who is in violation of legislative norms, the entire membership is likely to observe that behavior and offer such sanctions as embarrassment or ostracism. On the other hand, when a lawmaker violates party norms—such as deviating from a party vote—that monitoring of norm violation is most likely to come from the party leadership. We have previously presented information on the extent to which other members of the legislature are aware of an individual's behavior, including the extent to which lawmakers feel that leaders are aware of their behavior (Table 41).

The data for these monitoring agents suggest that a vast majority of members agree that other members and leaders are aware of what they do. The widespread agreement that other individuals are aware of behavior suggests that some type of monitoring or surveillance is likely.

Rewards and Punishments

An awareness of norms and the belief that there are monitoring devices in the legislature have no particular meaning unless there are actual sanctions—both positive and negative—to enforce behavior in conformity with norms. Although we can often think of norm violation only in terms of punishments, any legislative system is likely to have a mixture of both rewards and deprivations. That is, both chambers have means of encouraging conformity and means of discouraging nonconformity to norms. Although this distinction is meaningful, it is likely that most legislators think most in terms of negative sanctions—what they have to lose by not conforming. These negative sanctions are more visible and more immediate than the more long-term rewards and satisfactions of legislative life.

In order to measure the available sanctions in the Oklahoma legislature, individual respondents were asked the following questions: (1) "How was it made difficult for those members who do not follow these unwritten rules?"; and (2) "How was the member who carefully obeyed these unwritten rules rewarded?"

There is widespread belief in the Oklahoma House and Senate that negative sanctions are available. Indeed, only six members of the House and none of the Senators felt that things were not made difficult for them if they violated the unwritten rules of the game. Over half of the members of both chambers were able to identify two or more negative sanctions.[36]

Four areas of vulnerability to sanctions were most commonly mentioned. (1) The effectiveness of the member—more members of the legislature suggested that effectiveness was lost for violating unwritten rules. Most of them indicated that this had a very specific meaning—that it was more difficult for norm violators to get their legislation passed. (2) Personal relationships—the next most frequently mentioned punishment was a general deterioration of personal relationships with other members. This is a particularly important sanction since the passage of legislation involves not only cooperation, but mutual respect and personal interrelationships with colleagues. We have noted elsewhere that most members (two-thirds) agree that the likelihood of a bill's passage largely depends upon who is sponsoring it. The need for close personal regard and cooperation in light of this sponsorship factor is evident in the following comment from the floor: "A vote for this bill is a vote for Senator (the bill's sponsor). A vote against it is a vote against him" (the bill in question was immediately passed).[37] (3) Committee appointments—the third most frequently mentioned sanction was poor committee assignments in both the House and Senate. Such assignments are not only personally important to legislators, but they can have a significant impact on the passage of legislation. Memberships on key committees involve more power than other committees. Serving in a particular expertise area may be quite important for the individual who has certain substantive interests, and furthermore, his reelection and prestige may largely be based on such assignments. (4) Other sanctions mentioned often included those associated with the leadership. The leadership may personally ignore the wishes of norm violators, and it has special powers, particularly noticeable in the House, in the assignment of office space, secretarial assistance, and pages. In a recent study of reapportionment efforts, for example, it was found that particular "troublesome" legislators were given poor office space and only minimal secretarial assistance.[38]

Do Oklahoma legislators see any particular rewards for conformity? On the whole, members of both houses were less able to articulate such rewards, but when they did so, they corresponded to some of the negative sanctions or punishments. As with the negative sanctions, rewards were most commonly believed to involve an individual's effectiveness and influence, his personal relations in the chamber, and committee assignments. Substantial proportions of both the House and the Senate (approximately 40 per cent) mentioned that conformity to norms is rewarded by increased likelihood that one's own legislation will be passed. Similarly, 18 per cent of the House and 11 per cent of the Senate felt that a gain in overall effectiveness or influence resulted from norm conformity. Other Senators and House members felt that the reward for conformity was winning the respect of others, improving personal relationships, or obtaining better committee assignments. Gaining respect and improving interpersonal relationships appeared to be most important to senators, whereas committee assignments and favors from the leadership were more often cited as rewards in the House.

Sanctioning Agents

In addition to an awareness of norms, the monitoring of behavior, and the availability of sanctions, a legislative body must have people or agents capable of offering sanctions—either rewards or punishments. Just as "monitoring" should not imply a "big brother" atmosphere in the Oklahoma legislature, we should be particularly cautious in making assumptions about legislators' motives or intentions while achieving norm conformity. Legislators do not serve to "whip others into line," but they do react to others in ways not uncommon to everyday life. Much of it boils down to the fact that most of us are less likely to be friendly and helpful toward others whom we dislike—and the extent to which we "dislike" them is often based on the extent to which they agree with us. Therefore, some of the sanctioning that occurs in the legislature is based not only on nonconformity to norms, but on other more complex personal reasons.

In order to measure the sources or agents for sanctioning, legislators were asked the following question after the query requesting them to identify sanctions: "Without naming names, who is most likely to make things difficult for these (norm violating) members?" Individuals were therefore asked to identify others who impose negative sanctions—and this makes sense since most negative and positive sanctions were highly related to each other, as noted above. The responses to this question indicate that leadership was seen as the basic source of sanctions.[39] In the House, 28 per cent of the members made a general reference to leadership, and likewise, 31 per cent of the Senate also indicated that leadership generally provided sanctions. All in all, 50 per cent of the House and 43 per cent of the Senate made some mention of the leadership as an agent. Nevertheless, specific references to leaders showed noticeable differences between the chambers. A surprisingly large number of House members (21 per cent) specifically identified the speaker as a source of negative sanctions, whereas only 7 per cent of the senators indentified their corresponding formal leadership position (president pro tempore) as a source of "punishment." In addition, there is widespread belief in both chambers that the "membership as a whole" sanctions norm violators. Indeed, 50 per cent of the senators claimed that "everybody in the chamber" made it difficult for those who violate Senate norms, and in the House—where personal relationships appear to be less affected by sanctions—29 per cent of the members felt that the entire chamber acted as a sanctioning agent collectively. Important differences appear on other items that were mentioned. In the House, two particular "types" of legislators were mentioned as agents: committee chairmen (14 per cent) and senior members (10 per cent). On the other hand, only two individuals in the Senate mentioned seniority associated with sanctions, and no Senators mentioned committee chairmen as sanctioning agents. In general, members of the Senate have a more "diffuse" or generalized perception of sanctioning agents to include the leadership in general and the chamber as a whole, whereas House members tie those sanctions to specific individual leaders, older members, or committee chairmen.

In summary, the existence and importance of legislative norms for governing behavior are reinforced in the Oklahoma legislature by widespread awareness of norms, the availability of positive and negative sanctions, perceptions of "surveillance," and the actual enforcement of sanctions by certain individuals or the membership as a whole. Although there is considerable commonality between the sanctioning system in the Oklahoma House and Senate, senators appear to be most concerned with legislative effectiveness and personal relations as they may be affected by norm violations, and they are most likely to see sanctioning agents in more general terms.

CHAPTER 6

External Legislative Relationships: Constituents, Interest Groups, and the Press

The previous chapters have emphasized factors internal to the Oklahoma legislature, the rules and procedures associated with the passage of legislation, and the informal "rules of the game" relevant to everyday tasks. Yet those elected to serve as State senators and representatives do not exist in a legislative vacuum. Each legislator also relates to persons outside the respective chambers. These external relationships exist for three broad groups: constituents, pressure and interest groups and their representatives, and men and women from the press and news media. Since most of the contact between a legislator and someone outside the Senate or House relates to legislative business, the importance of positive relations so crucial to internal affairs extends beyond the walls of the state capitol. Most legislators understand the necessity for contact with "outsiders," both as a means for lawmaking and as a mechanism for buttressing a political career.

While it may be possible to argue over which group of these outsiders is most important to the legislator, most would place primary emphasis on constituents — those individuals who elected and will continue to elect or defeat a legislator. Yet a constituent may not often concern himself with a legislator's actions, and if he does, his perceptions of a representative may have little to do with direct contact. That is, other outsiders, such as news media and pressure groups have the capacity to influence constituents' views of legislators. Although each group will be treated in separate sections below, they form a complex system of interrelationships in the real political world.

CONSTITUENT RELATIONSHIPS

Most legislators view their constituents as a special group. If not in practice, at least in theory the legislator is responsible to those who elect him. Such political responsibility implies contact with, service for, and interaction with constituents, and it may occur in a variety of forms. Sometimes the interaction is promoted by the constituent, other times by the legislator himself. Among those contacts initiated by electors, the most frequent form of contact is letters written directly to representatives on an important issue before the legislature. Such letters will often suggest, demand, and attempt to persuade the legislator to follow a particular course of action on a bill. Some may even indicate that, if the legislator holds a differing view from that of the constituent, he will not vote for the legislator during the next election. Some of the constituents may also choose to contact a legislator by telephone, but whatever the mechanism of contact, the reply usually comes through similar channels. To insure the ability for elected representatives to communicate with constituents, each Senate and House member is allocated a supply of stamps and has access to statewide phone service. How they use their services to communicate with constituents depends upon the type of content of the communication received. If the constituent is voicing an opinion contrary to that of the legislator an immediate response usually follows. This may range from a simple acknowledgement to an in-depth explanation of why the legislator feels as he does. Most experienced legislators will have a better grasp of how to respond to such a situation than freshmen, and all types of considerations obviously come into play: the security of a legislator's district, the proximity of an election, and the shape of constituency opinion. These are just several of the many factors which enter the mind of a legislator when dealing with his constituents, but above all, his behavior and mode of response are structured to avoid the alienation of constituents.

Since the need for information and contact with constituents is a reciprocal process, all lawmakers initiate some form of contact. Under special circumstances a legislator may send out a questionnaire to his constituents. If the individual is an incumbent, this is most likely to occur prior to election time. The questionnaire is usually structured to obtain an idea of issues of the day which constituents feel are important. Since a proper stand on an important issue prior to an election is often a prerequisite for reelection, the legislator employs the questionnaire as a form of communication with constituents. The accuracy of any such poll depends on two criteria: (1) the structure of the sampling design, and (2) how much money the legislator can spend. A well structured sampling design will accurately reflect the opinions of all the constituents in a legislator's district, but it will also cost a great deal of money. Generally speaking, the legislator usually spends less money and obtains a less accurate sampling of how his constituents think. It is important that the results of any questionnaire be evaluated in reference to its reliability. It could be political disaster for a legislator to base a decision upon constituent opinions gathered from a biased sample. The technicalities of opinion polling need not concern us here, but it should be remembered that not all polls are accurate. The legislator must be keenly aware of the limitations inherent in opinion polling, and proceed from there to take whatever action toward his constituents he feels warranted. Since each legislator has to pay personally to have a poll conducted the questionnaire is not a commonplace means of communicating with constituents in Oklahoma. Yet as it grows in popularity, particular care must be taken to avoid biased results.

A somewhat less technical but more personal way legislators communicate with constituents is through a trip "back home." On weekends, during special events, or before elections the legislator often visits the towns in his district. This type of communication is positive and often essential. As one legislator said in this regard, "If they want to be reelected. . . they better stay in contact with their constituents." This feeling of importance attributed to personal contact with constituents is stated widely througout the legislature.

There are instances when a legislator may not be required to visit the "home folks" in order to be reelected. A few of the older and more established members may not visit or have much personal contact with their constituents. This, however, is rare, and these few men are usually considered to be "institutions" due to their personal attraction and solidarity at home with their constituents. In the language of legislative structures, these few men occupy *safe seats*—their districts are secure and reelection is virtually guaranteed regardless of what the legislator does. In Oklahoma, some of the leadership in the House and Senate have enjoyed this type of security. There have also been members from both chambers who have served upwards of twenty years in one or the other legislative bodies. To occupy such a position greatly simplifies the legislator's relations with all "outsiders."

A legislator, regardless of his status with the people back home, must at some time either run for reelection or retire from the legislative service. If the decision is made to retire or simply not to run for reelection again, the opinions of constituents need not affect the legislator at all. But to run for reelection necessitates some image in relation to constituents. Personal contact is an integral part of a successful image, but just how this image is developed depends upon those items deemed important by the legislator himself. He must find out through trial and error what pleases and offends his voters. Some may be required to spend more time in their home district than others, and some may find written communication an important aspect of this legislative image.

There are times when groups of constituents may simply want to visit the state capitol and their elected representative. These visitors may include such groups as high school civics classes, scouting groups, civic clubs, and other groups of interested citizens. Good relations between these visiting constituents and their legislator is vital to his legislative image. When these visitors arrive at the state capitol, the legislator representing them may do several things to develop good rapport between himself and his constituents. Many of these visiting groups may want a tour of the state capitol complex—this is usually arranged by the legislator, or if the day's business is less intense, he may conduct the tour himself. Most groups also want to witness the workings of the House and Senate. Galleries are available in both chambers where visitors may observe the actual proceedings of the legislature in action. Whether these constituents decide to visit the House or Senate chamber or both, they are usually recognized by their representative prior to the day's activities. This practice of recognizing a visiting group of constituents is not only a matter of courtesy, but an aspect of developing good relations with the people back home.

Although the above are insignificant gestures, they provide a positive forum from which the legislator can pursue a favorable image. At any given time, constituents may take a concerted look at their representative. In a real sense, an image tightrope is walked by each legislator. They must try to please as many people as possible while at the same time paying respect to their own feelings. Political viability is often dependent upon his conception of representation and how he sees his role as a representative.

REPRESENTATIONAL ROLES

The concepts of legislation and representation are closely intertwined througout classical political thinking. Lawmaking is accepted as legitimate only insofar as it is accomplished through a process which has widespread acceptance. Legislative bodies developed and grew out of pressing needs for the voice of the common man to be heard in the chambers of royal government. But beyond the simple notion that men shall elect others to represent them, the concept of representation is exceedingly complex. It is tied to notions of reponsibility and the ability to throw out old governments and elect new ones; to complex formulas and procedures for election; to notions of one man, one vote and reapportionment; to the equal weighting of votes in a legislative body; to notions that more than one legislator may represent the same individuals; to concepts of functional representation where a legislator may represent a single group; and to ideas of virtual representation where even an appointed official may be assumed to represent a certain constituency. Despite these complexities, the core of the representation issue is the extent to which a legislator reaches decisions in accord with demands and interests of the represented. Since the degreee to which this holds varies from individual to individual and constituency to constituency, we find that a legislator may assume one of a variety of styles of representation. These styles are inherent in his conception of a representational role.

Although substantial constituency influence over legislators seems to be a basic normative principle of American politics, the facts of legislative life are not nearly so simple. Indeed, this *delegate* role position was seriously questioned from the beginnings of parliamentary government. In the mid-eighteenth century, for example, we find the political philosopher Edmund Burke arguing that representatives should serve the constituency interests but not its will, that he should serve the interests of the nation and that he should not be bound by specific instructions. This *trustee* or *free-agent* conception of representation emphasizes the deliberative

function of the legislature, a wide interest rather than local purposes and prejudices, and a general good resulting from the general
reason of the whole. This issue of the free agent or trustee versus
the mandate or instructed-delegate theory (which emphasizes constituency consultation and instructions rather than independent
judgment) remains with us today. Certain legislators are more likely to see themselves in one of these primary roles than the other.
However, it is possible for them to combine role orientations with
some components of the trustee and some components of the
delegate. The latter is usually referred to as a *politico.*

The extent to which Oklahoma legislators adopt one of the three
basic representational roles—trustee, delegate or politico—is well
documented in fairly recent research. In 1967 and 1968 House and
Senate members were sampled and interviewed in order to ascertain
representational roles through the following questions:

1. How would you describe the job of being a state legislator — that is,
what are the most important things that you should be doing here?

2. How would you describe the atmosphere of the legislature?

3. I seldom have to sound out my constituents because I think so much like
them I know how to react to almost any proposal (agree-disagree).

4. My district includes so many different kinds of people that I often don't
know just what the people there want me to do (agree-disagree).

5. The legislator should consider the views of his constituents along with
his personal views when determining his position on an issue
(agree-disagree).[1]

The most prevalent representational role in the Oklahoma
legislature is clearly that of *trustee*—a finding in substantial congruence with results in four other states.[2] The findings presented in
Table 46 indicate that half of the Oklahoma House and nearly half
of the Senate view themselves as trustees or free agents. Although
these individuals claim to follow their own convictions and principles above and beyond constituency interests, there may be a
variety of underlying reasons for taking such a representational
role. Sometimes the trustee's ideas and attitudes are congruent with
those represented—or at least he perceives them to be—and since
there is harmony, he finds it unnecessary to pay attention to instructions from constituents. Other trustees may rely on their own
conscience in making decisions since the constituents, lobbyists and

TABLE 46.—Representational Role Orientations in Oklahoma and Four Other States

Representational Roles	Oklahoma		New Jersey	Ohio	California	Tennessee
	Senate	House				
Trustee	45.8%	50.0%	61.0%	56.0%	55.0%	81.0%
Politico	41.7	40.0	22.0	29.0	25.0	13.0
Delegate	12.5	10.0	17.0	15.0	20.0	6.0

other colleagues may not be trusted. Furthermore, the role of trustee should not necessarily imply that constituency interests are completely snubbed, for some representatives try to persuade their constituents that a certain position is relevant or correct. Other trustees may also assume that the electorate expects them to base legislative decisons on considered judgements and an assessment of facts not available to the ordinary citizen. Indeed, a trustee may follow his own judgment to avoid being influenced by others whom he considers ill informed. Even others may find it impossible to understand or discover constituency interests and preferences with regard to certain matters of policy. Any of the above reasons may be used as justification for the trustee role, and it is important to note that some representatives are willing to accept the political consequences of a refusal to be influenced by public opinion.

Evidence of these perceptions of a Burkean representational role is contained in the following scenario of comments from several members of the Oklahoma House:

I don't explain my vote to anybody. . . . What I do is my own decison. If they don't like it, then they don't have to send me back. . . .I am burned up about being misinformed by uninformed people. Quite often I vote my own conscience. . . . We have press conferences and a radio program. Here we tell them what we're doing. We usually don't ask what to do. . . . I can vote my true conscience and be elected.

Trustees in the Oklahoma Senate agree:

After elected, I represent all the people. I vote my own conscience as long as I am in the Senate. . . . I vote the way I want to do. If they don't like it, I won't be reelected. . . .As Edmund Burke said, "I am not a weathercock, turning my face to every fresh blowing breeze."

Although many citizens and political observers would expect the primary representational role to be delegate-oriented, data from Oklahoma and other states presented in the table indicate that it is the least popular representational role conception. These people feel that independent judgment or principles of conviction should not be the primary guiding force in decision making. But this does not always imply that legislators will follow instructions from any particular interest or constituency. Some merely consult constituents, while others explicitly ask for instructions on voting. In fact, some *delegates* even believe they should follow instructions when they are counter to the individual's own good judgment. Since it is rarely easy to follow any explicit instructions for voting from a complex constituency and set of interests, the delegate role is probably the most simplistic interpretation of the representation process. An example of verbatim responses from House and Senate members indicates the basic characteristics of the delegate role:

> If my people want it, it's my job to represent them — even over the governor's view or my personal view — even if it's not as good a bill that they favor. . . . Wish I could hear more to get a better idea of what they think. If you know what they want, you must vote as they say. . . . My job is to actively reflect what my people want. . . . Yes sir, that's my job, to know and do what my constituents want. . . . I have voted against a bill that I introduced becauce my constituents were against it later.

Since a substantial proportion of State legislators may hold more than one representational role orientation from time to time, allowances were made for an orientation somewhere between the delegate and trustee. The *politico* tends to vacillate from a delegate to a trustee orientation and back again, or, indeed, he may take both orientations simultaneously. Such an individual exhibits flexibility in his representational style, and such an interpretation usually relieves the tension and conflict caused by making conscious choices between the delegate and trustee conception. The politico therefore differs from other legislators in his awareness of conflicting choices, his flexibility in resolving conflicts, and his less dogmatic approach to role. The sample data from the late 1960's indicate that approximately 40 per cent of both houses of the Oklahoma legislature take the politico representation role. Comments from House members illuminate this position:

On things purely political you represent your constituents. Once you enter the floor of the House you represent the state. . . . I vote with the majority of my constituents. But sometimes they don't have an opinion — then I vote my convictions. . . . We need a balance between the state and local here.

And senators agree:

I vote what they want up to a certain point. . . . I vote for what my constituents want to a certain extent. Sometimes they do not have enough information, then I vote the way I think. . . . I generally go along with the idea of voting the way my constituents want. However, there are two other factors involved: state benefits and my personal principles.

Part of the model of the legislative system suggested in Chapter 1 indicates a few factors which may be associated with taking different representational roles. Although only a few of these factors have been examined for a sample of the Oklahoma House and Senate there are several apparent influences at work. It has been found that almost two-thirds of urban Senators are trustees, while the bulk of rural Senators are politicos. Although rural House members are equally divided between trustee and politico roles, urban House members are more likely to be trustees. These data suggest that urban environments are more likely to facilitate a free agent interpretation, and that a pure delegate or wavering politico role is particularly difficult to achieve in areas where inerests are complex and constituencies more diverse. It is apparently easier for representatives from urban areas to take the role of trustee and vote their own conscience. Although representational roles appear with few clear relationships to age, increasing years of legislative experience are apparently tied to the politico role. Less experienced members of both houses tend to vote their own conscience and those with more tenure adopt a flexible role between the trustee and delegate. Few partisan differences emerge between role types. However, Republicans are slightly more likely to be trustees than Democrats. There are also few links between educational level or occupation type, except that businessmen are less likely to vote their own conscience than lawyers. Since only a few clear patterns emerge from a comparison of background factors and representational role types, further research on the Oklahoma legislature should take other factors into account, as suggested in the role model in Chapter 1.

In order to assess more comprehensively the nature of representational roles in the Oklahoma House and Senate, we asked legislators a number of detailed questions about representation and constituency pressures.[3] Members of both the House and Senate were asked a series of nine questions to elicit their feelings about representation and their preceptions of constituents and other legislators. The responses to the questions listed in Table 47 generally reaffirm the predominance of a trustee role, and provide more specific information in a number of areas.

Although the first question listed in Table 47 has no particular reference point or basis for comparative judgments, the responses indicate that approximately 80 per cent of the Oklahoma legislature think their vote almost always reflects their own personal feelings. Although there is no reason to doubt legislator's honesty in responding to this question, it is difficult to judge what alternatives were in their own minds when they indicated that voting on issues is a reflection of personal feelings. A more accurate and specific indication of the trustee role appears in the responses to the second question in Table 47, and it comports with findings from the previously discussed role analyses of the Oklahoma House and Senate in the late 1960's. From 41 to 48 per cent of the legislature agrees that one should vote his own conscience even if it conflicts with the wishes of the people. Experience with research in other states suggests that this particular question, more so than any other, is probably a more accurate reflection of trustee roles.

Although previous studies of the Oklahoma legislature have not inquired about the areal roles mentioned in Chapter 1 (that is, whether one is district or state-oriented), the findings from an areal role question included in the most recent comprehensive analysis of the Oklahoma House and Senate are presented in Table 47. There is no doubt that areal roles and representational roles are closely intertwined. Other studies have found that individuals who view themselves as trustees or free agents are more likely to consider the good of the state when they cast their vote in the legislature rather than having a primary concern for the good of their own individual district. Indeed, the responses to this question indicate that a majority would vote for something good for the state even if their own legislative district were against it.

The remaining items in Table 47 attempt to measure a variety of perceptions and feelings about constituents. Although we have noted few differences in responses between House and Senate, an

TABLE 47.—Legislators' Attitudes About Representation

	Always		Almost Always	Seldom
Extent to which vote in the legislature is a true indication of *personal feelings* on an issue.				
House (N = 88)	13.6%		77.3%	9.1%
Senate (N = 43)	9.3		81.4	9.3

	Strongly Agree	Somewhat Agree	Somewhat Disagree	Strongly Disagree
A legislator should always vote according to the dictates of his conscience even if his vote conflicts with the wishes of the people.				
House (N = 90)	16.7%	24.4%	38.9%	20.0%
Senate (N = 42)	9.5	38.1	31.0	21.4
If something is good for the state, a legislator should support it even if the people back home don't like it.				
House (N = 90)	30.0	36.7	22.2	11.1
Senate (N = 42)	28.6	28.6	28.6	14.3
I seldom have to sound out my constituents because I think so much like them I know how to react to almost any proposal.				
House (N = 90)	20.0	53.3	22.2	4.4
Senate (N = 44)	18.2	36.4	27.3	18.2
It is extremely important that a legislator perform services for his constituents.				
House (N = 90)	65.6	30.0	3.3	1.1
Senate (N = 44)	81.8	15.9	2.3	0
A legislator cannot be effective if he is constantly concerned with reelection.				
House (N = 90)	53.3	25.6	11.1	10.0
Senate (N = 44)	54.5	31.8	11.4	2.3
My constituents are usually aware of my behavior here in the House (Senate).				
House (N = 90)	32.2	33.3	26.7	7.8
Senate (N = 44)	29.5	22.7	25.0	22.7
Generally speaking, I usually feel a great deal of pressure from my constituents to vote a particular way.				
House (N = 90)	8.9	18.9	43.3	28.9
Senate (N = 43)	2.3	14.0	51.2	32.6
Often legislators get so involved in affairs of the capitol that they lose touch with their constituents.				
House (N = 90)	12.2	40.0	31.1	16.7
Senate (N = 43)	18.6	44.2	20.9	16.3

interesting pattern appears when legislators are queried about the extent to which they must sound out constituents and the extent to which they perceive themselves as knowing constituency wishes. In discussing roles previously, we suggested that some legislators believe they have internalized the interests of their constituency or that they have a feel for the "collective will" of their electorate. In Oklahoma, 73 per cent of the House members agree that they seldom have to sound out constituents, since they know how to react to almost any proposal, while only 54 per cent of the Senate feel this way. Although both figures represent a majority of representatives, it is obvious that House members find it less essential to sound out their constituency. These members apparently have a better feel for their district; a finding which is certainly understandable, since those districts are smaller and often more homogeneous than Senate districts. In addition, legislators overwhelmingly agree that they should perform services for their constituents, yet approximately 80 per cent also feel that their effectiveness is diminished if they are constantly concerned with reelection. While they apparently feel that legislators should not devote an enormous amount of time to constant campaigning, a majority also think that other legislators often get so involved at the state capitol that they lose touch with their home base.

While district characteristics might make it easier for Oklahoma House members to "think" like their constituents, these House members apparently feel a greater degree of surveillance from their electorate. The data in Table 47 indicate that 65 per cent of the House agree that constituents are aware of their behavior, while this figure is somewhat lower for the Senate (53 per cent). Some observers of politics may claim that both of these figures are surprisingly low, yet data obtained from congressional constituencies in the United States show that even fewer voters are aware of legislative politics and behavior. In selected congressional districts in 1958, even that proportion of the public that was sufficiently interested to vote displayed little knowledge of congressional candidates: almost half of the voters (46 per cent) had read or heard nothing about either the Republican or Democratic candidate in districts where such partisan opposition was evident.[4] Although we have no comparable constituency data for Oklahoma, this national trend is somewhat reflected in a question on how much pressure representatives feel from constituents with regard to their vote. The data in Table 47 indicate that only small minorities in both houses feel a great deal of pressure, and House members apparently feel more pressure (28 per cent) than Senators (16 per cent).

In summary, the largest proportion of Oklahoma legislators view themselves as trustees, and a substantial segment (more than three-quarters) claim that their vote reflects their own personal feelings. A majority claim to vote for the good of the state over their district, and approximately 80 per cent feel their effectiveness is reduced if they are too concerned with reelection. Yet they see no basic conflict in their role, as a majority find it unnecessary to sound out constituents since they claim to think like them or know their interests. In spite of the predominant trustee orientation, a majority feel that other legislators often lose touch with their constituents, and that constituents are aware of their behavior, although few feel pressure to vote in a certain way. Differences between the House and Senate suggest that House members feel closer to their constituents in the sense that they claim to think for them and to have to contact them less often. They are also more likely to feel pressure from constituents and to perceive that voters are more aware of their behavior in the legislature.

ORGANIZED INTERESTS

A second major group of "outsiders" influential in the legislative process in Oklahoma includes a variety of organized interests and their official representatives. Altough the trustee role is prevalent in Oklahoma — suggesting that many legislators rely on individual judgment in voting and are less susceptible to group demands — such an orientation does not preclude the effective operation of organized interests or attention to selected groups within individual districts. Indeed, it can be argued that unorganized public opinion has little chance of influencing policy outcomes. The constituent's voice reaching a lawmaker has more influence and impact if that voice is channeled through an organized group. On the whole, organized interests have a much better chance of interacting with and influencing the legislator. Such a group is better equipped to approach a legislator than the single citizen, and it has been reported that approximately one-third of the American population belongs to one kind of interest group or another.[5]

An interest group is a shared-attitude group that makes certain claims upon other groups in society.[6] It is formed primarily for the attainment of common goals through direct communication with government decision makers. This sharing of related attitudes and common perspectives separates the interest group from other segments of society—its intention is a visible and active commitment to the furtherance of goals held in common by all members. One Oklahoma legislator concluded that the main function of the interest group was "perpetuating their common goals," and they do so by making claims on legislators and administrators—those who have "power" to act upon their requests. Technically, a *pressure group* is an interest group which applies direct or indirect pressure on government decision makers. The interest group per se may not be in the process of applying any particular pressure, yet it is still an organized group of individuals sharing common attitudes. For example, a local chapter of the Veterans of Foreign Wars (VFW) may rarely "pressure" legislators. However, at any given moment their common attitudes may be translated into common goals expressed by the group, and these common goals may become political goals. That is, the Veterans of Foreign Wars will move from the nonpolitical realm of an interest group into the political world of a pressure group.

Pressure groups vary from small, more local organizations with part-time lobbyists appearing only briefly and irregularly at the state capitol, to large state-wide organizations with professional staffs and several lobbyists who devote a major portion of their time to legislative work. Since many groups, by definition, focus on a narrow range of interests—whether state, local or national—the frequency and intensity of their contact with legislators depends on the presence of specific issues faced from time to time by lawmakers. Furthermore, their impact on policy making not only depends on their size, relevance, and ability to capture resources, but on their strength in certain legislative districts. Large statewide organizations, while undoubtedly powerful, are nonetheless diffuse—whereas certain large corporations or institutions employing a significant number of people within a single district tend to have a specific spokesman as their legislator. It is generally known that certain groups have their spokesmen at the state capitol, and these tend to be legislators from a district with unique interests (e.g., oil, higher education, prisons) or those whose occupations reflect particular group interests (e.g., farmers, teachers, doctors).

Lobbyists

The lobbyist is the individual who serves as a link between the pressure group and the legislature—he is the point of contact, the articulator of interests, and the focus for interaction with specific legislators. The interaction between the lobbyist and the lawmaker is an important exchange between the private and public sectors of Oklahoma society. He offers information and clarity on issues, and in effect, simplifies the choices faced by public officials. As one scholar of Oklahoma politics suggests, "the lobbyist's role is functional for the maintenance of the legislative system."[7]

There are a variety of styles and types of lobbyists, as well as a wide range òf legislative reactions to them. With regard to the latter, we mentioned in Chapter 1 that some legislators see their pressure group role as a facilitator—friendly toward pressure groups and lobbyists and knowledgeable about them—while others tend to be hostile and knowledgeable (resisters), or to have no strong attitude or knowledge about group activities (neutrals).

Studies of other states[8] indicate that facilitators readily recognize and solicit help and ideas from outside groups, that they tend to share the views of certain groups, and even to use lobbyists in drafting bills and developing support for their own bills. This tends to be the most prevalent pressure-group orientation in the United States, and data for Oklahoma suggest that it does not substantially diverge from findings in the four states studied most intensely. McCool classifies the bulk of Oklahoma legislators as facilitators rather than neutrals or resistors, since over half of those surveyed during the mid-1960's felt that lobbyists help them perform their duties, that their help provides improved service to the public, that lobbyists clarify issues, and that the absence of lobbyists would make their job more difficult.[9] However, this accommodating attitude may not be one of choice—rather one born of the necessity for information vital in the legislative process, Furthermore, there are two factors relevant to Oklahoma which implicitly suggest that facilitators are not overwhelming in number: (1) many legislators see themselves as free agents—voting their own conscience rather than representing specific interests; and (2) facilitator roles tend to be found mostly in populous states such as Ohio, New Jersey, and California where there is a greater degree of diversity and complexity of pressure groups.

In addition to the legislator's reaction, it is important to note the variety of styles of operation and types of lobbyists. Qualifications for such a job vary somewhat according to the goals of each group, yet a basic prerequisite is a thorough knowledge of group interests and the legislative process. In a major study of the relationships between legislators and lobbyists, Milbrath suggests that seven general rules are at work for successful lobbying:

1. be pleasant and nonoffensive;
2. convince the legislator that it is important for him to listen;
3. be well prepared and well informed;
4. be personally convinced with the case;
5. be succinct, well organized, and direct;
6. use the soft sell;
7. leave a short written summary of the case with the legislator.[10]

These seven rules for effective lobbying are sufficiently general to provide the lobbyist a broad framework from which to launch his campaign to influence the legislator. Also, these rules are based in part upon how congressmen view the job of the lobbyist. The rules therefore provide a guideline for lobbyists, but also serve as norms for acceptable lobbying behavior as determined by legislators. While these suggestions result from a study focusing upon the relationship between U.S. congressmen and Washington lobbyists, there is reason to believe that the roles and patterns of behavior between the Oklahoma legislator and lobbyists do not differ significantly from those observed at the national level.

Several basic types of lobbyists are at work in the state capitol. The *client-oriented* or *professional* lobbyist is one who hires himself out to an interest group for a fee, and his work is accomplished during the legislative session. The *permanent employee lobbyist* is one who is a full-time worker for the organization he represents. A third type is the *local* or *state employee* who represents respective local and state governmental agencies.

Another is the *amateur* who receives no salary for his efforts, but is rewarded by performing as an advocate of the "public interest". There are also *constituent* lobbyists who represent a group of electors and direct most of their attention to individual representatives.[11]

Studies focusing on legislator-lobbyist relations in Oklahoma are far from abundant. One attempt to discover the nature of these relationships and the existence of various lobbyist types is reflected in Patterson's analysis of data gathered from each individual registered to lobby in the Oklahoma House.[12] The kinds of individuals playing the lobbying role in Oklahoma vary considerably, but some general patterns are evident. Most lobbyists are professional staff members in their organizations, and very few of them have ever served in the legislature before. The personal characteristics of an average Oklahoma lobbyist depict him as a middle-aged male with fairly high education, high pay, and a residence in Oklahoma City. The types of groups represented suggest that business groups employ the highest proportion of lobbyists, and that labor groups have more experienced lobbyists at work for them. The latter undertake a majority of their efforts during the legislative session, while some other groups (i.e., farm and business) operate as pressure groups on a year-round basis.

Patterson also examined three types of lobbyist role orientations functioning in Oklahoma: the contact man, the informant, and the watchdog.

The *contact man* sees his job as one of developing and maintaining personal relations with legislators. By acquiring contacts and developing friendships with individual legislators he communicates directly with lawmakers and "persuades" in the "friendly" manner.

The *informant* lobbyist relies less on personal contact or friendships in securing his groups' goals; rather, he orients his approach to present a legislator with prepared information. Such "facts" may be distributed to the legislators by mail or delivered in person, but the lobbyist's goal is to use information to influence the lawmakers. Since he relies extensively upon data, his lobbying is often public rather than private. These informant lobbyists in Oklahoma tend to represent farm and professional groups —providing material on state and federal regulations, technical problems and other items relatively unknown to the average legislator. For example, the American Medical Association may oppose a proposed bill which would allow paramedics to perform abortions. To present their case the AMA lobbyist must "inform" the legislator of the medical reasons for opposing such a measure. The best way to transmit this highly specialized and technical information is by preparing data in factual form which is easily understood by all. The informants also address themselves to the appropriate legislative committees and provide testimony during the course of public hearings.

The *watchdog* lobbyist is the least visible of the three types in Oklahoma. He functions as a careful observer of the legislature's activities—and if at any time proposed legislation affects his group, the lobbyist alerts members to action. Whereas the contact and informant lobbyists spend much time at the state capitol, the watchdog rarely enters the legislative arena and rarely discusses his group's goals with individual legislators.

Regulation of Lobbying Activities

Many observers of the legislative process have noted the vital role played by pressure groups and their official representatives. The interactions between a legislator and lobbyist are important components of a diverse and pluralistic democratic society. The give and take which is part of these relationships provides a mechanism for groups to affect the course of legislation and a means by which issues are brought to the public's attention. As one observer of Oklahoma pressure group activities contends:

> The lobbyist is a very significant actor in the legislative system. His role complements that of the legislator. The legislator is indispensable to the lobbyist—his role is inconceivable without the legislator. Although perhaps to a lesser degree, the legislator depends a great deal on the lobbyist. . . . The lobbyist is an important link in the communication process within the legislative system, and he plays an essential representative role.[13]

Although the lobbyist provides important information to legislators, brings together public opinion on a particular matter, and is an important link in the legislative process, abuses resulting from such interactions are frequently noted by the public and the press. Some lawmakers—especially those who see their role as facilitators—are likely to be co-opted by one pressure group. That is, they act as that group's primary voice in the legislature, and their voting is highly influenced by pressure-group activities relevant to that group. While such a legislator may have a relatively narrow view of his job as a representative of the people, he does not necessarily engage in improper or illegal activities. More specific "abuses" are of greater concern, such as illegal campaign contributions or special considerations facilitated by the legislator. But for the most part, the responsibility for "proper" activities rests with the lobbyist himself—and attempts at regulation are directed to the pressure group and its lobbyist, rather than to the legislator.

While we have no specific studies of lobbying infractions in Oklahoma, studies in other states suggest these are most likely present in Oklahoma. One such study in North Dakota, for example, found that the most commonly mentioned "improper" activities—in the eyes of both legislators and lobbyists—included entertainment (buying dinners, sponsoring parties), lobbying on the floor of either chamber, and intimidation of legislators by lobbyists.[14] Over one-third of the legislators and lobbyists queried, however, were not aware of improper lobbying activities. But the fact that over one-fourth of the legislature viewed such activities as occurring "frequently" or "often," points to the need for public concern and continued regulation.

The response to the need for public control of lobbying activities has been widespread in the United States. Over two-thirds of the states require all lobbyists to register, and most of these states make reports on receipts and expenditures mandatory. It is widely recognized, however, that most states seldom enforce these laws strictly.[15] The close working relationship between legislators and lobbyists, as well as the number and complexity of pressure groups, automatically decrease the chances of strict enforcement. This is especially complicated in larger states where there may be 5,000 registered groups—as in Texas—compared to Oklahoma with only 112 lobbyists registered with the House in 1974. The Oklahoma law, however, is representative of those in other states. It defines lobbying in the following manner:

If any person, whether directly interested or not in any measure pending before or thereafter to be introduced in either branch of the legislature of this state, shall in any manner privately attempt to influence the act of vote of any member of the state legislature concerning such measure, he shall be deemed guilty of lobbying.[16]

Further enumeration of the above definition of lobbying is found in various sections of the Oklahoma statutes. More specifically, lobbyists may appear before a regular committee when it is in session only after (1) obtaining written permission from the presiding officer, and (2) each member of the house to be lobbied receives some written statement (for instance, newspaper, publication, written public address) concerning the matter at hand.[17] Application to lobby in the Oklahoma Senate or House must be submitted in writing to the presiding officer of each house. By law, the applicant must state his name, age, place of residence, and the name of the person, firm, company, or corporation he is representing. The amount of remuneration to be received "per day, week, or month" by the lobbyist must also be specified. The final decision on whether or not to recognize the "agent" of a group is governed by a majority vote of the chamber in which the application was received.

The employed lobbyist is prohibited by law from entering "the floor of the legislative hall reserved for the members thereof" while in session unless by invitation and a vote of the entire chamber.[18] For all practical purposes, this prohibits lobbying on the floor of the Senate or House. Violation is punishable by imprisonment in the county jail or by fine. Since the effectiveness of any law depends primarily upon the degree of enforcement, it is difficult to judge the Oklahoma law because there have been very few violations recorded. The sections on floor activity are clear, and violations are rather easy to define, but the surveillance of bribery by a lobbyist is more difficult. The law states that:

[no] person, firm or member of a firm, corporation, or association shall give or offer any money, position or thing of value to any member of the State Legislature to influence him to work or to vote for any proposition.[19]

The law also prohibits any legislator from accepting money, position, or promise of reward of anything of value for his action upon any proposed or pending legislation. Violations are specifically directed at lobbying practices occurring during and after bill consideration. That is, the law ties bribery to the actions of lobbyists and legislators at the time a bill is in the legislative domain (under consideration by a part of a chamber) and when it becomes part of the public domain (when it is voted upon). However, the law does not appear to exclude the giving of and/or receiving of "rewards" at other times besides when a bill is being considered or voted upon. The law is concerned with the time immediately surrounding legislation, rather than with actions transpiring months away. Indeed, in the event of bribery occurring at a distant or preceding point in time, it would be difficult for the body as a whole to "prove" a violation of the law. If violations are proven, however, punishment may be severe: imprisonment from two to five years and/or a fine of $1,000 to $5,000.[20]

While recent Senate rules changes require an annual report of lobbyists' income and expenditures, changes in state statutes governing lobbying activities are also possible in the near future—and have been considered by recent legislative sessions. Two general factors point to this possibility: (1) certain aspects of the existing law are either vague, difficult to enforce, or characterized by obvious loopholes; and (2) the public clamor for greater regulation is increasing. Oklahoma's legislature like many other state bodies, is being confronted by a public increasingly concerned with the "accountability" and "integrity" of elected officials and of influential individuals associated with them. Recent events at the national level have focused attention on the responsibility of the legislative system and the general trustworthiness of government—and the relationships between legislators and lobbyists are a key component in this controversy.

MEDIA RELATIONS

Legislating and representing is a reciprocal process—a two-way channel of communication exists between the legislator and the public. To this point in our discussion of "outsiders'" relationships to the legislative process we have emphasized incoming demands and supports from constituents and pressure groups. The primary mechanism for channeling outgoing information and images is the media. Although legislators may initiate some personal contacts with constituents, they rely heavily on press, television, and radio as a means of interaction and communication with the public.

Generally government officials at all levels have used the media as (1) a tool to facilitate a political career, (2) a sounding board for policy consideration, and (3) a means of facilitating the processes of government. The representatives of the media, on the other hand, view it as a broker between the politician and the people. As one Oklahoma governor said, "The great bold sunlight of the news media on the public officials is one of the major checks that we have on our government." If we accept this as one role of the media, it is then possible to view television, newspapers, or the radio as a viable force capable of enhancing or ruining the image of a legislator or any public official. Indeed, all legislators soon learn that the power of the media is an outside force to be reckoned with. Therefore, the development of positive press relations is usually of primary concern for all lawmakers. Some legislators may be considered "institutions" by their constituents, but the press and other media seldom recognize the sanctity of institutions—they may focus their "bold sunlight" on any legislator.

Good relations with the press are a vital canon of legislative life. Yet after his election a legislator may find that the media has little or no interest in him or his policy stands, that he is simply not newsworthy. Practically speaking, there is only a limited amount of news which can be printed in the state newspapers or shown on television. Often legislators feel that the press is treating them unfairly by not treating them at all—unless graft or corruption is the issue. A state senator recently told a gathering of freshman House and Senate members that they have probably decided that the press spends "too much time talking about the crooks, and the clown, and all the trivia. . . . they never treat the relevant issues with clarity and depth. . . ." This sounding was not a criticism of the press, but a statement of practical reality. Those in the press corps are interested in news. Although the press often has the power to define what is news, it is nevertheless true that news to a legislator may not be news to a representative of the media.

There is very little published information on the general relationship between state legislators and the press, and no systematic studies exist for Oklahoma. Nevertheless, it is possible to delineate two important components of the relationship between legislators and the media: (1) the elements of newsworthiness from the perspective of the media, and (2) the operating norms for successful interaction from the perspective of the legislator. Studies in other states suggest that state capitol reporters are primarily and sometimes exclusively interested in "significant" news. The media's definition of significance, therefore, takes on added importance to each legislator. With the perspective of the media in mind, individual lawmakers are capable of tailoring information to fit criteria for newsworthiness, and many are able to avoid complete frustration with—or even disdain for—the press. Previous research indicates that at least eight basic criteria govern the "significance" of news:

1. *Consequences.* The consequences of any news item are evaluated in terms of relevancy to the public. The result is that some determination must be made by the press as to what is relevant for the majority of the public, or relevant to important segments of the public. With the realities of limited time and space in mind, the legislator and the citizen should be aware that the consequences of news items are of primary importance to the press.

2. *Oddity.* The oddity component of information is a basic and readily understandable criterion as to what is considered newsworthy. The odd, the unusual, and the strange occurrences in the legislature are more newsworthy than commonplace events, and of course, such news items, while not always important to the legislator, may shape his image for constituents. The skillful legislator realizes this and is capable of capitalizing on relatively minor events to further his cause.

3. *Immediacy.* To the media, old news is no news. What occurred yesterday or the day before is not news, but history. Time is therefore crucial—to the news media personnel and to the legislator. If a lawmaker wants to call a news conference or make some announcement to the press, he oftens avoids complicating his chances of making the news by trying to compete with similar news items or outstanding news occurring at the same time. If the legislator has any control over the timing of news, it should be timed when there is no competition from other related sources. It is frustrating for a freshman legislator to make a statement on a particular bill only to be "out-newsed" by a senior legislator commenting on the same bill. Just how a legislator competes actively for legislative news depends upon his skill and knowledge of the process of news selection, of which immediacy is an important component.

4. *Proximity.* What is news in Oklahoma County may not be news in Adair County. A speech given by an Oklahoma County legislator may be important to those who live in Oklahoma County, but it may have little news value to citizens in other parts of the state. The legislator should expect legislative news of local interest to be presented to the locality which is affected—and this may or may not be his home district. There are times when a legislator will make the news outside his district, only to find that he was ignored by the media in his community.

5. *Suspense.* The often routine and uneventful occurrences in the legislature may emerge as suspenseful news items which capture the atten-

tion of the media. A seemingly unimportant bill may result in a complex system of debate and a high degree of interest, or a routine committee meeting may turn into a focal point of action which transcends the commonplace and yields an image of suspense. Very much like the odd or strange, the suspenseful occurrences also have a better chance of becoming news than the ordinary ones.

6. *Prominence.* Some public officials are obviously more newsworthy than others. A statement from the Senate or House leadership on the governor's State of the State message will receive more attention than a comment from a lesser-known legislator. It is true that those who are in the news make the news, and the higher ranking and more powerful legislators are in the news more often than others. This is often frustrating to individual lawmakers, since there is no guarantee that news personnel will choose to present the statements of a legislator in his district—instead, the pronouncements of other "more important" legislators will appear. As a practical consideration, the legislator should realize that his news may fall to the wayside when competing with other sources.

7. *Conflict.* We have all heard the criticism that the press tends to accentuate the violent and ignore the calm. There may be some truth to this, since news personnel believe that the public would rather read or hear about negative acts (violence, conflict, tensions, and so on) rather than mundane everyday events. In the legislative arena, news people will seek out those instances of tension and conflict. If the tension centers on partisan concerns, a power struggle between legislators, or verbal conflict on the floor or in committees, the media personnel will focus upon it. Such news has the capacity to cast a negative shadow upon a legislative image, since the public tends to remember the conflict rather than who won or lost.

8. *Emotion.* Many average citizens find some affinity with the emotional aspect of politics. They like to read about the "human" side of politicians. This does not mean that all emotional actions benefit the politician—on the contrary, emotional actions or reactions are often perceived negatively by the public. Like news of conflict and suspense, the public tends to consume this emotional news. Media personnel recognize this and will find many emotion-ladden events newsworthy. Thus, the skillful legislator realizes that emotional actions have a better-than-average chance of becoming news; and that such actions are often perceived negatively by constituents.[21]

The other major component of the relationship between legislators and the media is the lawmaker's perspective on effective operating guidelines. Since many legislators feel some antagonism toward the press—largely because of its power, particular editorial positions, frequent misquotations, or bothersome reporters—the issue of how to avoid angry confrontations is an important one.

While there are no perfect and lasting rules to govern this relationship, our discussions with individual lawmakers who see themselves as having good press relations and our observations of these legislators giving advice to others point to a set of general guidelines:

1. *Honesty.* A legislator must be completely honest when dealing with the news media—the slightest hesitation, innuendo, or vagueness may imply less than the truth. It is the reporter's task to "check out" and verify all information obtained. If news from a legislator is placed under speculation as to its validity, that individual is likely to be a target for reporters, and what a reporter thinks of the legislator is often more important than what the legislator thinks of the reporter.

2. *Cooperation.* There are instances when a legislator has the opportunity either to cooperate or to avoid the news spotlight. Just what to do in every situation is not always clear, yet skillful legislators are capable of creating an image of cooperation and non-avoidance. Such cooperation may necessitate disclosures to probing questions or simply a polite refusal to answer. Reporters are usually adept at recognizing attempts to be uncooperative, and the sincerity of the legislator becomes an important factor in this determination. They also recognize that some information cannot be divulged, and a simple statement to that effect is usually understood by media personnel who might otherwise view the legislator as obstinate.

3. *Promptness.* Although a lawmaker's schedule is more important and usually more hectic than a reporter's, when a legislator makes some arrangement to provide news to the media, the information should be given "on time." Being prompt is basically an act of politeness, and it recognizes that a reporter is usually on a tight schedule to process information for a deadline. The legislator who helps the reporter meet this deadline improves his image with the press corps and, indirectly, with the people of the state.

4. *Impartiality.* Even though reporters seem to show more interest in some legislators than others, lawmakers should not be partial to one or a few reporters to the exclusion of others. In fact, a legislator should avoid favoring one news source over another and should respect each reporter and news source equally. Being impartial will insure that a large number of reporters form positive feelings toward a legislator—to do otherwise is courting the wrath of the news media.

The above guidelines are based on norms favoring positive behavior. They all work to provide an open system of communication between the legislator and the reporter. Such guidelines are obviously flexible, due in part to the myriad of unspoken and unwritten rules of reporting. The reporter takes his job seriously, and he takes pride in the quality of his product. The legislator rarely has the time to know how the reporting business operates. He must therefore rely on behaving in such a way as to promote the confidence of the press, and at the same time remain independent from the "pressures" of the press. Effective legislating is not only carried out in committees and on the floor of the chambers, but in the news as well.

CHAPTER 7

Oklahoma In Comparative Perspective: A Postscript on Legislative Effectiveness

The preceding account of the legislative process in Oklahoma and its key participants is descriptive, factual, periodically analytical—and aims to be objective—in its search for explanations of behavior and decision making. We have consciously avoided dealing in personalities, prescriptive and postscriptive evaluations of good and bad behavior, and assessments of the capabilities of the institution and its members. The reader will no doubt find glimpses of normative preferences throughout the book, and even the casual reader will note a variety of provocative questions raised about how things ought to be in a representative, democratic system. But these skirt a major issue which we cannot presume to tackle comprehensively: Is the Oklahoma legislature a "good" legislature? The problems with such a question are obvious: one author's opinion may be as valid as another's; "good" implies different things to different people; and the legislature as a human institution obviously varies in character and quality according to its membership, to the socioeconomic and political conditions of the state, to the demands of the federal system, and according to political events. How can we begin to approach the nagging question of legislative effectiveness? The answer requires attention to goals and preferences for all state legislatures, a definition of the underlying dimensions of "effectiveness and capability," and analysis based on systematic comparisons among all legislatures in the United States. The latter implies that we can only know how "good" the Oklahoma legislature is by comparing it systematically with other lawmaking bodies.

MEASURING LEGISLATIVE EFFECTIVENESS

A major research effort which meets the above criteria was recently completed by the prestigious and nonpartisan Citizens Conference on State Legislatures (CCSL).[1] Although a variety of books and articles have been written on the topic of legislative reform and evaluation,[2] the CCSL study is undoubtedly the most comprehensive comparative analysis of legislative strengths and weaknesses in the various states, and clearly the most empirically based account of the technical capabilities of legislative decision making. It is a study of how decisions are made rather than which ones are or should be made. It therefore cautiously avoids major issues of public policy and partisanship.

The CCSL research on state legislatures was carried out in two general phases: the first established various criteria for evaluating legislatures, and the second phase involved the collection of data and the systematic analysis of findings in the various states. The criteria for evaluation were established through the work of a national panel of technical advisors who assisted in developing five general sets of objectives for legislative improvement and a total of 73 detailed subcriteria for measuring them. In addition, the panel provided assistance in ordering answers to questions related to these criteria, ranging from most to least desirable as judged by experts in the field. The result was a specific checklist of measures on which to judge each legislature according to a variety of ideal standards. Data were then collected on all of these measures, and fieldwork in 1969-1970 included interviews in all states with various legislators, legislative leaders, and staff.

The five general categories of objectives or dimensions of legislative effectiveness (capability) reflect the Citizen Conference's contention that "citizens should expect their legislatures to be functional, accountable, informed, independent, and representative."[3] These five criteria are viewed as ends in themselves rather than means to other ends. Each has several sub-components and specific indicators reflecting a variety of facts about each legislative institution. The FAIIR system of criteria follows.

Functionality

In order to carry out the basic tasks of lawmaking and deliberation, a state legislature needs adequate and flexible time for business, a multipurpose staff, proper physical facilities, structural features which enhance manageability (not too many members, not an excessive number of committees or committee assignments per member), procedures which expedite the flow of work, and good management and coordination. Each of the fifty state legislatures was analyzed and assigned values according to a host of specific measures reflecting this idea of functionality.

Accountability

A state legislature should be accountable. In order to achieve this objective, organizational structures must be understood by the public, there must be public access and availability of information about the legislature, and there must be some degree of internal accountability. These various aspects of accountability are facilitated by (and in turn measured by) the existence of conditions such as the following: single member districts, where there is only one legislator per group of constituents; explicit rules and procedures known to the public; advance notice of committee meetings; open meetings; available voting records; no impediments to media coverage; and the availability of information about legislator's personal interests and lobbyists' activities. Furthermore, accountability within the legislative institution implies that there shall be no small oligarchy which rules the day-to-day affairs of legislative life or a highly centralized leadership with few restraints on its power. It implies opportunities for minority leadership, and in general, an opportunity for individual members to have responsibility so that individuals may be held accountable.

Information-Handling Capability

Any state legislature is an information processing system which handles a variety of demands from citizens and multiple pieces of information essential for decision making. Proper handling of such information is facilitated by the following conditions: adequate time, including presession activities; proper use of standing committees and procedures to solicit testimony; the availability of staff; activities between sessions; and fiscal review powers. This dimension measures factors which encourage information gathering, analysis and quick access by legislators, plus the availability of information from a diversity of sources (neither the executive branch solely nor a particularly influential lobbyist).

Independence

Another aspect of legislative effectiveness is independence: autonomy in legislative activity, independence from the executive branch, legislative oversight of the executive branch, regulations on lobbyists, and a lack of conflicting interests which dilute a legislator's concerns. The above are all factors which enable the legislature to be independent of the executive branch, lobbyists, and private and occupational interests of individual members. This dimension is measured by such factors as budget and auditing powers, veto relationships, lobbying registration procedures, control over the duration and frequency of sessions, and laws which prohibit holding multiple public offices.

Representativeness

The Citizens Conference argues that legislatures will be more representative if constituents and members can identify and communicate with one another, if legislative composition reflects diversity in the states, and if members are effective and capable of making identifiable contributions. Examples of some of the measures of representativeness employed in the study include the following: liberality of qualifications for office (to ensure its openness to more people); the presence of single member districts (which give constituents one legislator); and legislative size (if the institution is too large, individual effectiveness will be hampered).

On the basis of the above criteria, each state legislature was assigned five specific scores (as well as an overall score) reflecting its position on the various indicators. The final result was a set of rankings for each state on the various dimensions.

HOW OKLAHOMA FARES

When final rankings were calculated across all five FAIIR dimensions, the Oklahoma legislature stood fourteenth in the nation compared to all other state legislatures. This high ranking is especially boosted by high positions on representativeness (8) and functionality (9). Although the overall rank is high, there is some unevenness across measures of effectiveness as noted by midpoint rankings on independence (22), information (24), and accountability (27). This indicates a mixture of good and bad features for the Oklahoma legislature. Neverthless, its overall position in comparison to other states is unusually favorable.

Since regional comparisons are often useful in matters of social and political concern, reflecting common historical and cultural traditions, the map in figure 5 indicates the relative position of Oklahoma with regard to other states.

With the exception of New Mexico, Oklahoma's legislature ranks considerably higher than that of any adjacent state. The map also suggests that region is not a primary influential factor for overall legislative effectiveness; that is, common migration patterns, historical and cultural similarities, and information flow between adjacent states does not necessarily create homogeneous pockets of "good" and "bad" legislative institutions throughout the country. Nevertheless, the obvious low quality of deep South state legislatures is present in Figure 5, as well as the relative high quality of institutions in typically more reform-oriented, upper midwest and north central states. Since Oklahoma is often classified as a "border" state, given its similarity in tradition to other states outside the deep South and Southwest, it is useful to note that it stands in relatively favorable position to such other border states as Tennessee, Kentucky, West Virginia and Virginia.

Why is Oklahoma so high? Although we will investigate this question in greater detail in the following pages of this chapter, the most obvious answer is that the state legislature scores "high" on a variety of measures judged as critically important by the Citizens Conference on State Legislatures and its technical advisory panel. The CCSL study cites as salient features some of the following: (1) the legislature meets in annual session which is only limited to 90 legislative days rather than calendar days, apparently giving more than usual time for deliberation in comparison to other states; (2) the various committees of each house were comparable at the time of the study in function and responsibility, coming together as joint interim committees to work between sessions; (3) at the time of the study, only a few House members had more than three committee assignments, and no Senate members had more than four committee assignments; (4) individual offices and physical facilities are more prevalent than in many other states; (5) bills not finally defeated or passed during a session are carried over to the second session of the legislature; and (6) a small but effective legislative staff provided an extensive number of services to the individual members.

The most elaborate, and probably the most basic, dimension of legislative effectiveness is the category of functional capability, under which a number of criteria are subsumed. As noted above, Oklahoma ranks ninth on this functional dimension. One primary reason why Oklahoma stands so high nationally is that the most important subcriteria for the functional dimension reflect various indicators of committee structure, including the number of standing committees, standing committees with interim status, and the number of committee assignments. Oklahoma fares very well on all of these committee structure measures,[4] and also has very high scores on two other heavily weighted subcriteria: the management of time resources, and leadership power and continuity. The latter, of course, is partially reflective of high House leadership continuity under Representative J. D. McCarty.

The Oklahoma legislature is by no means free of difficulties and obstacles to effective legislating: its independence is limited, its information handling capability is modest, and its level of accountability is below average. As a result of these general deficiencies, the Citizens Conference offered a variety of recommendations for reform and improvement, including some of the following:

1. Strengthen the minority party role generally, especially as reflected in committee positions (particularly the Rules Committee).
2. Publish uniform committee rules, specific committee jurisdictions, and roll calls for votes taken in committees.
3. Encourage more committee hearings, prohibit secret committee meetings, and provide for more effective notice of committee meetings.
4. Committees should be required to report on all bills and they should be balanced in their composition so that they are more reflective of the overall characteristics of members in each chamber.
5. Amend the Oklahoma constitution to permit the legislature to convene special sessions and to permit more flexibility in setting the agenda for special sessions called by the governor.
6. Expand the audit function of the legislature to improve oversight of executive agencies.
7. Strengthen staff support, including specific assistance for legislative

leaders and rank-and-file members, plus improved staffing of committees on a permanent and year-round basis.
8. The legislature should partially support district offices for individual members to improve effective representation.[5]

It should be noted that some progress has been made recently toward the achievement of specific goals.[6] We indicated earlier that the functional and numerical comparability between standing committees in the House and Senate has been dismantled, yet there is a slightly higher degree of comparability evident in the 35th Legislature compared to the 34th (1973-74). Most important, a number of specific changes address the CCSL recommendations: there has been a considerable expansion in the size of the Legislative Council staff in the research, fiscal, and legal areas; several House and Senate committees now have staff assistance; and committee votes (as well as those in Committee of the Whole) are recorded with greater frequency under modified rules.

While, on balance, some progress has been made toward a more effective legislative system in Oklahoma, it is relevant to inquire about the prospects for substantial reform. Although specific attention to weaknesses in Oklahoma and to the possibility of making specific changes are beyond the scope of our concern, we should note the difficulty of legislative reform throughout most of the United States. The prospects for reform have always been less than encouraging—this fact alone led to the establishment of the Citizens Conference on State Legislatures in 1965. Yet when some thought is given to the nearly insurmountable obstacles to reform in the states, the amount of change in the last ten years is quite remarkable.

First of all, many practices and procedures necessary for reform are tied to specific provisions in state constitutions, which by their nature are very difficult to change. As an example, the Oklahoma legislature has recently been characterized as a "weakly developed institution," reflecting low legislative independence and weak gubernatorial powers—both of which depend upon constitutional provisions.[7] Also, Oklahoma's constitution is one characterized by a proliferation of unnecessary specifics, and constitutional amendments are usually difficult to pass; convention reform is even more difficult.[8]

Secondly, many matters are easier to change than those embedded in a state constitution, such as committee procedures and

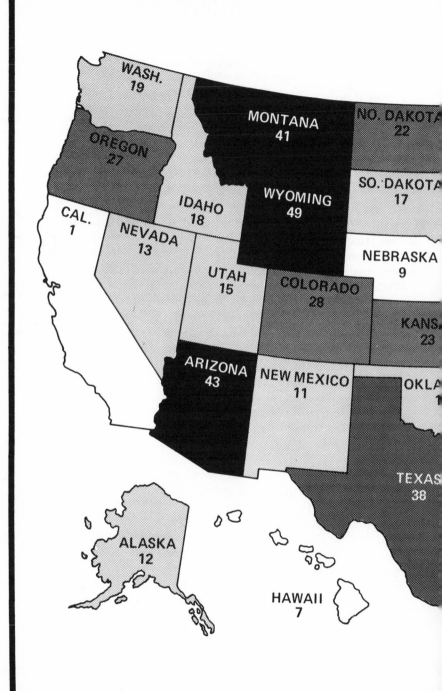

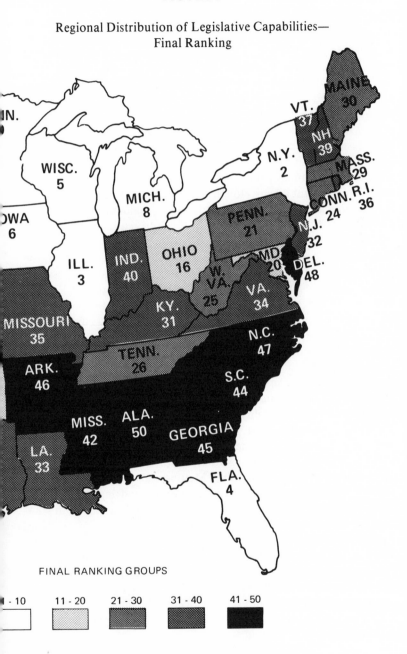

FIGURE 5

Regional Distribution of Legislative Capabilities—
Final Ranking

IN.

VT. 37

MAINE 30

NH 39

N.Y. 2

WISC. 5

MICH. 8

MASS. 29

CONN. 24 R.I. 36

PENN. 21

N.J. 32

OWA 6

ILL. 3

IND. 40

OHIO 16

MD 20 DEL. 48

W. VA. 25

VA. 34

KY. 31

MISSOURI 35

TENN. 26

N.C. 47

ARK. 46

S.C. 44

MISS. 42

ALA. 50

GEORGIA 45

LA. 33

FLA. 4

FINAL RANKING GROUPS

- 10   11 - 20   21 - 30   31 - 40   41 - 50

rules—yet those changes are extremely sensitive for a variety of reasons. Matters of partisanship become relevant in many instances; changes in rules are seen as group power plays (and often are); internal modifications are sometimes seen as the sole prerogative of the legislative body, of little interest to "outsiders", and are indeed obscure to the general public. In general, matters of procedure which facilitate information handling or accountability or any of the other objectives discussed earlier, are often seen as dull matters, lacking in the excitement of more usual public policy concerns. The Citizens Conference study claims that "There is, of course, little drama in these matters; they are the dull details that hardly anyone but a legislator thinks about—and he has no choice. But it is precisely because hardly anyone has paid much attention to the dull details that, in the middle of the 20th century, many of our legislatures are still entrapped in 19th century structures."[9] In addition, when procedural matters are brought to public attention, the mobilization of public opinion is difficult, if not impossible. Citizens groups such as Common Cause, the League of Women Voters, and special local organizations may change the picture and facilitate the mobilization of public opinion on matters usually seen as more obscure.

In addition to the above categories of obstacles, legislative reform faces a host of other problems.[10] There is often press indifference to reform considerations. It is generally known that state legislative bodies are poorly covered by the media. Gubernatorial indifference and hostility are prevalent. Internal legislative obstacles frequently exist reflecting the attitudes of individual members. Indications of the latter are evident in low institutional loyalty and high turnover in state legislatures—where lawmaking is often viewed as a part-time job.[11] Members also have a tendency to see their legislature and its tasks as unique and incomparable to other states; and in truth, they are not much concerned with what goes on elsewhere.

Although all of the above are not necessarily characteristic obstacles to reform in Oklahoma at any one point in time, they all play a potential role in the consideration of any particular reform. On the whole, gubernatorial hostility is more relevant for constitutional changes than internal procedural changes, individual legislator's attitudes are more relevant for changes in internal mechanisms, and popular opinion may be more relevant for issues of openness, accountabilty, and representation.

FACTORS INFLUENCING LEGISLATIVE EFFECTIVENESS

It is not sufficient to claim that levels of legislative effectiveness are due to disproportionately higher scores in one area of effectiveness versus another. Rather, it is essential to search for underlying reasons for levels of effectiveness and to do so across all fifty states. Once factors influencing legislative effectiveness are isolated, Oklahoma can be examined in greater detail to discover the extent to which it varies from national standards.

A search for relevant influential factors necessitates brief attention to other research in comparative state politics. The policy-analysis perspective relies heavily on the political science version of "systems theory" or "input-output analysis."[12] This approach suggests that social, economic, and political characteristics in the environment of every state influence political structures and decision making to result in final decisions about the allocations of resources and values. These decisions are "public policies" made by various authoritative agencies that act within state environments characterized by different levels of social, economic, and political development. In other words, legislative effectiveness reflects the quality of socioeconomic and political characteristics in the states, and in turn influences the character of public policy, much of which is directly tied to legislative actions. An example of the "system" would include the elements in Figure 6.

Research utilizing a systems perspective has been both empirical (based on observable and measurable indicators) and comparative in an attempt to explain variations in public policy among the states. This was a radical departure from older, more reformist, and prescriptive studies, most popular before the Second World War. Although the research field is complex and large, several basic findings and controversies have emerged. Some of the earliest studies suggested that socioeconomic influences—such as level of education, income, and industrialization—influence public policy much more than do political factors—such as voter participation, legislative malapportionment, and interparty competition.[13]

FIGURE 6

A General Political System Model for Oklahoma

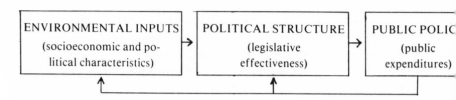

Since these early findings considerable controversy has occurred over the conclusions, especially among political scientists pondering the role of political institutions and partisan characteristics in shaping public policy among different states. There has been subsequent controversy over what "policies" are, how to identify relevant political characteristics, and how to measure each of them.[14] The research arguments led to improvements by measuring services, in addition to spending levels, on the policy output side of the model,[15] and to expanding the consideration of various political factors which may be relevant, for instance, historical and cultural traditions, interest group activity, and executive powers.[16] As a consequence, political factors now appear to be less important in shaping levels of taxation and spending in America, yet they exert significant influence on the distribution of burdens and benefits.[17] In addition, it has been noted that certain political factors are crucial in specific policy areas—that the impact of political factors varies with the type of policy.[18]

While the "system" perspective utilized in comparative state policy analysis provides some clues to factors shaping levels of legislative effectiveness, the analysis presented here is limited to the study of legislative effectiveness. It in no way attempts to solve the controversy over the relevance of socioeconomic versus political and structural characteristics, and it is not an examination of the causes of differences in policy among the states. Meeting the latter objectives would require substantial technical and measurement capability, as well as sophisticated multivariate statistical analysis well beyond the scope of this chapter. One of the immediate goals is to examine the role of legislative effectiveness in the general policy system by focusing on: (1) the relationship between selected socioeconomic and political characteristics on the one hand, and legislative capability on the other; (2) the linkage between the level of legislative effectiveness and the nature of selected public policy outputs in the American states; and (3) the extent to which Oklahoma deviates from these linkages and relationships generalized from an analysis of all states. Since items (1) and (2) above have been briefly addressed by the Citizens Conference on State Legislatures, the findings reported here will be derived and adapted from their data and analysis, with some additional original analysis essential for more focused attention on Oklahoma.

The CCSL study isolated four influential factors in the socioeconomic and political environment of the American states that are relevant and statistically powerful in explaining levels of legislative capability.[19] These factors include two socioeconomic characteristics of the states and two basic political indicators. The socioeconomic measures are *affluence,* as reflected in educational levels, personal income in the various states, property values, and literacy levels[20]; and *metro-urbanism,* as a measure of large metropolitan areas, population density, wealth, and ethnicity.[21] Among other factors, the CCSL study predicts or hypothesizes that legislative effectiveness is related to levels of affluence and metro-urbanism to the degree that more effective states are ones more likely to be characterized by higher levels of urbanism and population affluence.

The political factors include measures of *partisanship* and *political culture.* Partisanship is measured in terms of the Democratic proportion of the vote for governor, the Democratic percentage of seats in the state legislature, and the degree of Democratic control of the governorships, state houses, and Senates.[22] Political culture reflects migration and settlement patterns throughout the United States and includes orientations among the public and politicians toward political participation, bureaucracy, government intervention, and policy innovation. As originally developed by Elazar and modified by Sharkansky,[23] the political-culture measure suggests a continuum ranging from moralistic, to individualistic, to traditionalistic orientations toward politics. Certain states are more moralistic and characterized by

higher levels of citizen participation, professionalization of government, government intervention for the common good, and innovative programs. On the other extreme, traditionalistic political
cultures are those characterized by limited participation, restraint
on bureaucracy, opposition to government intervention except for
the maintenance of political elites, and resistance to innovation.

Table 48 presents data on the relationship between these four influential environmental conditions and legislative effectiveness, as
well as Oklahoma's rank on each measure and the quantitative difference between that rank and Oklahoma's standing on legislative
capability. For all states, the relationship between environmental
factors and ranking on legislative effectiveness is measured by
Spearman's rho correlation coefficient with a range of + 1 to -1. A
higher positive correlation represents the co-occurrence of environmental factors with higher levels of legislative effectiveness.
Although the Citizens Conference investigated a large number of
other environmental conditions potentially influential for
legislative effectiveness, the four reported in Table 48 were the only
ones statistically significant at the .01 level, which implies that the
likelihood of a chance occurrence at that level between each pair of
factors is only one in 100.

In addition to the four primary indicators, however, two related
political characteristics were also influential for legislative effectiveness: (1) political party integration,[24] as a measure of competition and cohesiveness in the political parties of the states; and (2)
partisan competition and voting turnout,[25] as measures of party
competitiveness in legislative and gubernatorial elections, of participation in gubernatorial elections, and of suffrage law liberality.
Each of these measures exhibit a .3 correlation with state rankings
on legislative effectiveness.

While the correlation coefficients in Table 48 represent only the
relationship between pairs of characteristics rather than a complex
statistical analysis with controls for other factors, they are sug-
gestive of basic relationships between the socioeconomic and
political environment in the American states and the subsequent
measures of legislative effectiveness. The overall state ranking is
the only measure analyzed here, with minor variations being evident for each of the various five dimensions contributing to the
overall effectiveness score. Since each of the correlation coeffi-

TABLE 48.—A Comparison of Oklahoma's Legislative Effectiveness with Selected Environmental Indicators

Environmental Indicator[a]	Rank order Correlation (rho) Between Effectiveness Rank and Environmental Indicator Rank for All States	Oklahoma Environmental Rank	Difference Between Oklahoma Environmental Rank and Legislative Effectiveness Rank
Affluence Factor	.42	26	12
Political Culture	.42	43	29
Metro-Urbanism Factor	.38	22	8
Partisanship Index[b]	.36	39	25

[a]Environmental socioeconomic and political indicators correlated with legislative effectiveness rank at .01 level, statistically significant. Adopted and calculated from Citizens Conference on State Legislatures, *State Legislatures: An Evaluation of Their Effectiveness* (New York: Praeger, 1971), pp. 40, 60-62, 70-71.

[b]The reported rank order correlation was -.36; Oklahoma's rank was reversed to reflect a positive correlation comparable to the other measures.

cients is moderate, we can conclude that the presence of these various characteristics occurs with higher levels of legislative capability, for all of the states as a whole. The CCSL study summarizes the finding as follows:

Those state legislatures ranking high in technical capability tend to be wealthy states whose citizens live predominantly in urban areas. The political culture in such states tends to encourage innovation, popular political participation, bureaucratic efficiency, and government activism. Citizens in these states are generally well-educated, politically active, and involved in public affairs. The political systems in such states tend to have strong governors, professional legislatures, competitive and cohesive political parties, and strong local governments. Finally, these states tend to lack rigid stratification by income class.[26]

Since the discerning and informed reader will readily note that these environmental characteristics are ones not common to even more generous interpretations of Oklahoma politics, two logical questions follow: Where does Oklahoma stand on these important environmental indicators? What explains the Oklahoma legislature's relative high standing on effectiveness in comparison with the state's overall low standing on factors influential for effectiveness according to an analysis of *all* states? The first inquiry is addressed in Table 48. It contains Oklahoma's ranking on the four most crucial environmental characteristics—each of which is substantially lower than Oklahoma's ranking on political effectiveness. A measure of the difference between the state's ranking on environmental characteristics and its ranking (14th) on legislative effectiveness is presented in the last column of Table 48.

Although an analysis of all states yields modest to high correlation coefficients between environmental conditions and the overall measure of legislative effectiveness, Oklahoma's low ranking on the environmental characteristics suggests that it is a deviant case. The Oklahoma legislature is clearly more effective that it "should" be given the state's low to moderate level of affluence and urbanism, and especially given its traditionalistic political culture, Democratic one-party dominance, and lower party competition, cohesiveness and electoral turnout. Deviance on the latter measures is supported by 20 and 21 point differences respectively for indicators of party integration and competition-turnout. Of all measures, Oklahoma's political culture is one most incongruent with legislative capability: high legislative effectiveness is found among more moralistic, participation-oriented, interventionist, and innovative states, yet Oklahoma ranks 43rd on the traditionalist end of the scale. Although each item could be analyzed separately, among the four most influential factors shaping legislative effectiveness across all fifty states, Oklahoma stands 8 to 29 rankings below its position on overall legislative effectiveness. Oklahoma, of course, is not the only deviant case—for if there were none, all correlation coefficients would approximate 1.0. Florida, for example, is traditionalistic in its political culture and high on legislative capability; and New Jersey is high in affluence, yet low in legislative effectiveness. Indeed, causal language is especially difficult. For Oklahoma few of the four factors appear to be necessary conditions for legislative effectiveness.

PUBLIC POLICY LINKAGES

Perhaps the most intriguing question suggested by the systems model inquires about the linkages between legislative effectiveness and public policy consequences in the American states. What are some measurable policies more likely found in states with effective legislatures? Such a sweeping inquiry cannot be answered comprehensively here, yet it is possible to investigate selected policies in the same manner as we investigated environmental influences. The CCSL study selected five policy indicators for analysis: (1) welfare-education—an index on which high scores represent higher state and local government welfare payments, a larger proportion of people completing high school, and more success on military mental examinations, as well as a host of other factors largely associated with welfare (more than education);[27] (2) per capita general revenue of state and local government; (3) an innovation index reflecting the speed with which state governments adopt innovations across a variety of areas;[28] (4) expenditures per pupil in average daily attendance; and (5) scope of government—on which higher scores indicate greater per capita state and local taxes, higher spending per capita, and more per capita governmental employment, among others.[29]

In addition to the above policies analyzed by the Citizens Conference, Table 49 reports data for five additional important policies included in Morgan's *Handbook of State Policy Indicators*. These measures include an indication of tax effort (measured as tax collections as a percentage of tax capacity), and various per capita and per-student expenditures in the areas of education, health, highway, and criminal justice policy.

Table 49 reports rank-order correlation coefficients between measures in the ten policy areas and rankings on the overall CCSL measure of state legislative effectiveness; plus an indication of Oklahoma's rank in the various policy areas, and a ranking point difference between policy position and Oklahoma's location on the

TABLE 49.— A Comparison of Oklahoma's Legislative Effectiveness with Selected Policy Consequences

Policy Outputs	Rank order correlation (rho) between effectiveness rank and policy rank for all states	Oklahoma policy rank	Difference between Oklahoma policy rank and legislative effectiveness rank
Policies Analyzed by CCSL [a]			
Welfare-Education Factor	.55	13	1
Per Capita State and Local General Revenue	.46	24	10
Innovation Index	.37	44	30
Expenditure Per Pupil	.33	44	30
Scope of Government	.21	16	2
Additional Policies[b]			
Per Capita State/Local Expenditures for Police Protection	.47	36	22
Tax Effort Index	.38	47	33
Per Capita State/Local Expenditures for Health and Hospitals	.29	35	21
Per Capita State/Local Expenditures for Highways	.14	30	16
Per Student State Tax Funds for Higher Education	.06	50	36

[a]Adapted and calculated from Citizens Conference on State Legislatures, *State Legislatures: An Evaluation of Their Effectiveness* (New York: Praeger, 1971), pp. 40, 60-62, 78.

[b]Adapted and calculated from David R. Morgan, *Handbook of State Policy Indicators* (Norman, Bureau of Government Research, University of Oklahoma, 1971), pp. 30, 46, 62, 68, 74.

legislative effectiveness scale. Although all of the policies are not exclusively tied to state legislative decision making, the state legislature is obviously central to most of the policy considerations. Particular caution in interpretation is necessary; especially since the policy making system is exceedingly complex and involves substantial input from the federal government in selected policy areas. The policies analyzed in the CCSL study are presented in the top half of Table 49 in descending order based on the strength of correlations with legislative effectiveness. The second or bottom half of the table reports five additional policies, largely of a taxing and spending variety in several areas not covered by the CCSL analysis.

The overall results presented in Table 49 suggest that states characterized by more effective legislatures are also likely to tax and spend more in a variety of areas, especially welfare, education, police protection, and health. In addition, the CCSL authors conclude that "highly capable legislatures tend to be generally innovative in many different areas of public policy, generous in welfare and education spending services and 'interventionist' in the sense of having powers and responsibilities of broad scope."[30] In addition, the original study reported similar data for each of the five FAIIR dimensions of legislative effectiveness, and concluded that there was only a weak relationship between independence and representativeness of legislatures on one hand, and public policy outputs on the other: "These two dimensions of legislative capability are evidently more important in determining how laws are made than which laws are made."[31]

Where does Oklahoma stand on these measures and how does its level of effectiveness influence public policy? Of all the indicators reported in Table 49 Oklahoma ranks "higher" only on the "welfare-education" factor, which is largely a measure of expenditures and effort in the welfare area, plus successful completion of high school. For each of the other policy measures Oklahoma stands up to 36 ranks away from its position on legislative effectiveness—all of which are "lower." A more thorough analysis of Oklahoma's standing on public policy among the various states can be found in the *Handbook of State Policy Indicators*—it shows that among 45 policies measured during the same period as the legislative effectiveness study, Oklahoma ranks more favorably than other states in only a few policy areas: percentage of state and local revenue from the federal government, four measures of welfare effort, and total highway mileage.[32] In sum, Oklahoma appears to be a deviant cast with regard to the relationship between legislative effectiveness and public policy, as well as a deviant case in terms of the mechanisms by which environmental social and political characteristics are translated into higher legislative capabilities.

Characterizing Oklahoma as a "deviant case" by definition implies that it is difficult, if not impossible, to explain its widely divergent positions on legislative effectiveness, public policy, and socioeconomic development. On the average, the processes and mechanisms in other states which link the environment with legislative effectiveness and levels of public policy output apparently do not hold for Oklahoma as a single case. At least, it is considerably removed from the average equation for all the states.

A comprehensive understanding of the forces at work requires considerably more comparative state research and the application of multivariate statistics to assist in isolating the mediating role of the legislature. In this regard, two recent excursions approaching the issue are helpful: the findings indicate that (1) the linkage between party competition and welfare expenditures is greater for more "professional" legislatures;[33] and (2) levels of legislative openness (including the CCSL effectiveness score) influence expenditure policies independent of socioeconomic and political variables.[34] Although deviant cases cannot be explained without recourse to other measures, such as factors not included in the original CCSL study, or without more comprehensive knowledge of the interaction between the three primary system components, the question of linkage between legislative effectiveness and policy is sufficiently important to warrant several educated guesses for Oklahoma's deviance.

First of all, it should be obvious that effectiveness of legislatures does not necessarily lead to "good" policy, in comparison with other states. One person's measure of "good" policy may differ widely from another's. Indeed, the disparity for Oklahoma may result from a legislature strong on representation (as suggested by the CCSL study) and reflective of constituents who are not in favor of increased governmental activity, greater use of resources, or innovation; plus a host of other characteristics more normally associated with traditionalist political cultures. In a sense, the legislature may merely reflect the environment in such a way that the main linkage in the systems model is direct from that environment to various measures of policy, with very little unique impact for legislative effectiveness. In certain circumstances legislative effectiveness may have little to do with public policy, especially when the socioeconomic and political environment is not conducive to greater support of those policies in the first place.

The above suggests a second general explanation. The policy system as discussed earlier is exceedingly complex: the linkage between political structures and policy outputs includes relationships between multiple political structures involving legislative decision making, administrative channels, and various bureaucracies on one hand, and multiple outputs and various policies, plus federal involvement on the other. In addition, the environmental linkage to the political system and its structural characteristics is complex given the variety of structures and a host of potentially important environmental conditions, some of which may vary from time to time. As an example of this complexity, consider the variety of functions performed by any legislature—only a few of which result in concrete or even controversial policy measures. In some states, legislative oversight of the executive branch consumes considerable effort, and in many, legislative actions are often validating, nonsubstantive and unanimous. Procedural matters are included in many legislative roll calls, a tenth to a fifth of all substantive action involves pro forma validation of actions taken by others, and unanimous decisions may comprise more than half of all roll calls.[35] In general, there is much more decisional activity in a legislative body that is represented by "policy consequences."

Other more specific explanations may be subsumed under the above category. Further analysis may indicate that in a state characterized by a high percentage of earmarked taxes, where budgets are already largely dedicated to specific policy purposes, there is less room for legislative impact and discretion in certain policy areas. This is potentially relevant for the Oklahoma case, since the latest comparative state study ranked Oklahoma 41st on a measure of legislative "discretion" or "fluid resources" available to legislative decision makers and capable of being translated into public policy.[36] Although the fluidity of resources is not empirically related to legislative effectiveness across all states (-.04),[37] there may be a linkage between legislative effectiveness and policy which is strong for states with more fluid resources and weaker for those with less legislative discretion (as in Oklahoma).

Finally, there may be certain components of the legislative effectiveness measure which are unduly inflated for the Oklahoma aspect of the study. Such an explanation would discount the importance of legislative leadership, or continuity, and low committee membership ratios which were important in determining "functionality" as discussed earlier. Dwelling on such minor "inflating" characteristics is difficult, especially when most other states would have been exposed to similar circumstances along several of the effectiveness dimensions.

There is a relationship between legislative effectiveness and selected socioeconomic and political characteristics in the American states, as well as a linkage between that effectiveness and the quality and quantity of public policy consequences. While Oklahoma has a high-ranking legislative body, it neither meets minimum environmental criteria for encouraging such a body, nor produces public policies which are typical of such "effective" decision making institutions. This should not imply that the Oklahoma legislature and its effectiveness are irrelevant to public policy, nor that a decrease in effectiveness through a variety of maneuvers would in any way "improve" public policy. Indeed, it may be essential to further improve effectiveness if policy consequences comparable to other states are desirable. Unfortunately, the area of linkages between effectiveness and policy is an especially difficult one. Sometimes it is more important than at others, and certain policy consequences are more likely to reflect effectiveness than are others. In general, legislative analysts and researchers have only begun to scratch the surface for relevant linkages and measures. If we can expand our concepts of public policy and continue to move beyond measures of taxing and spending, we are likely to discover several policy areas that are even more closely linked with legislative effectiveness and more likely to reflect on the quality of legislation. When knowledge of this sort emerges, the likelihood of reform impact heightens. The success of such efforts, however, rests not only with members of the legislative body, but also with an informed and intelligent citizenry who no longer look askance at legislative life. This book is dedicated to those means and to an enlightened dialogue which furthers the goals of representative government.

Senate Rules Study Guide — Selected Review Questions on Senate Rules

I. The Senate in General

1. What voting majority is required to amend or suspend the Senate rules?

    Amendments to the rules require a two-thirds majority of those elected to and constituting the Senate.

2. Under what conditions shall the reading of the Journal be dispensed?

    The Journal of the preceding day shall be read, and any mistakes made in the entries corrected. The reading of the Journal shall not be suspended unless by unanimous consent and when any motion shall be made to amend or correct the same, it shall be deemed a privileged question and proceeded with until disposed of.

3. What voting majority is required for final passage of a bill and for reconsideration of a final vote?

    A simple majority of the membership.

4. How may the Senate instigate an investigation of a state agency? In what 2 ways may this be done?

    The Oklahoma State Senate by simple resolution, or the duly elected President Pro Tempore, may initiate a study, inquiry or investigation of any state agency, department or institution or any other matter of state government. Such study, inquiry or investigation shall be referred by the duly elected President Pro Tempore, at his discretion to either (1) the appropriate Standing Committee, or

---

Author's note: The House and Senate Rules Study Guides contained in the Appendices were organized to facilitate review of the Rules by progressing down each page with a note card or cover sheet concealing the correct answer.

(2) a special Committee on Research and Investigation, the membership of which shall be appointed by the duly elected President Pro Tempore.

5. What voting majority is required for adjournment, adoption of an amendment or appeal from the decision of the Chair?

A simple majority of those voting.

6. Who may call for a quorum?

If, at any time during the daily sessions of the Senate, a question shall be raised by any Senator as to the presence of a quorum, the Presiding Officer shall forthwith direct the Secretary to call the roll and announce the result and these proceedings shall be without debate.

7. When no quorum exists and absent members are being located, what motions can be made?

Whenever upon such roll call it shall be ascertained that a quorum is not present, a majority of the Senators present may direct the Sergeant-at-Arms to request and, when necessary, to compel the attendance of the absent Senators, which order shall be determined without debate; and pending its execution and until a quorum shall be present, no debate nor motion except to adjourn shall be in order.

8. What voting majority is required for an emergency clause; overriding the Governor's veto; or for placing a bill or resolution, under second reading, on calendar without reference to a committee?

Two-thirds (⅔) of the Senate membership.

9. Under what conditions may the Senate operate under the Call of the Senate?

The Senate may operate under the Call of the Senate, upon a majority vote of the members present. The roll shall be called and the Sergeant-at-Arms directed to compile the attendance of absentees. No Senator shall be excused, except by unanimous consent. While the absentees are being notified to attend, the Senate shall have the power to proceed with the business of the Senate.

10. Under Call of Senate, what is the procedure if a present Senator does not answer roll call?

After the Call of the Senate has been ordered, any Senator, who having been thereafter recorded present and not having been excused by unanimous consent, shall be recorded as voting "NO" on the final passage of any measure taken during the Call of the Senate, if such Senator fails to answer roll call.

11. What voting majority is required to pass a bill over veto if it is an Emergency measure?

Three-fourths (3/4) of the Senate membership.

II. Committees

12. Under what conditions may a member of a Standing Committee be dropped?

A member of any Standing Committee failing to attend three consecutive meetings of any Committee of which he is a member shall be automatically dropped from the roll of said Committee unless he be excused on proper showing by the Chairman or a majority of the members of said Committee.

13. Under what conditions may a sub-committee report be given?

The Chairman shall appoint such sub-Committees as recommended by the Committee on Rules to expedite the work of the Committee. When ready to report to the parent Committee, the sub-Committee Chairman shall prepare a written committee report for presentation to the parent Committee. Such report must meet the approval of the majority of the members of the sub-Committee.

14. Which committee shall have leave to sit at any time?

No Committee shall sit during a session of the Senate without leave, except the Committee on

Engrossed and Enrolled Bills and the Committee
on Rules, and they shall have leave to sit or report
at any time.

15. What committee is in charge of printing Bills, Calendars, and Resolutions?

All Bills, Calendars, Orders, Stationery and
Resolutions ordered printed shall be in charge and
under control of the Committee on Employment
and Printing regardless of former references, and
printed under its direction.

16. How may a Bill be withdrawn from Committee?

Any bill or resolution may be withdrawn from
Committee to which referred by a 2/3 majority
vote of those elected to and constitution the
Senate.

17. Under what conditions may executive sessions of a committee be called?

Executive sessions of the Committee or Sub-
Committee may be held upon majority vote of the
membership of the Committee present.

18. Under what conditions may additions be made to a standing committee?

No additions shall be made to a Standing Committee except when a two-thirds (2/3) majority of the
Senate agrees thereto.

19. How many members are on the Rules committee and
how are they selected?

The Committee on Rules, in all future organizations of the Senate in subsequent sessions, shall
have a total membership of fourteen and the three
members of the Senate with the most seniority
shall be members of this Committee and the eleven
remaining members shall be elected.

20. Who presides in Committee of the Whole?

In forming a Committee of the Whole, the President shall leave the Chair. The President Pro Tempore, or any Senator designated by him, shall

preside, subject to the rights of the Senate to select its own Chairman.

21. What may be considered in Committee of the Whole?
All bills and resolutions may be considered in the Committee of the Whole.

22. What is the procedure concerning debates in Committee of the Whole?
Debates in the Committee of the Whole, by any member of the Senate, shall be limited to five (5) minutes on any one motion or subject, and no Senator shall speak more than once upon any question, expect the proposer of the motion or amendment, who shall have the right to open and close the debate.

III. Consideration of a Bill

23. How does a Senator introduce a bill?
A Senator desiring to introduce a bill or resolution shall rise at his desk and address the Presiding Officer and when he has obtained recognition shall publicly notify the Presiding Officer that he desires to introduce a bill or resolution; or he may deposit all the bills he desires to introduce in a basket on the Secretary's desk, provided for that purpose, and when the order of business for the introduction of bills has been reached, the reading clerk shall take from such basket all bills contained therein and publicly read the titles thereof, numbering the bills consecutively in the order read.

24. How many readings must a bill have to pass?
Three.

25. What happens to a bill or resolution following second readings?
When a bill or resolution is read a second time, it shall be referred to a Committee, unless otherwise ordered by unanimous consent of those present or

by a 2/3 vote of the members elected to and constituting the Senate.

26. How many readings must a bill have before it is committed or amended?

No bill or joint resolution shall be committed or amended until it shall have been twice read.

27. What is the procedure for referring appropriations bills to committee?

All bills carrying appropriations which are referred for consideration to any Committee other than the Committee on Appropriations and Budget shall, immediately upon a favorable report by the Committee to which referred or upon the rejection by the Senate of any unfavorable report by such Committee thereon, be referred to the Committee on Appropriations and Budget for consideration of the appropriation features, and no appropriation shall be considered by the Senate until the Committee on Appropriations and Budget has reported in accordance with the rules of the Senate.

28. How shall amendments be offered to bills under the heading of General Order?

Bills under consideration under the heading General Order must not be interlined or defaced but all amendments offered shall be in writing and duly entered upon a separate piece of paper and shall be entered in the Journal.

29. How may a subject be made a "special order"?

Any subject may, by a majority of the Senators elected to the Body, be made a Special Order; and when the time fixed for its consideration arrives the Presiding Officer shall lay it before the Senate. If it is finally disposed of on that day, it shall take its place on the Calendar under the heading of Special Orders in the order of time at which it was made special.

30. In what form must a "question" be set?

The Presiding Officer shall rise to put a question, but may state it sitting. All questions shall be put in this form to-wit: "As many as are in favor (as the question may be) indicate 'AYE' as many as are opposed indicate 'NO'; except when the yeas and nays are ordered, then question shall be put thus: "As many as are in favor (as the question may be) will indicate 'AYE'; as many as are opposed will indicate 'NO'.

31. On a question in debate, which motion may be debated?

If the question in debate contains several propositions, any Senator may have the same divided, except a motion to strike out and insert, which shall not be divided; but the rejection of a motion to strike out and insert one proposition shall not prevent a motion to strike out and insert a different proposition, nor shall it prevent a motion simply to strike out; nor shall the rejection of a motion to strike out prevent a motion to strike out and insert. But, pending a motion to strike out and insert, the part to be stricken out and the part to be inserted shall each be regarded for the purpose of amendment as a question and motions to amend the part to be stricken out shall have precedence.

32. When may a question be "interrupted?"

A question regularly before the Senate can be interrupted only by call for the Previous Question, for amendment, postponement, commitment, to lay on the table, or adjournment.

33. When may a question of order be raised?

A question of order may be raised at any stage of the proceedings except when the Senate is divided and shall be decided by the Presiding Officer, without debate, subject to an appeal to the Senate. When an appeal is taken, any subsequent question of order which may arise before the decision on such appeal, shall be decided by the Presiding Officer without debate; and any appeal may be laid on the table without prejudice to the pending proposition and thereupon shall be held as affirming the decision of the Presiding Officer.

34. When is a bill "engrossed"?

After a measure has been considered as provided under General Order, the next proceedings shall be by motion, non-debatable, to advance said measure to engrossment, and after said measure has been so advanced it shall appear on the Calendar under the heading "Bills on Third Reading" and not subject to amendment, except by unanimous consent.

35. On third reading, what is the regulation concerning the electric voting machine?

When the yeas and nays are ordered, the Presiding Officer shall order the electric voting machine to be activated; and each Senator shall, without debate, indicate his assent or dissent to the question unless excused by the Senate; and no Senator shall be permitted to vote or change his vote after the decision shall have been announced by the Presiding Officer. No motion to suspend this rule shall be in order, nor shall the Presiding Officer entertain any request to suspend it by unanimous consent.

36. When considering bills on General Order, how much time may a Senator consume without unanimous consent of the Senate?

When considering bills on General Order, no Senator shall consume more than ten minutes without the unanimous consent of the Senate.

37. Who may make a motion to reconsider an amendment and what is the vote required?

A motion to reconsider any vote on the adoption or rejection of an amendment to or section of a bill must be made by a Senator who voted in the majority and disposed of on the same day on which the vote was taken, or before advancement of such measure to engrossment. The motion to

reconsider shall be decided by a majority vote of
those present and may be laid on the table without
affecting the question in reference to which same
is made, which shall be a final disposition of the
motion.

38. When is a motion to adjourn not in order?
A motion to adjourn shall always be in order except when the motion shall have been the last
voted on and no business transacted thereafter, or
when the Previous Question shall have been
ordered now put, or when a member has the floor,
and it shall be decided without debate.

IV. Senate Ethics and Decorum

39. What is done when a rule of Senate Decorum is
violated?
If any Senator, in speaking or otherwise,
trangresses the Rules of the Senate, the Presiding
Officer shall, or any Senator may, call him to
order. When any Senator shall be called to order,
he shall sit down and not proceed except in order.

40. In questions of privilege, what is the order of consideration?
Question of privilege shall be: 1st, affecting the
rights of the Senate collectively, its safety, dignity,
and the integrity of its proceedings; 2nd, the
rights, reputation and conduct of members individually in their representative capacity, only,
and shall have precedence of all other questions
except motion to adjourn. Provided, however,
that privileges of the floor may not be invoked
during consideration of a question before the
Senate.

41. What are the duties of the Sergeant-at-Arms?
The Sergeant-at-Arms shall, under the direction of
the Committee on Rules, have charge of all property of the Senate, and receive from the printer
all matters printed for the use of the Senate; and

shall keep a record of the time of the reception of each document and the number of copies received, and cause a copy to be placed on the desk of each member under orders of the Senate. The Sergeant-at-Arms shall keep the front and rear lobbies to the Senate cleared at all times, and no person unless authorized may be admitted to the Senate Lounge or either lobby when the Senate is in session. The Sergeant-at-Arms shall serve all processes and shall enforce the rules of the Senate subject to the directions of the President Pro Tempore. The Sergeant-at-Arms, when directed to, shall indicate vote at voting station of Senator presiding, other than President Pro Tempore.

42. What must one do in order to Lobby before the Senate?
     He shall be required to make application to the Senate, under oath, for permission to lobby or appear as a representative in legislative meetings. He shall reveal to the Senate the person, firm, organization or corporation which he represents and the remuneration or compensation he is to receive.

43. Who besides a Senator may discuss a matter with a Senator on the floor:
     Only a state officer.

44. How may guests enter the Press Gallery?
     Guests may be admitted to the press gallery with the permission of the President Pro Tempore and the Chairman of the Capitol Press Association or his representative at the press gallery.

V. House and Senate

45. How is a joint session of the Senate and House convened?
     When any business shall require a joint session of the Senate and House of Representatives, the Senate preceded by its officers shall be conducted into the bar of the House and there be seated, the

President of the Senate taking a seat by the side of the Speaker of the House, at his right.

46. Who are the officers of a joint session?

The President of the Senate shall be the presiding officer of the joint session and the Secretary of the Senate shall call the roll of the Senate, to be announced by the President of the Senate. The Clerk of the House shall call the roll of the House, which shall be announced by the Speaker of the House. Both the Secretary of the Senate and the Clerk of the House shall keep a report of the proceedings to be entered on the Journals of their respective houses.

47. Where do revenue bills originate?

All bills for raising revenue shall originate in the House of Representatives. The Senate may propose amendments to revenue bills. No revenue bill shall be passed during the last five days of the session.

48. Who shall sign bills when passed and when must he sign it?

The presiding officer of each house shall in the presence of the house over which he presides, sign all bills and joint resolutions passed by the Legislature immediately after the same shall have been publicly read at length.

49. Who constitutes a conference committee?

A conference Committee shall consist of three members of the Senate and three members of the House, unless otherwise specified, to be appointed by the President Pro Tempore of the Senate and the Speaker of the House. In all cases, the first-named member of the house in which the bill originated shall be chairman of the Conference Committee.

50. What ensues following failure of either house to adopt the Conference Report?

In the event of the failure of either house to adopt the Conference Report, the bill or resolution as reported by the Conference Committee shall be considered lost, the papers to remain with the house of origin, except that further conferences may be requested and the original or new conferees appointed for the further consideration of amendments.

51. How are joint rules adopted?

Joint rules shall be adopted in joint session by a majority vote of the membership of each house. Thereafter said rules may be amended, modified or repealed only by the adoption of a concurrent resolution by a two-thirds vote of the membership of each house.

52. What happens to any bill or joint resolution pending at the close of the 1st session?

Any bill or joint resolution pending in the Legislature at the final adjournment of the first regular session of a legislative term shall carry over to the second regular session with the same status as if there had been no adjournment; provided, however, that this Rule shall not apply to bills and resolutions pending in a Conference Committee at the time of said adjournment.

53. May either house consider in the 2nd session a bill defeated in the 1st?

Any bill or joint resolution pending at the time of final adjournment and to be carried over into the second regular session, and which is not in committee at the time of said adjournment, is referred automatically to the standing committee from which it was last reported.

54. How are bills numbered in second session?

Bills and resolutions (a) prefiled for introduction, and (b) introduced in the second regular session of a Legislature shall be numbered consecutively with

the last bill and resolution, respectively, introduced in the first regular session of the same
Legislature.

55. Under what conditions may joint hearings be held?
     With the concurrence of the Speaker and the
     President Pro Tempore, joint hearings before cor-
     responding subject-matter committees of the two
     houses may be held upon agreement of the
     chairmen of said committees, when in their judg-
     ment the interests of legislation or the expedition
     of business will be better served thereby.

House Rules Study Guide — Selected Review Questions on House Rules

1. In the absence of the Speaker, who may be designated to preside over the House from "day to day?"
    A. The Speaker Pro Tempore only
    B. Any member of the House
    C. Majority floor leader
    D. The senior House member

    Answer:
    B.

2. The Speaker may at any time change employees to another department, remove or discharge any of the employees for incompetency, negligence, disorderly conduct or for any other cause with. . .
    A. A simple majority of the House
    B. Concurrence by a special committee
    C. His discretion
    D. At no time

    Answer:
    C.

3. According to the House rules the Speaker is...
    A. An ex officio member of all standing committees
    B. Chairman of all standing committees
    C. A full member of all standing committees
    D. None of the Above

    Answer:
    A.

4. According to the House rules, who is chairman of the Committee on Rules?
    A. The senior House member

B. Speaker Pro Tempore
C. Someone appointed by the Speaker
D. Speaker of the House

Answer:
D.

5. The right to appeal from the decision of the Chair by any member of the House is decided by...
    A. The Speaker Pro Tempore
    B. A roll call with debate by the House
    C. A roll call without debate by the House
    D. A roll call with 5 minutes allowed for the person making the appeal to state his reasons

    Answer:
    D.

6. A roll call may be demanded for any proposition by...
    A. The author of a bill
    B. The Speaker of the House
    C. Committee of the Whole
    D. None of the above

    Answer:
    B.

7. In perfecting a bill or resolution before the House membership, what is the limit placed on debate for each member?
    A. No longer than five (5) minutes, except by consent of the House
    B. Ten (10) minutes
    C. Five (5) minutes
    D. Ten (10) minutes, except by consent of the House

    Answer:
    A.

8. Who has custody and responsibility for the safekeeping

of all official papers, records, reports, and testimony?
A. The Speaker of the House
B. Committee on Records
C. Chief Clerk of the House
D. None of the above

Answer:
C.

9. The Sergeant-at-Arms does which of the following...
A. Executes the commands of the House as directed by the Chair
B. Maintains control over pages
C. Assists committee chairman in maintaining order during committee hearings
D. All of the above

Answer:
A.

10. The first reading of a bill includes the...
A. Number only
B. Title only
C. Number and author
D. Number and title

Answer:
B.

11. Amendment and debate may occur during which of the following stages?
A. First reading
B. Second reading
C. Introduction
D. None of the Above

Answer:
D.

12. During the third reading a bill is...

A. Open to debate
B. May not be subject to amendment
C. May carry an emergency clause
D. All of the above

Answer:
D.

13. If final action is taken on a bill, at what time may a similar bill having the same effect and covering the same specific subject matter be considered by the House?
A. Fifteen (15) days after the final action
B. During the second session of the Legislature
C. Not until the next new legislative session
D. Never

Answer:
C.

14. Which of the following constitutes final action?
A. If a motion to reconsider the vote on a bill fails to prevail
B. Adoption of Committee of the Whole Report of "Do not pass"
C. Failure to adopt the conference committee report
D. All of the above

Answer:
D.

15. What is the debate time for joint resolutions?
A. Not to exceed 20 minutes on each side
B. Not to exceed 30 minutes on each side
C. No debate is allowed
D. No time limit on joint resolutions

Answer:
A.

16. Some resolutions may not be taken up the same day they

are introduced. Which of the following type of resolution must lie over one day or be referred to committees for consideration?
A. Resolutions giving rise to debate
B. Resolutions relating to business immediately before the House
C. Resolutions relating to business of the day on which they may be offered
D. Resolutions relating to adjournment or recess

Answer:
A.

17. Debate on all resolutions is limited to how much time?
A. Thirty (30) minutes to each side
B. Twenty (20) minutes to each side
C. Thirty (30) minutes to the "Aye" side and twenty (20) minutes to the "Nay" side
D. None of the above
Answer:
B.

18. Resolutions authorizing investigations of any officer or department of the State of Oklahoma will not be considered unless...
A. The Attorney General requests it
B. The Governor requests it
C. A report of the Committee on Rules and Procedures has been made
D. A report of the Joint Committee on Rules and Procedures has been made

Answer:
C.

19. The recommendation "do pass" may come from which of the following?
A. The Speaker of the House
B. Any standing or special committee
C. Only a standing committee
D. Only a special committee

Answer:
B.

20. When a "Do not Pass" recommendation is made, what action can be taken to halt final House action?
A. The filing of majority and minority committee reports
B. Request of the author
C. A majority vote of the House
D. No action is possible

Answer:
A.

21. Amendments to any bill approved by a standing committee shall...
A. Not be incorporated into the printed bill
B. Be incorporated into the printed bill
C. Be incorporated into the printed bill but kept in record form by the engrossing department
D. None of the above

Answer:
C.

22. Standing committees are appointed by:
A. The Governor
B. The Committee on Committees
C. Legislative Council
D. Speaker of the House

Answer:
D.

23. In order to reassign a bill from one committee to another which item(s) must be followed?
A. Debate
B. Two-thirds vote of those elected to the House
C. All of the above
D. None of the above

Answer:
C.

24. The Rules and Procedures Committee is chaired by:
A. Speaker Pro-Tempore
B. Majority Floor Leader
C. An appointee of the Speaker
D. Speaker of the House

Answer:
D.

25. Standing committee reports must be reported to the House during each session. In the first session, what is the final date for reporting House bills and joint resolutions from committees?
A. The 27th day is the final date
B. The 27th legislative day is the final date
C. There is no final day
D. None of the above

Answer:
B.

26. During the second session of each Legislature, what is the final date for reporting House bills and joint resolutions from committee?
A. There is no deadline
B. The 47th legislative day
C. The 25th legislative day
D. The 41st legislative day

Answer:
C.

27. What is the composition of a Conference Committee and how are members selected?
A. Three members from each house appointed by the President Pro Tempore and Speaker
B. All members of the House and Senate Committee

which originally considered the bill in question
C. The majority and minority leaders of both houses
D. Two members of each house chosen by the
Governor

Answer:
A.

28.   The adoption of a Conference Committee report is
      achieved by...
      A. A two-thirds vote of those present
      B. A quorum and a two-thirds vote of those present
      C. A majority of those present
      D. A quorum and a majority of those present

      Answer:
      D.

29.   Debate may be extended in the House Committee of the
      Whole by...
      A. Any member and a majority vote of those present,
      with a quorum
      B. Any member with consent by the Chairman
      C. Only by the Chairman
      D. None of the above

      Answer:
      A.

30.   "All bills and resolutions having received a favorable
      report from any standing committee shall be placed on
      the calendar under the heading "General Order," and
      shall be referred to the:"
      A. Ways and Means Committee
      B. Committee of the Whole
      C. Speaker of the House
      D. Floor

      Answer:
      B.

31. The Speaker at his discretion may preside as chairman of...
A. Subcommittees
B. Interim Committees
C. Committee of the Whole
D. None of the above

Answer:
C.

32. Which of the following, according to the House Rules, is the Committee of the Whole *not* entitled to perform...
A. Rise and report
B. Make any matters "Special Order"
C. Perfect the title to conform to the body of the bill
D. All of the above

Answer:
B.

33. A motion that when the Committee of the Whole rise to report it recommend that a bill "Do pass" shall be in order...
A. Immediately after a discussion of a motion
B. Only prior to the motion debate
C. At any time
D. Only after all committee business has been eliminated

Answer:
C.

34. A motion that the Committee of the Whole recommend that a bill "Do not Pass" shall be in order...
A. So long as there are no suggested amendments on the Clerk's desk
B. At any time
C. Only immediately after a discussion of a motion
D. None of the above

Answer:
A.

35. When a division is called for in the Committee of the Whole the affirmative and negative votes are counted by...
A. The Speaker
B. The Chairman
C. The senior committee member
D. The Clerk

Answer:
D.

36. Passage of a motion to reconsider (by the Committee of the Whole) shall require...
A. A simple majority of those voting
B. A two-thirds majority of those voting
C. A two-thirds majority of the total membership
D. Committee of the Whole cannot pass a motion to reconsider

Answer:
B.

37. A motion to "rise and report" or a motion to report progress and request leave to sit again shall be decided...
A. After 5 minutes of debate
B. Without debate
C. At the Speaker's discretion
D. At request of the committee chairman

Answer:
B.

38. Which of the following committees may sit during Committee of the Whole without special leave?
A. Ways and Means
B. Budget Committee

C. Rules Committee
D. None of the above

Answer:
D.

39. According to the House Rules a Division of the Question may be requested...
A. By any member if seconded by 15 members
B. By the Speaker
C. By the Speaker at any member's request
D. By any member if seconded by 20 members

Answer:
A.

40. Conduct during roll call provides that...
A. No member shall speak unless recognized
B. No member shall leave unless given permission
C. No member shall leave his place or speak while roll is being called
D. Any member may leave if called away

Answer:
C.

41. According to House rules, until the completion of the roll call and the announcement of the result, no member shall be recognized and no other business shall be transacted, except...
A. To request debate
B. To be recognized for the purpose of changing one's vote
C. To request permission to leave the floor
D. None of the above

Answer:
B.

42. While ayes and nays are being called, who may visit or remain by the Clerk's desk?

A. The Governor
B. The Speaker
C. The Clerk's aid
D. No member or other person

Answer:
D.

43. A roll call upon any proposition may be demanded by a minimum of...
A. One-fifteenth (1/15) of the members present (with a quorum)
B. A majority of those present
C. Two-thirds (2/3) of the membership
D. Two-thirds (2/3) of those present

Answer:
A.

44. If it has been ascertained that a quorum is not present those members present on the floor may...
A. Debate only the items last considered
B. Vote on any motion
C. Ask for a roll call
D. Adjourn to a day and time specified

Answer:
D.

45. Call of the House may be moved with which minimum condition?
A. At any time by the Speaker
B. At any time by 15 or more members
C. At any time by a majority of those members present
D. Only after 12:00 noon by the Speaker

Answer:
B.

46. According to the House Rules, in all cases where an absent member shall be sent for and fails to attend in obe-

dience to the summons, the report of the messenger...
A. Shall be given to the Speaker
B. Shall be entered upon the Journal
C. Shall be given to the Lt. Governor
D. None of the above

Answer:
B.

47. Who is entitled to lobby on the floor of the House?
A. Any registered lobbyist
B. Any member of the Senate
C. No person
D. The Speaker

Answer:
C.

48. Applications to lobby are referred to the...
A. Committee of the Whole
B. Committee on Lobbyists
C. Committee on House Affairs
D. Rules Committee

Answer:
D.

49. Permission to lobby must first obtain committee approval, then minimum approval from...
A. One-fifteenth (1/15) of the members present
B. A majority of the members present and voting
C. A two-thirds (2/3) majority
D. A majority of the total membership

Answer:
B.

50. In the absence of a quorum, how is adjournment handled?

A. The Speaker with three (3) members shall be a sufficient number to adjourn
B. The Speaker may adjourn
C. No member may call for an adjournment
D. None of the above

Answer:
A.

51. House citations may be issued under special circumstances. Which of the following situations is not appropriate?
A. To a particular person, or on a particular occasion, specified in the motion
B. To be used in lieu of resolutions for Commendations, Congratulations, and Condolences, or to give recognition to an important event
C. For procedural matters
D. All of the above

Answer:
C.

52. Previous questions are not applied in...
A. A debatable question before the House
B. Committee of the Whole
C. Both of the above
D. None of the above

Answer:
B.

53. The motion to recommit may be made at what time?
A. During the first reading
B. During the second reading
C. During the third reading
D. None of the above

Answer:
C.

54. The motion to recommit is...
A. Debatable and amendable
B. Debatable
C. Debatable for 10 minutes only
D. Neither debatable nor amendable

Answer:
D.

55. If a motion to reconsider when called up fails to prevail,
or if the motion to table prevails, it shall be...
A. Referred to Committee of the Whole
B. Referred to the original committee
C. Deemed a final disposition of the matter
D. Reconsidered the next day

Answer:
C.

Notes

CHAPTER 1

1. From John W. Wood, "The Oklahoma Legislature," in Alex B. Lacy, ed., *Power in American State Legislatures* (New Orleans, Tulane University, 1967), p. 157; another helpful source on legislative power and organization is Jack W. Strain, *An Outline of Oklahoma Government* (Norman: Rickner's Book Store, 1972), Chapter 3, plus previous editions by H. V. Thornton.

2. Stephen V. Monsma, "Integration and Goal Attainment as Functions of Informal Legislative Groups," *Western Political Quarterly*, Vol. 22 (March, 1969), 19-28. For a study of Congress see Herbert B. Asher, "The Learning of Legislative Norms," *American Political Science Review*, Vol. 67 (June, 1973), 499-514.

3. See Frank J. Sorauf, *Party and Representation: Legislative Politics in Pennsylvania* (New York: Atherton Press, 1963).

4. Generally see Samuel A. Kirkpatrick, David R. Morgan and Thomas G. Kielhorn, *The Oklahoma Voter: Politics, Elections, and Political Parties in the Sooner State* (Norman: University of Oklahoma Press, 1977).

5. Wilder Crane, Jr., and Meredith W. Watts, Jr., *State Legislative Systems* (Englewood Cliffs: Prentice-Hall, Inc., 1968), Chapter 3.

6. See John C. Wahlke, *et al., The Legislative System* (New York: John Wiley & Sons, Inc., 1962), p. 96; and Duane Lockard, "The State Legislator," in Alexander Heard ed., *State Legislatures in American Politics* (Englewood Cliffs: Prentice-Hall, Inc., 1966), pp. 109-110.

7. Crane and Watts, *State Legislative Systems*, pp.44-45.

8. Sorauf, *Party and Representation*, Chapter 4.

9. U.S. Department of Commerce, Bureau of the Census, *Census of Population, 1960, General Population Characteristics, Oklahoma*, Table 16; and U.S. Department of Commerce, Bureau of the Census, *Census of Population, 1970, General Population Characteristics, Oklahoma*, Table 20.

10. These and other personal data were compiled from the various issues of *Who is Who is the Oklahoma Legislature* (Oklahoma City: Oklahoma Department of Libraries, Legislative Reference Division).

11. Crane and Watts, *State Legislative Systems*, p. 47.

12. U.S. Department of Commerce, Bureau of the Census, *1970 Census of Population, General Social and Economic Characteristics, Oklahoma*, Table 51.

13. Wahlke, *et al., The Legislative System*, p. 488.

14. Lockard, "The State Legislator," p. 121.

15. See Heinz Eulau and John D. Sprague, *Lawyers in Politics* (Indianapolis: Bobbs-Merrill Co., Inc., 1964).

16. David R. Derge, "The Lawyer as Decision-Maker in the American State Legislature," *Journal of Politics*, Vol. 21 (August, 1959), 408-433.

17. "The State Legislator," pp. 122-123.

18. Donald R. Matthews, *U.S. Senators and Their World* (New York: Vintage Books, 1960).

19. See Philip E. Converse, "Religion and Politics: The 1960 Election," in Angus Campbell, *et al.*, eds., *Elections and the Political Order* (New York: John Wiley & Sons, Inc., 1966), pp. 96-125.

20. See David R. Morgan and Samuel A. Kirkpatrick, "Urbanism and Oklahoma Politics," *Oklahoma Business Bulletin*, Vol. 40 (January, 1972), 10-14.

21. Much of the following discussion is drawn from David R. Morgan and Samuel A. Kirkpatrick, "Legislative Reapportionment and Urban Influence in the Oklahoma Legislature," *Oklahoma Business Bulletin*, Vol. 40 (March, 1972), 5-9.

22. Bureau of Government Research, *The Apportionment Problem in Oklahoma* (Norman: University of Oklahoma, 1959). For general historical treatments of the apportionment problem in both chambers see Lionel V. Murphy, "Legislative Apportionment in Oklahoma," *Southwestern Social Science Quarterly*, Vol. 13 (June, 1932), 1-8; Bureau of Government

Research, *Legislative Apportionment in Oklahoma* (Norman: University of Oklahoma, 1951); Bureau of Government Research, *Legislative Apportionment-1960* (Norman: University of Oklahoma, 1960); Bureau of Government Research, *Apportionment Acts of the Legislature, Twenty-Eighth Session, 1961* (Norman: University of Oklahoma, 1961); Joseph C. Pray and George J. Mauer, *The New Perspective of Legislative Apportionment in Oklahoma* (Norman: Bureau of Government Research, University of Oklahoma, 1962); and Jack R. Noble, Dale G. Parent, and Teresa Ramirez, *Oklahoma's Thirtieth Legislature* (Norman: Bureau of Government Research, University of Oklahoma, 1966).

23. Bureau of Government Research, *The Apportionment Problem in Oklahoma* , p. 10

24. Richard D. Bingham, *Reapportionment of the Oklahoma House of Representatives: Politics and Process* (Norman: Bureau of Government Research, University of Oklahoma, 1972), p. 3.

25. *Ibid.*, p. 6.

26. *Ibid.*, p. 7.

27. *Ibid.*, p. 8.

28. *Ibid.*, p. 15.

29. *Ibid.*

30. *Ibid.*

31. *Ibid.*, p. 21.

32. Bureau of Government Research, *The Apportionment Problem in Oklahoma*, p. 11.

CHAPTER 2

1. The role typology is suggested by John C. Wahlke, *et al., The Legislative System* (New York: John Wiley and Sons, Inc., 1962).

2. An exception is *Ibid.*, Chapters 3-6.

3. The categories are developed by William C. Mitchell, "Occupational Role Strains: The American Elective Public Official," in Samuel A. Kirkpatrick and Lawrence K. Pettit eds., *The Social Psychology of Political Life* (Belmont, Calif.: Duxbury Press, 1972), pp. 87-97.

4. Wahlke, *et al., The Legislative System* , Chapter 16.

5. *Ibid.*, Chapter 11.

6. Emil Lee Bernick and Holly Kinkade, *A Study of the Role Orientations of the Oklahoma House of Representatives, 31st Legislature* (unpublished paper, University of Oklahoma, 1967); and Emil Lee Bernick, *A Study of The Role Orientations of the Oklahoma Senate, 31st-32nd Legislatures* (unpublished paper, University of Oklahoma, 1968).

7. From *Ibid.*, Table II; and Wahlke, *et al., The Legislative System* , p. 259.

8. The various comments which follow are from Bernick and Kinkade, *A Study of the Role Orientations of the Oklahoma House of Representatives* and Bernick, *A Study of the Role Orientations of the Oklahoma Senate, passim.*

9. From the "Oklahoma Legislative Study" conducted by the Bureau of Government Research, University of Oklahoma, 1972.

10. Bernick and Kinkade, *A Study of the Role Orientations of the Oklahoma House of Representatives* and Bernick, *A Study of the Role Orientations of the Oklahoma Senate.*

11. These data from the "Oklahoma Legislative Study" are appearing here for the first time. Codebooks, interview schedules and other descriptive material are available from the Bureau of Government Research, University of Oklahoma.

12. The measures were originally developed by Wahlke, *et al., The Legislative System* , pp. 474-75.

13. See for example, Donald Matthews, *U.S. Senators and Their World* (New York: Vintage Books, 1960).

14. Charles S. Hyneman, "Tenure and Turnover of Legislative Personnel," *Annals of the American Academy of Political and Social Science*, Vol. 195 (January, 1938), 21-31.

15. James David Barber, *The Lawmakers: Recruitment and Adaptation to Legislative Life* (New Haven: Yale University Press, 1965), p. 8.

16. Wahlke, *et al., The Legislative System*, p. 122.

17. Allan Rosenthal, "Turnover in State Legislatures," *American Journal of Political Science* , Vol. 18 (August, 1974), 611.

18. Jeff Fishel, "Ambition and the Political Vocation: Congressional Challengers in American

Politics," *Journal of Politics*, Vol. 33 (February, 1971), 26.

19. See Wilder Crane, Jr., and Meredith W. Watts, Jr., *State Legislative Systems* (Englewood Cliffs: Prentice-Hall, Inc., 1968), p. 49.

20. Rosenthal, "Turnover in State Legislatures."

21. *Ibid.*, p. 615.

22. See Barber, *The Lawmakers*; Joseph A. Schlesinger, *Ambition and Politics* (Chicago: Rand McNally, 1966); Fishel, "Ambition and the Political Vocation"; Kenneth Prewitt and William Nowlin, "Politican Ambitions and the Behavior of Incumbent Politicians," *Western Political Quarterly*, Vol. 22 (June, 1969), 298-308; and John W. Soule, "Future Political Ambitions and the Behavior of Incumbent State Legislators," *Midwest Journal of Political Science* , Vol. 13 (August, 1969), 439-54.

23. Soule, "Future Political Ambitions and the Behavior of Incumbent State Legislators," p. 440.

24. *Ambition and Politics*, p. 10.

25. Soule, "Future Political Ambitions and the Behavior of Incumbent State Legislators," p. 443.

26. Barber, *The Lawmakers*, p. 8.

27. Soule, "Future Political Ambitions and the Behavior of Incumbent State Legislators," p. 442.

28. Adapted from Wahlke, *et al., The Legislative System*, p. 129.

29. Schlesinger, *Ambition and Politics*, p. 73.

30. Soule, "Future Political Ambitions and the Behavior of Incumbent State Legislators."

31. Harold D. Lasswell, *Power and Personality* (New York: Norton, 1948).

32. Wahlke, *et al., The Legislative System*, p. 121.

33. Schlesinger, *Ambition and Politics*, p. 2.

34. Kenneth Prewitt, "Political Ambitions, Volunteerism, and Electoral Accountability," *American Political Science Review*, Vol. 64 (March, 1970), 5-18.

35. Barber, *The Lawmakers* , Chapter 1.

36. *Ibid .*, p. 20.

37. *Ibid* .

38. For a summary, see *Ibid .*, pp. 214-16.

39. *Ibid .*, p. 249.

CHAPTER 3

1. William J. Siffin, *The Legislative Council in the American States* (Bloomington: Indiana University Press, 1959).

2. Joseph E. McCool, Jr., *The Oklahoma Legislative Council: Pressure Group Participation in the Legislative Process* (unpublished Master's Thesis, Oklahoma State University, 1968), p. 41.

3. For a general treatment see Jack A. Rhodes, "The Legislative Council: A Program for Planning and Research," *Southwestern Social Science Quarterly* , Vol. 27 (June, 1946), 54-61.

4. For a general description see Jack W. Strain, *An Outline of Oklahoma Government* (Norman: Rickner's Bookstore, 1972), pp. 41-42.

5. 74 O.S. 1971, sec. 452

6. See Malcolm E. Jewell and Samuel C. Patterson, *The Legislative Process in the United States*, 2d ed. (New York: Random House, 1973), p. 250; Wilder Crane, Jr., and Meredith W. Watts, Jr., *State Legislative Systems* (Englewood Cliffs: Prentice-Hall, Inc., 1968), p. 67; and Duane Lockard, "The State Legislator," Alexander Heard, ed., *State Legislatures in American Politics* (Englewood Cliffs: Prentice-Hall, Inc., 1966), pp. 114-115.

7. The following relies heavily on a presentation by Attorney General Larry Derryberry at the Oklahoma Presession Legislative Conference, University of Oklahoma, December, 1972.

8. John C. Wahlke, "Organization and Procedure," in Heard ed., *State Legislatures in American Politics*, pp. 141-143.

9. Jewell and Patterson, *The Legislative Process in the United States*, p. 250; and Crane and Watts, *State Legislative Systems*, p. 61.

10. Malcolm E. Jewell, *The State Legislature: Politics and Practice*, 2d ed. (New York: Random House, 1969), p. 52.

11. Crane and Watts, *State Legislative Systems*, pp. 62-63.
12. Jewell, *The State Legislature*, p. 53.
13. Thomas R. Dye, "State Legislative Politics," in Herbert Jacob and Kenneth Vines eds., *Politics in the American States*, 2d ed. (Boston: Little, Brown and Company, 1971), p. 189.
14. William J. Keefe and Morris J. Ogul, *The American Legislative Process: Congress and the States*, 3d ed. (Englewood Cliffs: Prentice-Hall, Inc., 1973), p. 392.
15. Wayne Francis, *Legislative Issues in the Fifty States* (Chicago: Rand McNally, 1967), pp. 74-75.
16. Crane and Watts, *State Legislative Systems*, p. 61.

CHAPTER 4

1. Malcolm E. Jewell, *The State Legislature: Politics and Practice*, 2d ed. (New York: Random House, 1969), p. 106.
2. A similar model guides Randall Ripley, *Congress: Process and Policy* (New York: W.W. Norton & Company, Inc., 1975), p. 70.
3. Jewell, *The State Legislature* , pp.106ff.
4. Hugh L. LeBlanc, "Voting in State Senates: Party and Constituency Influences," *Midwest Journal of Political Science*, Vol. 13 (February, 1969), 33-57.
5. Robert H. Salisbury, *Missouri Politics and State Political Systems* (Columbia: Bureau of Government Research, University of Missouri, 1959).
6. See Jewell, *The State Legislature* , pp. 118-119; Allan P. Sindler, *Huey Long's Louisiana* (Baltimore: Johns Hopkins Press, 1956); and Malcolm E. Jewell, *Kentucky Politics* (Lexington: University of Kentucky Press, 1968).
7. LeBlanc, "Voting in State Senates."
8. Donald R. Matthews and James A. Stimson, "Decision-Making by U.S. Representatives: A Preliminary Model," in S. Sidney Ulmer ed., *Political Decision-Making* (New York: Van Nostrand Reinhold Co., 1970), pp. 14-44.
9. H. Owen Porter, "Legislative Experts and Outsiders: The Two-Step Flow of Communication," *Journal of Politics*, Vol. 36 (August, 1974), 703-731.
10. In Kansas, the impact of party affiliation exceeds urban-rural influences; see John G. Grumm, "The Kansas Legislature: Republican Coalition," in Samuel C. Patterson ed., *Midwest Legislative Politics* (Iowa City: Institute of Public Affairs, The University of Iowa, 1967), 37-67.
11. Robert S. Friedman, "The Urban-Rural Conflict Revisited," *Western Political Quarterly*, Vol. 14 (June, 1961), 481-495.
12. David R. Derge, "Metropolitan and Outstate Alignments in Illinois and Missouri Legislative Delegations," *American Political Science Review*, Vol. 52 (December, 1958), 1051-1065.
13. Frank J. Sorauf, *Party and Representation: Legislative Politics in Pennsylvania* (New York: Atherton, 1963).
14. Thomas A. Flinn, "Party Responsibility in the States: Some Causal Factors," *American Political Science Review*, Vol. 58 (March, 1964), 60-71.
15. Thomas R. Dye, "A Comparison of Constituency Influences in the Upper and Lower Chambers of a State Legislature," *Western Political Quarterly*, Vol. 14 (June, 1961), 473-480.
16. Robert W. Becker, *et al.*, "Correlates of Legislative Voting: Michigan House of Representatives, 1954-1961," *Midwest Journal of Political Science* , Vol. 6 (November, 1962), 384-396.
17. Wilder W. Crane, Jr., "Do Representatives Represent?" *Journal of Politics* , Vol. 22 (May, 1960), 295-299.
18. Robert J. Huckshorn, "Decision-Making Stimuli in the State Legislative Process," *Western Political Quarterly*, Vol. 18 (March, 1965), 164-185.
19. See Alan Rosenthal, "Contemporary Research on State Legislatures: From Individual Cases to Comparative Analysis," in *Political Science and Local Government* (Washington: The American Political Science Association, 1973), pp. 62-64.
20. Thomas R. Dye, "Malapportionment and Public Policy in the States," *Journal of Politics*, Vol. 27 (August, 1965), 586-601; and Richard I. Hofferbert, "The Relation Between Public Policy and Some Structural and Environmental Variables in the American States," *American Political Science Review*, Vol. 60 (March, 1966), 73-82.

21. William deRubertis, "How Apportionment With Selected Demographic Variables Relates to Policy Orientation," *Western Political Quarterly*, Vol. 22 (December, 1969), 904-920; Brett Hawkins and Cheryl Whelchel, "Reapportionment and Urban Representation in Legislative Influence Positions: The Case of Georgia," *Urban Affairs Quarterly*, Vol. 3 (March, 1968), 69-80; C. Richard Hofstetter, "Malapportionment and Roll Call Voting in Indiana, 1929-1963: A Computer Simulation," *Journal of Politics*, Vol. 33 (February, 1971), 92-111; and Richard Lehne, *Reapportionment of the New York Legislature: Impact and Issues* (New York: National Municipal League, 1972).

22. Malcolm E. Jewell, "State Legislatures in Southern Politics," *Journal of Politics*, Vol. 26 (February, 1964), 177-196.

23. Wayne L. Francis, *Legislative Issues in the Fifty States: A Comparative Analysis* (Chicago: Rand McNally, 1967).

24. Ralph Eisenberg, "Reapportionment and A Legislature: Some Observations on the Virginia Experience," in *Reports and Recommendations of the Duke University Assembly on State Legislatures* (Durham: Duke University, 1967), pp. 7-31.

25. William B. Buchanan, *Legislative Partisanship: The Deviant Case of California* (Berkeley: University of California Press, 1963).

26. Francis, *Legislative Issues in the Fifty States* .

27. Wayne L. Francis, "A Profile of Legislator Perceptions of Interest Group Behavior Relating to Legislative Issues in the States," *Western Political Quarterly* , Vol. 24 (December, 1971), 702-712.

28. See Hugh L. LeBlanc and D. Trudeau Allensworth, *The Politics of States and Urban Communities* (New York: Harper and Row, 1971), pp. 35-44.

29. *Legislative Issues in the Fifty States* , p. 15.

30. Samuel C. Patterson, "Dimensions of Voting Behavior in a One-Party State Legislature," *Public Opinion Quarterly* , Vol. 26 (Summer, 1962), 185-200.

31. Aage Clausen, *How Congressmen Decide: A Policy Focus* (New York: St. Martin's Press, 1973).

32. Warren E. Miller and Donald E. Stokes, "Constituency Influence in Congress," *American Political Science Review* , Vol. 57 (March, 1963), 45-56.

33. John W. Kingdon, *Congressmen's Voting Decisions* (New York: Harper and Row, 1973).

34. "Dimensions of Voting Behavior in a One-Party Legislature."

35. This section draws heavily form E. Lee Bernick and F. Ted Hebert, "Emergent Partisanship and the Dimensions of Roll Call Voting" (unpublished manuscript, University of Oklahoma, 1973).

36. See Malcolm E. Jewell, "Party Voting in American State Legislatures," *American Political Science Review* , Vol. 49 (September, 1955), 773-791; and Duane Lockard, "Legislative Politics in Connecticut," *American Political Science Review* , Vol. 48 (March, 1954), 166-173.

37. See Malcolm E. Jewell and Samuel C. Patterson, *The Legislative Process in the United States* (Random House, 1966), pp. 416-426; Flinn, "Party Responsibility in the States."

38. Exceptions include Harlan Hahn, "Leadership Perceptions and Voting Behavior in a One-Party Legislative Body," *Journal of Politics* , Vol. 32 (February, 1970), 140-155; Charles W. Wiggins, "Party Politics in the Iowa Legislature," *Midwest Journal of Political Science* , Vol. 11 (February, 1967), 86-97; and John G. Grumm, "A Factor Analysis of Legislative Behavior," *Midwest Journal of Political Science* , Vol. 7 (November, 1963), 336-356.

39. From Bernick and Hebert, "Emergent Partisanship and the Dimensions of Roll Call Voting," Table 2.

40. *Ibid* ., pp. 4-5.

41. *Ibid* ., Table 4.

42. *Ibid* ., p. 8.

43. E. Lee Bernick, "The Impact of the Governor on the Voting Behavior of State Legislators: An Examination of Four States" (presented at the Annual Meeting of the Southwestern Political Science Association, San Antonio, Texas, March 27-29, 1975).

44. *Ibid* ., pp. 23-24.

45. E. Lee Bernick, *Legislative Voting Patterns and Partisan Cohesion in a One-Party Dominant Legislature* (Norman: Bureau of Government Research, Legislative Research Series, University of Oklahoma, 1973).

46. Friedman, "The Urban-Rural Conflict Revisited"; David Derge, "Urban-Rural Conflict: The Case of Illinois," in John Wahlke and Heinz Eulau eds., *Legislative Behavior* (Glencoe, Ill.: Free Press, 1959), pp. 218-227; and Murray Havens, *City vs. Farm* ? (University, Alabama:

University of Alabama Press, 1957).

47. William J. Keefe, "Comparative Study of the Role of Political Parties in State Legislatures," *Western Political Quarterly* , Vol. 9 (June, 1956), 726-742; and Flinn, "Party Responsibility in the States."

48. Duncan MacRae, Jr., "The Relation Between Roll Call Votes and Constituencies in the Massachusetts House of Representatives," *American Political Science Review* , Vol. 46 (December, 1952), 1046-1055; Samuel C. Patterson, "The Role of the Deviant in the State Legislative System: The Wisconsin Assembly," *Western Political Quarterly* , Vol. 14 (June, 1961), 460-472; and Flinn, "Party Responsibility in the States."

49. Patterson, "The Role of the Deviant in the State Legislative System," p. 466.

50. From Bernick, *Legislative Voting Patterns and Partisan Cohesion in a One-Party Dominant Legislature* , Table 3, p. 17.

51. From *Ibid* ., Table 4, p. 20.

52. *Ibid* ., p. 22.

53. "Dimensions of Voting Behavior in a One-Party State Legislature."

54. David R. Morgan and Samuel A. Kirkpatrick, "Urban-Rural Divisions Within the Oklahoma Legislature," *Oklahoma Business Bulletin*, Vol. 40 (April, 1972), 5-10.

55. From *Ibid*., Table 2, p. 7.

56. Gary N. Parent, "The Reapportionment Decade in the Oklahoma House" (unpublished paper, University of Oklahoma, 1975).

57. See Clara Penniman, "The Politics of Taxation," in Herbert Jacob and Kenneth Vines eds., *Politics in the American States*, 2d ed. (Boston: Little, Brown & Co., 1971), p. 520; and Leon D. Epstein, *Votes and Taxes* (Madison: Institute of Government Affairs, University of Wisconsin, 1964), p. 14.

58. E. Lee Bernick, *Legislative Decision-Making and the Politics of Tax Reform: The Oklahoma Senate* (Norman: Bureau of Government Research, Legislative Research Series, University of Oklahoma, 1975).

59. Patton N. Morrison, "Legislative-Constituency Interaction in Oklahoma: A Study of Legislative Referenda Voting" (unpublished paper, University of Oklahoma, 1975).

CHAPTER 5

1. Samuel A. Kirkpatrick and Lawrence K. Pettit, *The Social Psychology of Political Life* (Belmont Calif.: Duxbury Press, 1972), p. 73.

2. Lelan E. McLemore, *The Structuring of Legislative Behavior: Norm Patterns in a State Legislature* (unpublished Ph.D. dissertation, University of Oklahoma, 1973), pp. 7-8.

3. Samuel A. Kirkpatrick and Lawrence K. Pettit, *Legislative Role Structures, Power Bases and Behavior Patterns: An Empirical Examination of the U.S. Senate* (Norman: Bureau of Government Research, Legislative Research Series, University of Oklahoma, 1973), pp. 4-5.

4. Ralph K. Huitt, "The Outsider in the Senate: An Alternative Role," in Ralph K. Huitt and Robert L. Peabody eds., *Congress: Two Decades of Analysis* (New York: Harper and Row, 1969), p. 113.

5. Donald R. Matthews, *U.S. Senators and Their World* (New York: Vintage Books, 1960), pp. 92-102.

6. John C. Wahlke, *et al., The Legislative System* (New York: John Wiley & Sons, 1962), p. 165.

7. *Ibid* ., p. 168.

8. Samuel C. Patterson, "The Role of the Deviant in the State Legislative System: The Wisconsin Assembly," *Western Political Quarterly* , Vol. 14 (June, 1961), 460-472.

9. Kirkpatrick and Pettit, *The Social Psychology of Political Life* , p. 75.

10. Samuel C. Patterson, "Patterns of Interpersonal Relations in a State Legislative Group," *Public Opinion Quarterly* , Vol. 23 (Spring, 1959), 101-109.

11. *Ibid* ., p. 109.

12. The 1972 Oklahoma Legislative Study directed by the author contained a substantive proportion of material on legislative norms subsequently reported in McLemore, *The Structuring of Legislative Behavior: Norm Patterns in a State Legislature*, from which the following analysis draws heavily. Related materials include the following: Samuel A. Kirkpatrick and Lelan E.

McLemore, "Evaluative and Perceptual Dimensions of Legislative Norms: An Analysis of Congruence and Conflict" (presented at the Annual Meeting of the Midwest Political Science Association, Chicago, May 1-3, 1975); McLemore, "Norms and the Structuring of Partisan Behavior" (presented at the Annual Meeting of the Southwestern Political Science Association, Dallas, March 28-30, 1974); McLemore, *Task-Related Norms in a State Legislature: The Case of Oklahoma* (Norman: Bureau of Government Research, Legislative Research Series, University of Oklahoma, 1973); and McLemore, *Behavioral Orientations Toward Party Leadership and System Norms: An Exploratory Analysis* (Norman: Bureau of Government Research, Legislative Research Series, University of Oklahoma, 1975).

13. A mere sharing of beliefs may not be sufficient for analyzing legislative norms, since it is also important to examine the extent to which legislators share that others share their beliefs. That is, all norms have a subjective or preferential component as well as an objective or perceptual component, and the two are closely interrelated.See Kirkpatrick and McLemore, "Evaluative and Perceptual Dimensions of Legislative Norms."

14. Lewis Froman, Jr. and Randall Ripley, "Conditions for Party Leadership: The Case of the House Democrats," *American Political Science Review*, Vol. 59 (March, 1965), 52-63.

15. Matthews, *U.S. Senators and Their World*; and James D. Barber, "Leadership Strategies for Legislative Party Cohesion," *Journal of Politics*, Vol. 28 (May, 1966), 347-367.

16. McLemore, *The Structuring of Legislative Behavior*, p. 76.

17. Patterson, "The Role of the Deviant in the State Legislative System."

18. Wahlke, *et al., The Legislative System*, p. 150.

19. McLemore, *The Structuring of Legislative Behavior*, p. 125.

20. Matthews, *U.S. Senators and Their World*.

21. Wahlke, *et al., The Legislative System*, p. 157.

22. *Ibid*., pp. 141-169; and Patterson, "The Role of the Deviant in the State Legislative System."

23. McLemore, *The Structuring of Legislative Behavior*, p. 138.

24. Patterson, "The Role of the Deviant in the State Legislative System," p. 464; and Wahlke, *et al., The Legislative System*, pp. 146-147.

25. Matthews, *U.S. Senators and Their World*; and Wahlke, *et al., The Legislative System*.

26. See Malcolm E. Jewell and Samuel C. Patterson, *The Legislative Process in the United States*, 2nd ed. (New York: Random House, 1973), p. 392; and Wahlke, *et al., The Legislative System*, p. 214.

27. James D. Barber, *The Lawmakers: Recruitment and Adaptation to Legislative Life* (New Haven: Yale University Press, 1965).

28. McLemore, *The Structuring of Legislative Behavior*, p. 201.

29. *Ibid*., p. 210.

30. For more details see *Ibid*., pp. 108 and 220.

31. Wahlke, *el al., The Legislative System*, p. 143.

32. *Ibid*., p. 154; and Matthews, *U.S. Senators and Their World*.

33. McLemore, *The Structuring of Legislative Behavior*, pp. 223-224.

34. Barber, *The Lawmakers*.

35. McLemore, *The Structuring of Legislative Behavior*, p. 226.

36. For detailed data see *Ibid*., p. 239-240.

37. *Ibid*., p. 242.

38. Richard D. Bingham, *Reapportionment of the Oklahoma House of Representatives: Politics and Process* (Norman: Bureau of Government Research, Legislative Research Series, University of Oklahoma, 1972).

39. McLemore, *The Structuring of Legislative Behavior*, p. 253.

CHAPTER 6

1. E. Lee Bernick and Holly Kinkade, *A Study of the Role Orientations of the Oklahoma House of Representatives, 31st Legislature* (unpublished paper, University of Oklahoma, 1967); and E. Lee Bernick, *A Study of the Role Orientations of the Oklahoma Senate, 31st-32nd Legislatures* (unpublished paper, University of Oklahoma, 1968).

2. John C. Wahlke, *et al., The Legislative System* (New York: John Wiley and Sons, Inc.,

1962), Chapter 12; also see Ronald D. Hedlund and H. Paul Friesema, "Representatives' Perceptions of Constituency Opinion," *Journal of Politics* , Vol. 34 (August, 1972), 730-753 for the finding that Iowa "trustees" offer more accurate predictions of how constituents will vote on referenda than "delegates."

3. These items were part of the Bureau of Government Research, Oklahoma Legislative Study in 1972.

4. Donald E. Stokes and Warren E. Miller, "Party Government and the Saliency of Congress," *Public Opinion Quarterly* , Vol. 26 (Winter, 1962), 531-546.

5. David Saffell, *The Politics of American National Government* (Cambridge: Winthrop Publishers, Inc., 1973), p. 59.

6. David B. Truman, *The Governmental Process* , 2d ed. (New York: Alfred A. Knopf, Inc., 1971), p. 33.

7. Samuel C. Patterson, "The Role of the Lobbyist: The Case of Oklahoma," *Journal of Politics* , Vol. 25 (February, 1963), p. 72.

8. Wahlke, *et al., The Legislative System* , p. 327.

9. Joseph E. McCool, Jr., *The Oklahoma Legislative Council: Pressure Group Participation in the Legislative Process* (unpublished Master's Thesis, Oklahoma State University, 1968), pp. 57-62.

10. Lester Milbrath, *The Washington Lobbyists* (Chicago: Rand McNally, 1963), pp. 220-227.

11. See Charles W. Wiggins, *The Iowa Lawmakers* (Ames: Iowa State University, 1970), pp. 88-90.

12. "The Role of the Lobbyist."

13. *Ibid* ., pp. 72-73; also see Lester Milbrath, "Lobbying as a Communication Process," *Public Opinion Quarterly* , Vol. 24 (Spring, 1960), 32-53.

14. Larry Dreyer, *Legislator and Lobbyist's Views of Improper Lobbying in North Dakota* (Grand Forks: Bureau of Government Affairs, University of North Dakota, 1974).

15. Edgar Lane, *Lobbying and the Law* (Berkeley: University of California Press, 1964), pp. 141-152.

16. 21 O.S. 1971, § 313.

17. 21 O.S. 1971, § 316.

18. 21 O.S. 1971, § 316.

19. 21 O.S. 1971, § 318.

20. 21 O.S. 1971, § 320.

21. Carl Warren, *Modern News Reporting* , 3d. ed. (New York: Harper and Row, Publishers, 1959), p. 15; also see Ronald D. Hedlund and Wilder Crane, Jr., *The Job of the Wisconsin Legislator* (Washington, D.C.: Americal Political Science Association, 1971), pp. 90-113.

CHAPTER 7

1. Findings from the study are reported in Citizens Conference on State Legislatures, *Summary Report: An Evaluation of the Fifty State Legislatures* (Kansas City, Mo.: Citizens Conference on State Legislatures, 1971); CCSL, *The Sometime Governments: A Critical Study of the Fifty American Legislatures* (New York: Bantam Books, 1971); and CCSL, *State Legislatures: An Evaluation of Their Effectiveness* (New York: Praeger Publishers, 1971). Follow-up data appear in CCSL, *Legislatures Move to Improve Their Effectiveness* (Kansas City, Mo.: CCSL, 1972). It should be noted that as of 1976 the CCSL changed its name to Legis 50/The Center for Legislature Improvement. Publications prior to 1976 still carry the former name.

2. See Donald Herzberg and Alan Rosenthal (eds.) *Strengthening the States: Essays on Legislative Reform* (New York: Doubleday & Company, Inc., 1971) and Donald Herzberg and Jess Unruh, *Essays on the State Legislative Process* (New York: Holt, Rinehart and Winston, Inc., 1970).

3. CCSL, *State Legislatures: An Evaluation of Their Effectiveness* , p. 11.

4. Subsequent to the major study, Oklahoma increased the number of its standing committees. It was therefore one of the few states which regressed from CCSL standards from mid-1970 to late 1971. See CCSL, *Legislatures Move to Improve Their Effectiveness* , pp. 5 and 41.

5. CCSL, *State Legislatures: An Evaluation of Their Effectiveness* , pp. 282-286.

6. For a description of the legislature's apparent unfriendliness to the press, partially reflecting historic conflict with the metropolitan newspapers, see CCSL, *The Sometime Governments* , p. 94.

7. Eugene R. Declerq, "Gubernatorial Power and Legislative Independence in the Fifty States" (unpublished paper presented at the Annual Meeting of the Midwest Political Science Association, Chicago, May 1-4, 1975).

8. See David R. Morgan and Samuel A. Kirkpatrick, *Constitutional Revision: Cases and Commentary* (Norman: Bureau of Government Research, University of Oklahoma, 1970).

9. CCSL, *The Sometimes Governments* , p. 4.

10. For a compendium of obstacles see John C. Wahlke, "Organization and Procedure," in Alexander Heard ed., *State Legislatures in American Politics* (Englewood Cliffs: Prentice-Hall, Inc., 1966), pp. 126-154; Alexander Heard, "Reform: Limits and Opportunities," in *Ibid* ., pp. 154-163; and Herzberg and Rosenthal, *Strengthening the States* , part three.

11. See Alan Rosenthal, "Turnover in State Legislatures," *American Journal of Political Science* , Vol. 18 (August, 1974), 609-616.

12. For an overview see David R. Morgan, *Handbook of State Policy Indicators* (Norman: Bureau of Government Research, University of Oklahoma, 1971), pp. 1-18; and for more details on the systems perspective see David R. Morgan and Samuel A. Kirkpatrick, *Urban Political Analysis: A Systems Approach* (New York: Free Press, 1972), pp. 1-28.

13. Richard E. Dawson and James A. Robinson, "Inter-Party Competition, Economic Variables and Welfare Policies in the American States," *Journal of Politics* , Vol. 25 (May, 1963), 265-287; and Thomas R. Dye, *Politics, Economics, and the Public* (Chicago: Rand McNally, 1966).

14. Ira Sharkansky,"Environment, Policy, Output, and Impact: Problems of Theory and Method in the Analysis of Public Policy," in Sharkansky (ed.), *Policy Analysis in Political Science* (Chicago: Markham, 1970).

15. Ira Sharkansky, *Spending in the American States* (Chicago: Rand McNally, 1968).

16. Herbert Jacob and Michael Lipsky, "Outputs, Structures, and Power: An Assessment of Changes in the Study of State and Local Politics," *Journal of Politics* , Vol. 30 (May, 1968), 510-538.

17. Brian R. Fry and Richard F. Winters, "The Politics of Redistribution," *American Political Science Review* , Vol. 64 (June, 1970), 508-522.

18. For a list of numerous studies see Morgan, *Handbook of State Policy Indicators* , pp. 7, 16.

19. See *State Legislatures: An Evaluation of Their Effectiveness* , Chapter 5.

20. The original measure appears in Richard Hofferbert, "Socioeconomic Dimensions of the American States: 1890-1960," *Midwest Journal of Political Science* , Vol. 12 (August, 1968), 401-419.

21. Originally developed by John Crittenden, "Dimensions of Modernization in the American States," *American Political Science Review* , Vol. 61 (December, 1967), 989-1002.

22. See Austin Ranney, "Parties in State Politics," in Henry Jacob and Kenneth Vines eds., *Politics in the American States* (Boston: Little, Brown and Co., 1965).

23. Daniel J. Elazar, *American Federalism: A View from the States* (New York: Thomas Crowell, 1966) and Ira Sharkansky, "The Utility of Elazar's Political Culture: A Research Note," *Polity* , Vol. 2 (Fall, 1969), 66-83.

24. From Duane Lockard, "State Party Systems and Policy Outputs," in Oliver Garceau ed., *Political Research and Political Theory* (Cambridge, Mass.: Harvard University Press, 1968).

25. From Ira Sharkansky and Richard Hofferbert, "Dimensions of State Politics, Economics, andd Public Policy," *American Political Review* , Vol. 63 (September, 1969), 876-879.

26. *State Legislatures: An Evaluation of Their Effectiveness* , p. 72.

27. From Sharkansky and Hofferbert, "Dimensions of State Politics, Economics, and Public Policy."

28. From Jack Walker, "The Diffusion of Innovations Among the American States," *American Political Science Review* , Vol. 63 (September, 1969), 880-900.

29. From Crittenden, "Dimensions of Modernization in the American States."

30. *State Legislatures: An Evaluation of Their Effectiveness* , p. 77.

31. *Ibid* .

32. Morgan, *Handbook of State Policy Indicators* , pp. 29, 52, 53, 54, 58, 71.

33. Edward G. Carmines, "The Mediating Influences of State Legislatures on the Linkage Between Interparty Competition and Welfare Policies," *American Political Science Review,* Vol.

68 (September, 1974), 1118-1125.

34. Michael A. Baer and Dean Jaros, "Participation as Instrument and Expression: Some Evidence from the States," *American Journal of Political Science* , Vol. 18 (May, 1974), 365-385.

35. See John Wahlke, "Policy Determinants and Legislative Decisions," in Sidney Ulmer ed., *Political Decision-Making* (New York: Van Nostrand Reinhold Company, 1970), 76-120.

36. Tax Foundation, Inc., *Earmarked State Taxes* (New York: Tax Foundation, Inc., 1965).

37. *State Legislatures: An Evaluation of Their Effectiveness* , p. 70.

Glossary of Legislative Procedure

ADJOURN — to close the session of the Legislative Day.

AMENDMENT — any change in a bill or resolution.
Committee amendment — amendment action in a committee meeting.
Floor amendment — amendment action during the session of the legislature.

AUTHOR — a member of the legislature who introduces a bill for consideration by the legislature.

BILL — a proposed law.

CALENDAR — a list of bills and other items for consideration by the legislature.

CAUCUS — a closed meeting of a group of people belonging to the same political party to select leaders or decide policy.

CONCURRENT RESOLUTION — a resolution passed by both houses of the legislature.

CONSTITUENT — one of a group of persons who elects a legislator.

CONVENE — to assemble, as the legislature.

DEBATE — free discussion of matters before the legislature.

EMERGENCY CLAUSE — a provision that allows a measure to become effective immediately upon the signature of the governor.

ENGROSSED — a verified copy of the bill or resolution as introduced with amendments, executed before third reading and subsequently as needed.

ENROLLED — a final copy of the identical bill passed by both houses, ready for the governor's signature.

EXECUTIVE NOMINATION — nominations made by the governor to the Senate for members of State Boards and Commissions.

EXECUTIVE SESSION — a closed meeting of the Senate for the purpose of confirming executive nominations.

FILIBUSTER — a prolonged debate for the purpose of delaying or preventing action by the legislature.

FIRST READING — introduction of a bill and the reading of its title for the first time.

GENERAL ORDER — any measure on the calendar pending action by the legislature.

JOINT RESOLUTION — a resolution passed by both houses of the legislature which has the effect of law if signed by the governor.

JOURNAL — the official record of the legislative proceedings.

LAW — a bill which has passed both houses of the legislature, been signed by the governor, and therefore is binding upon the citizens.

LEGISLATIVE DAY — a day on which the legislature meets.

LOBBYIST — a person representing any individual, organization, or corporation before the legislature.

MAJORITY — more than half.

MESSAGE TO/FROM THE HOUSE — communication from the Senate to the House, or vice versa.

MINORITY — less than half.

MOTION — proposition presented for action by a legislative body.

OVERRIDE — to reconsider a bill after the governor's veto and pass it again by an extraordinary majority.

POCKET VETO — no bill shall become a law after the sine die adjournment of the legislature unless approved by the governor within fifteen days after such sine die.

PRIVILEGE — matters which relate to the legislature or its members and affect proper functioning.

QUORUM — a majority of the members of each house.

RECONSIDER — to consider again a vote on any action previously taken by the legislature.

RESOLUTION — an order of a legislative body which expresses policies and purposes.

RULES — provisions for the procedure, organization, officers, and committees of the legislature.

SECOND READING — title of a bill read for second time and referred to committee.

SESSION — a series of connected meetings of the legislature for the purpose of transacting business.

SINE DIE — the close of a session.

STATUTE — a law enacted by the legislature.

TABLE — to remove a measure from consideration indefinitely.

THIRD READING — bill read at length before a vote of the legislature is taken.

TITLE — a heading which is a brief statement of the subject of the act.

UNANIMOUS CONSENT — action taken when no member objects.

VETO — when governor does not sign a bill and sends it back to the legislature with his objections.

Bibliography

Asher, Herbert B. "The Learning of Legislative Norms," *American Political Science Review* , 67 (June, 1973): 499-514.

Baer, Michael and Dean Jaros. "Participation as Instrument and Expression: Some Evidence Form the States," *American Journal of Political Science* , 13 (May, 1974): 365-385.

Barber, James D. *The Lawmakers: Recruitment and Adaptation to Legislative Life* . New Haven: Yale University Press, 1965.

——— "Leadership Strategies for Legislative Party Cohesion," *Journal of Politics* , 28 (May, 1966): 347-367.

Becker, Robert W., *et al* . "Correlates of Legislative Voting: Michigan House of Representatives, 1954-1961," *Midwest Journal of Political Science* , 6 (November, 1962): 384-396.

Bernick, E. Lee. *A Study of the Role Orientations of the Oklahoma Senate, 31st-32nd Legislatures* . Unpublished paper. University of Oklahoma, 1968.

——— *Legislative Voting Patterns and Partisan Cohesion in a One-Party Dominant Legislature* . Norman: Bureau of Government Research, Legislative Research Series, University of Oklahoma, 1973.

——— "The Impact of the Governor on the Voting Behavior of State Legislators: An Examination of Four States." Presented at the Annual Meeting of the Southwestern Political Science Association, San Antonio, Texas, March 27-29, 1975.

——— *Legislative Decision-Making and the Politics of Tax Reform: The Oklahoma Senate* . Norman: Bureau of Government Research, Legislative Research Series, University of Oklahoma, 1975.

——— and F. Ted Hebert. "Emergent Partisanship and the Dimensions of Roll Call Voting." Unpublished manuscript. University of Oklahoma, 1973.

——— and Holly Kinkade. *A Study of the Role Orientations of the Oklahoma House of Representatives, 31st Legislature* . Unpublished paper. University of Oklahoma, 1967.

Bingham, Richard D. *Reapportionment of the Oklahoma House of Representatives: Politics and Process* . Norman: Bureau of Government Research, Legislative Research Series, University of Oklahoma, 1972.

Buchanan, William B. *Legislative Partisanship: The Deviant Case of California* . Berkeley: University of California Press, 1963.

287

Bureau of Government Research. *Legislative Apportionment in Oklahoma* . Norman: University of Oklahoma, 1951.

——— *The Apportionment Problem in Oklahoma* . Norman: University of Oklahoma, 1959.

——— *Legislative Apportionment-1960* . Norman: University of Oklahoma, 1960.

——— *Apportionment Acts of the Legislature, Twenty-Eighth Session, 1961* . Norman: University of Oklahoma, 1961.

Carmines, Edward G. "The Mediating Influence of State Legislatures on the Linkage Between Interparty Competition and Welfare Policies," *American Political Science Review* , 68 (September, 1974): 1118-1125.

Citizens Conference on State Legislatures. *The Sometime Governments: A Critical Study of the Fifty American Legislatures* . New York: Bantam Books, 1971.

——— *State Legislatures: An Evaluation of Their Effectiveness* . New York: Praeger Publishers, 1971.

——— *Summary Report: An Evaluation of the Fifty State Legislatures* . Kansas City, Mo.: Citizens Conference on State Legislatures, 1971.

——— *Legislatures Move to Improve Their Effectiveness* . Kansas City, Mo.: Citizens Conference on State Legislatures, 1972.

Clausen, Aage. *How Congressmen Decide: A Policy Focus* . New York: St. Martin's Press, 1973.

Converse, Philip E. "Religion and Politics: The 1960 Election," in *Elections and the Political Order,* edited by Angus Campbell et al. New York: John Wiley & Sons, 1966.

Crane, Wilder W., Jr. "Do Representatives Represent?," *Journal of Politics* , 22 (May, 1960): 295-299.

——— and Meredith W. Watts, Jr. *State Legislative Systems* . Englewood Cliffs: Prentice-Hall, Inc., 1968.

Crittenden, John. "Dimensions of Modernization in the American States," *American Political Science Review* , 61 (December, 1967): 989-1002.

Dawson, Richard E. and James A. Robinson. "Inter-Party Competition, Economic Variables and Welfare Policies in the American States," *Journal of Politics* , 25 (May, 1963): 265-287.

Declerq, Eugene R. "Gubernatorial Power and Legislative Independence in the Fifty States." Unpublished paper presented at the Annual Meeting of the Midwest Political Science Association, Chicago, May 1-4, 1975.

Derge, David R. "Metropolitan and Outstate Alignments in Illinois and Missouri Legislative Delegations," *American Political Science Review* , 52 (December, 1958): 1051-1065.

———"The Lawyer as Decision-Maker in the American State Legislature," *Journal of Politics* , 21 (August, 1959): 408-433.

———"Urban-Rural Conflict: The Case of Illinois," in *Legislative Behavior* , edited by John Wahlke and Heinz Eulau. Glencoe, Ill.: Free Press, 1959.

deRubertis, William. "How Apportionment With Selected Demographic Variables Relates to Policy Orientation," *Western Political Quarterly* , 22 (December, 1969): 904-920.

Dreyer, Larry. *Legislator and Lobbyist's Views of Improper Lobbying in North Dakota* . Grand Forks: Bureau of Government Affairs, University of North Dakota, 1974.

Dye, Thomas R. "A Comparison of Constituency Influences in the Upper and Lower Chambers of a State Legislature," *Western Political Quarterly* , 14 (June, 1961): 473-480.

———"Malapportionment and Public Policy in the States," *Journal of Politics* , 27 (August, 1965): 586-601.

———*Politics, Economics, and the Public* . Chicago: Rand McNally, 1966.

———"State Legislative Politics," in *Politics in the American States* . 2d ed., edited by Herbert Jacob and Kenneth Vines. Boston: Little, Brown and Co., 1971.

Eisenberg, Ralph. "Reapportionment and A Legislature: Some Observations on the Virginia Experience," in *Reports and Recommendations of the Duke University Assembly on State Legislatures* . Durham: Duke University, 1967.

Elazar, Daniel J. *American Federalism: A View From the States* . New York: Thomas Crowell, 1966.

Epstein, Leon D. *Votes and Taxes* . Madison: Institute of Government Affairs, University of Wisconsin, 1964.

Eulau, Heinz and John D. Sprague. *Lawyers in Politics* . Indianapolis: Bobbs-Merrill Co., Inc., 1964.

Fishel, Jeff. "Ambitions and the Political Vocation: Congressional Challengers in American Politics," *Journal of Politics* , 33 (February, 1971): 25-57.

Flinn, Thomas A. "Party Responsibility in the States: Some Causal Factors," *American Political Science Review* , 58 (March, 1964): 60-71.

Francis, Wayne L. *Legislative Issues in the Fifty States: A Comparative Analysis* . Chicago: Rand McNally, 1967.

————."A Profile of Legislator Perceptions of Interest Group Behavior Relating to Legislative Issues in the States," *Western Political Quarterly*, 24 (December, 1971): 702-712.

Friedman, Robert S. "The Urban-Rural Conflict Revisited," *Western Political Quarterly*, 14 (June, 1961): 481-495.

Froman, Lewis, Jr. and Randall Ripley. "Conditions for Party Leadership: The Case of the House Democrats," *American Political Science Review*, 59 (March, 1965): 52-63.

Fry, Brian R. and Richard F. Winters. "The Politics of Redistribution," *American Political Science Review*, 64 (June, 1970): 508-522.

Grumm, John G. "A Factor Analysis of Legislative Behavior," *Midwest Journal of Political Science*, 7 (November, 1963): 336-356.

————."The Kansas Legislature: Republican Coalition," in *Midwest Legislative Politics* , edited by Samuel C. Patterson. Iowa City: Institute of Public Affairs, The University of Iowa, 1967.

Hahn, Harlan. "Leadership Perceptions and Voting Behavior in a One-Party Legislative Body," *Journal of Politics* , 32 (February, 1970): 140-155.

Havens, Murray. *City vs. Farm* ? University, Ala.: University of Alabama Press, 1957.

Hawkins, Brett and Cheryl Welchel. "Reapportionment and Urban Representation in Legislative Influence Positions: The Case of Georgia," *Urban Affairs Quarterly* , 3 (March, 1968): 69-80.

Heard, Alexander, "Reform: Limits and Opportunities," in *State Legislatures in American Politics* , edited by Alexander Heard. Englewood Cliffs: Prentice-Hall, 1966.

Hedlund, Ronald D. and Wilder Crane, Jr. *The Job of the Wisconsin Legislator* . Washington, D.C.: American Political Science Association, 1971.

———— and H. Paul Friesema. "Representatives' Perceptions of Constituency Opinion," *Journal of Politics*, 34 (August, 1972): 730-753.

Herzberg, Donald and Alan Rosenthal, eds. *Strengthening the States: Essays on Legislative Reform* . New York: Doubleday & Co., Inc., 1971.

———— and Jess Unruh. *Essays on the State Legislative Process* . New York: Holt, Rinehart and Winston, Inc., 1970.

Hofferbert, Richard I. "The Relation Between Public Policy and Some Structural and Environmental Variables in the American States,"

American Political Science Review , 60 (March, 1966): 73-82.

———."Socioeconomic Dimensions of the American States: 1890-1960," *Midwest Journal of Political Science* , 12 (August, 1968): 401-419.

Hofstetter, Richard. "Malapportionment and Roll Call Voting in Indiana, 1923-1963: A Computer Simulation," *Journal of Politics* , 33 (February, 1971): 92-111.

Huckshorn, Robert J. "Decision-Making Stimuli in the State Legislative Process." *Western Political Quarterly* , 18 (March, 1965): 164-185.

Huitt, Ralph K. "The Outsider in the Senate: An Alternative Role," in *Congress: Two Decades of Analysis* , edited by Ralph K. Huitt and Robert L. Peabody. New York: Harper and Row, 1969.

Hyneman, Charles S. "Tenure and Turnover of Legislative Personnel," *Annals of the American Academy of Political and Social Science* , 195 (January, 1938): 21-31.

Jacob, Herbert and Michael Lipsky. "Outputs, Structures and Power: An Assessment of Changes in the Study of State and Local Politics," *Journal of Politics* , 30 (May, 1968): 510-538.

Jewell, Malcolm E. "Party Voting in American State Legislatures," *American Political Science Review* , 49 (September, 1955): 773-791.

———. "State Legislatures in Southern Politics," *Journal of Politics* , 26 (February, 1964): 177-196.

———. *Kentucky Politics* . Lexington: University of Kentucky Press, 1968.

———. *The State Legislature: Politics and Practice* . 2d ed. New York: Random House, 1969.

——— and Samuel C. Patterson. *The Legislative Process in the United States* . New York: Random House, 1966.

———. *The Legislative Process in the United States* . 2d ed. New York: Random House, 1973.

Keefe, William J. "Comparative Study of the Role of Political Parties in State Legislatures," *Western Political Quarterly* , 9 (June, 1956): 726-742.

——— and Morris J. Ogul. *The American Legislative Process: Congress and the States* . 3d ed. Englewood Cliffs: Prentice-Hall, Inc., 1973.

Kingdon, John W. *Congressmen's Voting Decisions* . New York: Harper and Row, 1973.

Kirkpatrick, Samuel A. and Lelan E. McLemore. "Evaluative and Perceptual Dimensions of Legislative Norms: An Analysis of Congruence and Conflict." Presented at the Annual Meeting of the Midwest Political

Science Association, Chicago, May 1-3, 1975.

——— and Lawrence K. Pettit. *The Social Psychology of Political Life* . Belmont, Cal.: Duxbury Press, 1972.

———. *Legislative Role Structures, Power Bases and Behavior Patterns: An Empirical Examination of the U.S. Senate* . Norman: Bureau of Government Research, Legislative Research Series, University of Oklahoma, 1973.

———, David R. Morgan, and Thomas G. Kielhorn. *The Oklahoma Voter: Politics, Elections, and Political Parties in the Sooner State* . Norman: University of Oklahoma Press, 1977.

Lane, Edgar. *Lobbying and the Law* . Berkeley: University of California Press, 1964.

Lasswell, Harold D. *Power and Personality* . New York: Norton, 1948.

LeBlanc, Hugh L. "Voting in State Senates: Party and Constituency Influences," *Midwest Journal of Political Science* , 13 (February, 1969): 33-57.

——— and D. Trudeau Allensworth. *The Politics of States and Urban Communities* . New York: Harper and Row, 1971.

Lehne, Richard. *Reapportionment of the New York Legislature: Impact and Issues* . New York: National Municipal League, 1972.

Lockard, Duane. "Legislative Politics in Connecticut," *American Political Science Review* , 48 (March, 1954): 166-173.

———. "The State Legislator," in *State Legislatures in American Politics* , edited by Alexander Heard. Englewood Cliffs: Prentice-Hall, 1966.

———. "State Party Systems and Policy Outputs," in *Political Research and Political Theory* , edited by Oliver Garceau. Cambridge, Mass.: Harvard University Press, 1968.

MacRae, Duncan, Jr. "The Relation Between Roll Call Votes and Constituencies in the Massachusetts House of Representatives." *American Political Science Review* , 46 (December, 1952): 1046-1055.

Matthews, Donald R. *U.S. Senators and Their World* . New York: Vintage Books, 1960.

——— and James A. Stimson. "Decision-Making by U.S. Representatives: A Preliminary Model," in *Political Decision-Making* , edited by S. Sidney Ulmer. New York: Van Nostrand Reinhold Co., 1970.

McCool, Joseph E., Jr. *The Oklahoma Legislative Council: Pressure Group Participation in the Legislative Process* . Unpublished Master's Thesis, Oklahoma State University, 1968.

McLemore, Lelan E. *The Structuring of Legislative Behavior: Norm Patterns in a State Legislature* . Unpublished Ph.D. dissertation, University of Oklahoma, 1973.

―――. *Task-Related Norms in a State Legislature: The Case of Oklahoma* . Norman: Bureau of Government Research, Legislative Research Series, University of Oklahoma, 1973.

―――. "Norms and the Structuring of Partisan Behavior." Presented at the Annual Meeting of the Southwestern Political Science Association, Dallas, March 28-30, 1974.

―――. *Behavioral Orientations Toward Party Leadership and System Norms: An Exploratory Analysis* . Norman: Bureau of Government Research, Legislative Research Series, University of Oklahoma, 1975.

Milbrath, Lester, "Lobbying as a Communication Process," *Public Opinion Quarterly,* 24 (Spring, 1960): 32-53

―――. *The Washington Lobbyists* . Chicago: Rand McNally, 1963.

Miller, Warren E. and Donald E. Stokes. "Constituency Influence in Congress," *American Political Science Review* , 57 (March, 1963): 45-56.

Mitchell, William C. "Occupational Role Strains: The American Elective Public Official," in *The Social Psychology of Political Life,* edited by Samuel A. Kirkpatrick and Lawrence K. Pettit. Belmont, Cal.: Duxbury Press, 1972.

Monsma, Stephen V. "Integration and Goal Attainment as Functions of Informal Legislative Groups," *Western Political Quarterly* , 22 (March, 1969): 19-28.

Morgan, David R. *Handbook of State Policy Indicators* . Norman: Bureau of Government Research, University of Oklahoma, 1971.

――― and Samuel A. Kirkpatrick. *Constitutional Revision: Cases and Commentary* . Norman: Bureau of Government Research, University of Oklahoma, 1970.

―――. "Legislative Reapportionment and Urban Influence in the Oklahoma Legislature." *Oklahoma Business Bulletin* , 40 (March, 1972): 5-9.

―――. "Urbanism and Oklahoma Politics." *Oklahoma Business Bulletin* , 40 (January, 1972): 10-14.

―――. *Urban Political Analysis: A Systems Approach* . New York: Free Press, 1972.

―――. "Urban-Rural Divisions Within the Oklahoma Legislature," *Oklahoma Business Bulletin* , 40 (April, 1972): 5-10.

Morrison, Patton N. "Legislative-Constituency Interaction in Oklahoma:

A Study of Legislative Referenda Voting." Unpublished paper, University of Oklahoma, 1975.

Murphy, Lionel V. "Legislative Apportionment in Oklahoma," *Southwestern Social Science Quarterly* , 13 (June, 1932): 1-8.

Noble, Jack R, Dale Parent, and Teresa Ramirez. *Oklahoma's Thirtieth Legislature* . Norman: Bureau of Government Research, University of Oklahoma, 1966.

Parent, Gary N. "The Reapportionment Decade in the Oklahoma House." Unpublished paper, University of Oklahoma, 1975.

Patterson, Samuel C. "Patterns of Interpersonal Relations in a State Legislative Group," *Public Opinion Quarterly* , 23 (Spring, 1959): 101-109.

———. "The Role of the Deviant in the State Legislative System: The Wisconsin Assembly," *Western Political Quarterly,* 14 (June, 1961): 460-472.

———. "Dimensions of Voting Behavior in a One-Party State Legislature," *Public Opinion Quarterly* , 26 (Summer, 1962): 185-200.

———. "The Role of the Lobbyist: The Case of Oklahoma," *Journal of Politics* , 25 (February, 1963): 72-92.

Penniman, Clara. "The Politics of Taxation," in *Politics in the American States* , 2d ed., edited by Kenneth Vines. Boston: Little, Brown & Co., 1971.

Porter, H. Owen. "Legislative Experts and Outsiders: The Two-Step Flow of Communication," *Journal of Politics* , 36 (August, 1974): 703-731.

Pray, Joseph C. and J. Mauer. *The New Perspective of Legislative Apportionment in Oklahoma* . Norman: Bureau of Government Research, University of Oklahoma, 1962.

Prewitt, Kenneth. "Political Ambitions, Volunteerism, and Electoral Accountability," *American Political Science Review* , 64 (March, 1970): 5-18.

——— and William Nowlin. "Political Ambitions and the Behavior of Incumbent Politicians," *Western Political Quarterly* , 22 (June, 1969): 298-308.

Ranney, Austin. "Parties in State Politics," in *Politics in the American States* , edited by Henry Jacob and Kenneth Vines. Boston: Little, Brown and Co., 1965.

Rhodes, Jack A. "The Legislative Council: A Program for Planning and Research," *Southwestern Social Science Quarterly* , 27 (June, 1946): 54-61.

Ripley, Randall. *Congress: Process and Policy* . New York: W.W. Norton

& Co., 1975.

Rosenthal, Alan. "Contemporary Research on State Legislatures: From Individual Cases to Comparative Analysis," in *Political Science and Local Government* . Washington: The American Political Science Association, 1973.

――――. "Turnover in State Legislatures," *American Journal of Political Science* , 18 (August, 1974): 609-616.

Saffell, David. *The Politics of American National Government* . Cambridge: Winthrop Publishers, Inc., 1973.

Salisbury, Robert H. *Missouri Politics and State Political Systems* . Columbia, Mo.: Bureau of Government Research, University of Missouri, 1959.

Schlesinger, Joseph A. *Ambition and Politics* . Chicago: Rand McNally, 1966.

Sharkansky, Ira. *Spending in the American States* . Chicago: Rand McNally, 1968.

――――. "The Utility of Elazar's Political Culture: A Research Note," *Polity* , 2 (Fall, 1969): 66-83.

――――. "Environment, Policy, Output, and Impact: Problems of Theory and Method in the Analysis of Public Policy," in *Policy Analysis in Political Science* , edited by Ira Sharkansky. Chicago: Markham, 1970.

―――― and Richard Hofferbert. "Dimensions of State Politics, Economics, and Public Policy," *American Political Science Review* , 63 (September, 1969): 867-879.

Siffin, William J. *The Legislative Council in the American States* . Bloomington: Indiana University Press, 1959.

Sindler, Allan P. *Huey Long's Louisiana* . Baltimore: Johns Hopkins Press, 1956.

Sorauf, Frank J. *Party and Representation: Legislative Politics in Pennsylvania* . New York: Atherton Press, 1963.

Soule, John W. "Future Political Ambitions and the Behavior of Incumbent State Legislators." *Midwest Journal of Political Science* , 13 (August, 1969): 439-454.

Stokes, Donald E. and Warren E. Miller. "Party Government and the Saliency of Congress," *Public Opinion Quarterly* , 26 (Winter, 1962): 531-546.

Strain, Jack W. *An Outline of Oklahoma Government* . Norman: Rickner's Book Store, 1972.

Tax Foundation, Inc. *Earmarked State Taxes* . New York: Tax Foundation, Inc., 1965.

Truman, David B. *The Governmental Process* . 2d ed. New York: Alfred A. Knopf, Inc., 1971.

U.S., Department of Commerce, Bureau of the Census. *Census of Population, 1960, General Population Characteristics, Oklahoma* .

————. *Census of Population, 1970, General Population Characteristics, Oklahoma* .

————. *Census of Population, 1970, General Social and Economic Characteristics, Oklahoma* .

Wahlke, John C. "Organization and Procedure," in *State Legislatures in American Politics* , edited by Alexander Heard. Englewood Cliffs: Prentice-Hall, 1966.

————. "Policy Determinants and Legislative Decisions," in *Political Decision-Making* , edited by Sidney Ulmer. New York: Van Nostrand Reinhold Co., 1970.

————, et al., *The Legislative System* . New York: John Wiley & Sons, Inc., 1962.

Walker, Jack. "The Diffusion of Innovations Among the American States," *American Political Science Review* , 63 (September, 1969): 880-900.

Warren, Carl. *Modern News Reporting* . 3d ed. New York: Harper and Row, 1959.

Who is Who in the Oklahoma Legislature . Oklahoma City: Oklahoma Department of Libraries, Legislative Reference Division.

Wiggins, Charles W. "Party Politics in the Iowa Legislature," *Midwest Journal of Political Science* , 11 (February, 1967): 86-97.

————. *The Iowa Lawmakers* . Ames: Iowa State University, 1970.

Wood, John W. "The Oklahoma Legislature," in *Power in American State Legislatures* , edited by Alex B. Lacy. New Orleans: Tulane University, 1967.

Index

Adair County: 221
Adaptation, legislator styles of: 88-92
American Medical Association: 216
Appropriations: 140, 157
Attorney General's Office: 101-103, 135
Attorneys in legislature: 31

Baker v. *Carr:* 42, 47
Bartlett, Governor Dewey: 151
Bible belt, Oklahoma: 35
Bills: 104, 115, 123-25, 134-35; veto of, 7, 109, 116-19; introduction in House or Senate, 105, 110; first reading, 105; second reading, 105; amendments, 105-106; and committee action, 105-107; and emergency clause, 109; carry-over, 116
Board of Legislative Compensation: 9
Budget-balancing amendment of 1941: 7
Budget Office: 103
Bureaucracy: 100
Bureau of Government Research, University of Oklahoma: 43, 169
Bureau of Government Research Oklahoma Legislative Study: 123, 129-30
Burke, Edmund: 203, 206
Businessmen in legislature: 33

Caucus meetings: 13, 14
California legislature: 61, 182, 214; interest groups, 143
Citations: 110
Citizens Conference on State Legislatures: study, 225;

measurement of legislative effectiveness, 225-26; and FAIIR system of criteria, 226-28, 243; Oklahoma rating, 228-35; recommendations, 230-31; and factors in legislative effectiveness, 235-41; and public policy, 241-43
Code of Federal Regulations: 101
Committee on Constitutional Revision and Regulatory Services: 43
Committees: 17, 95, 169, 176; agricultural, 37; appropriations, 37, 128-29; finance and commerce, 37; judiciary, 37, 128-29; revenue and taxation, 37, 128; roads and highways, 37, 128; rules, 37, 128, 131; of Legislative Council, 95-97, 134; bills referred to, 105; motions on bills, 106; Committee of the Whole, 105-106, 133; standing, 120-21, 125-26, 129, 131; and assignment shifts, 122; appointment of, 122-23, 127; functions, 123-25; and "sunshine rule" changes, 124; number of, 126-28; assignments, 128-30; appointment of chairmen, 130-31; powers and duties of chairmen, 131-32; procedure, 132-34; interim and special, 134; jurisdiction, 134-35; Ways and Means, 134-35
Common Cause: 234
Compromise: 4, 5
Concurrent resolutions: 110
Congressional Clearing House
Congressional Index: 101
Congressional Monitor: 101

Congressional Quarterly: 101
Congressional Record: 101
Connecticut legislature: 77, 88, 90-91, 193
Conservation: 152
Constituents: 49, 53, 137, 142, 144, 155-60, 199, 204-10; demands on legislators, 48, 68; influences on roll call votes, 142, 144; and legislator interaction, 200-203
Constitution, Oklahoma: 5, 6, 14, 43-44, 46-47, 93, 98, 231
Council Executive Committee: 9-10
Courts: 4

Davis v. *Mann:* 43
Democrats: 14, 25-29, 36, 45, 50, 66-67, 78, 80, 151, 153-55, 184, 186, 207; and legislative dominance, 20-22, 45, 49; governors, 119; and decision making, 139; and roll call voting, 147; on judicial reform, 149; on labor, 150; on racial integration, 150

Education: 50; legislators', 55, 84
Effectiveness, legislative: measurement of, 225-26; FAIIR system of criteria, 226-28, 243; how Oklahoma fares, 228-35; and factors in, 235-41; and public policy, 241-46
Elections: of legislators, 11; of legislative officers, 16; and public school measures, 145
Executive branch: 4, 5; *see also* governor

Farmers in legislature: 31-32
Federal reporter: 101
Feedback: 16, 56
Floor leaders: 14, 37
Florida legislature: 240
Forces in decision making: political party, 137-40; cues from colleagues, 137-38, 140-41; rules and procedures, 137;

socioeconomics, 49, 55, 137, 139, 158, 225, 246; constituency influences, 142, 144, 155-60; environment, 142-43; and interest groups, 143; gubernatorial, 143-44, 146-52; partisan factors, 146-52; non-party influences on party, 152-55; legislators' political beliefs, 160-61; *see also* roll call voting

Galleries: 202
Governor, Oklahoma: 6, 98, 100, 110, 137, 141, 150-51, 169, 187-88, 234; State of the State message of, 16; action on bills, 7, 109, 116-19; Democrat, 119; Republican, 120; influence on roll call voting, 143-52; *see also* executive branch

Hall, Governor David: 151, 158
Handbook on State Policy Indicators: 241, 243
Health and welfare: 140
Highway Department, Oklahoma: 36, 103
House of Representatives, Oklahoma: 7, 15, 19, 36, 47, 60-66, 69-77, 83, 87, 91, 104-16, 126-30, 134, 146, 150-51, 155-57, 167, 169-70, 173-75, 183-84, 186-87, 193-98, 201-10, 220; qualifications, responsibilities, compensation, 8-9, 68; officers, 10-11, 14; party membership, 20-22; reapportionment, 37-46; tenure and turnover, 78
House rules study guide: 260-74

Idaho legislature: constituency influence, 142; and interest groups, 142
Impeachment: 7
Indiana legislature: 33
Initiative petitions: 6

Insurance men in legislature: 30-32
Interest groups: 57, 124, 143, 199; organized, 211; unorganized, 211; and lobbyists, 213-19; *see also* pressure groups
Inter-Local Cooperative Act: 36

Joint resolutions: 110, 115, 124
Jones v. *Freeman:* 41-42

Kentucky: 140, 229

Labor unions: 139
Lawmakers: *see* legislators
League of Women Voters: 234
Legislation: course of, 104-109; types of measures, 109-20
Legislative Council, Oklahoma: 10, 15, 42, 65, 103-104, 134-35, 193; development of, 94-95; as part of legislative body, 95; duties, 95, 97-98; and executive committee, 95; committees of, 96-98; divisions of, 97; publications, 99-100
Legislative Council Committee on Interstate Cooperation: 98
Legislators, freshman: 11, 17, 104, 169, 177, 180; frustrations, 67-68
Legislators, Oklahoma: 3, 4, 31, 98, 136, 179, 188; as lawmakers, 4; as representatives, 4; as counselors, advisers, 4; as overseers of executive branch, 5; duties, 5, 11-13; powers and restraints, 6, 7; organization and composition, 7-11; presession activities, 13-15; oath of office, 15-16; background characteristics, 22-35, 52, 55; self views, 54-77; frustrations, pressures, 67-72, 77, 85; rewards, 69-70, 74-77; job satisfaction, 70, 77; efficacy, 72-74; perception of power structure, 74-77; career perspectives, 77-88; political ambition, 81-85; activity and involvement, 85-88;

see also religious affiliations and self views of legislators
Legislators, rural: 145, 152, 155
Legislature, Oklahoma: 3, 4, 26, 33, 36, 52, 58, 62, 64-66, 83-84, 88, 90-91, 97, 104, 111, 120-22, 125-27, 135, 140, 144, 147, 171, 177-81, 189-90, 192, 195, 197-98; sessions, 8, 68, 81, 109, 114; convening of, 15; first week of, 16-18; political, social makeup of, 18-35; bills, 104-105, 123-25, 134-35; informal rules, 162-70; external relationships, 199-224; perceptive, 225; rating among states, 228-35; factors influencing effectiveness, 235-41; and public policy, 241-46
Lieutenant governor: 10
Lobbyists: 100, 124-25, 165, 186, 204, 212, 228; kinds of, 214-16; regulation of, 216-19; defined, 217-18
Louisiana: 140

McCarty, Representative J. D.: 230
Majority leaders: 9-10
Malapportionment: 42, 48, 143, 152
Memorials: 110
Metro-urban districts: 21, 237
Michigan legislature: 141
Mid-Atlantic states: 139
Middle West: 139
Minority leaders: 10
Missouri: 139
Moral issues: 156, 159
Moss v. *Burkhart:* 42

New England: 139
New Jersey legislature: 61, 77, 181, 214, 240
News media: 199, 219-21; news significance criteria, 221-22; and guidelines of legislators, 223-24
New York State: 139

Norms, legislative: 53, 162–70, 214; partisan, 170–72; and procedural voting, 172–74; and substantive voting, 174–75; committee action, 175–76; floor behavior, 176–77; publicity, 177–79; and floor speaking, 179–81; and personalities, 180–81; specialization, 181–84; interest groups, 185–87; and governor, 185, 187–89; and shared beliefs, 189–91; sanctions of, 191–93; awareness of, 193–94; monitoring of, 194–95; rewards and punishments, 195–97; and sanctioning agents, 197–98
North Dakota: 217

Occupations of legislators: 31–32, 50
Officers, legislative: 9–11
Ohio legislature: 61, 214; constituency influences, 142
Oklahoma: 20–23, 26, 29, 47, 49, 52, 61–62, 65–66, 78, 80, 83–84, 90, 92, 101–103, 109, 122, 137, 143–44, 146–47, 150; party organization, 139; constituencies, 139, 200–203; lobbyists, 213–19
Oklahoma City, Oklahoma: 36–37, 39
Oklahoma County: 9, 22, 37–39, 41, 160, 221
Oklahoma Department of Libraries: 100–101, 135
Oklahoma Gazette: 101
Oklahoma session laws: 117
Oklahoma, University of: 15, 110, 193
Opinion polls: 201

Pennsylvania legislature: 142
Pocket veto: 7, 109, 119
Presession Legislative Conference: 15
President pro tempore, Senate:

9–10, 14, 17, 37, 126–28, 130–31, 134, 192; and committee appointments, 122–23
Public-policy enactment: 93; information inputs, 93–94; and Legislative Council, 93–100, 103–104; and Oklahoma Department of Libraries, 100–101, 103; and Attorney General's Office, 101–103; Tax Commission, 103; budget office, 103; department of highways, 103

Real estate men in legislature: 30–32
Reapportionment: 3, 7–8, 19, 21, 24–25, 32, 35–37, 50–51, 80–81, 143, 146, 156, 203; House of Representatives, 37–46; Senate, 46—-49
Religious affiliations, legislators': 33–35, 50, 55; see also Oklahoma legislators
Reports, legislative committee: on bills, 133–34
Republicans: 14, 25–29, 36, 45, 50, 66, 78, 80, 151, 153–55, 186, 207; as legislative minority, 20–22, 49; and decision making, 139; and roll call voting, 147; and judicial reform, 149; on labor, 150; on racial integration, 150
Reynolds v. Sims: 8, 43, 47
Roll call voting: 53, 93, 132, 135, 172, 245; internal forces on, 137–41; external forces, 141–44; mix of internal and external forces, 144; influences on, 145–61; see also forces in decision making

Secretary of state: 16, 117
Self views, legislators': roles, 53; as tribune, 54, 60, 62–64, 66; ritualist, 54, 59, 61–62, 66; broker, 54, 57, 60, 64, 66; inventor or innovator, 54, 57, 60,

65–67; trustee, 54, 57, 84, 203–208; delegate of constituency, 54, 203–207; politico, 54, 204, 206–207; in areal role, 54; structural position, 54; facilitator, 54, 57, 213–14; resister, 54, 213; neutral, 54; party man, 54, 66, 176; maverick, 54ferent to party, 54; and role conflict, 57–59; and purposive roles, 59–66; tribune inventor, 60; perception of power and privilege, 74–77; free agent, 203–204, 208, 214; *see also* Oklahoma legislators

Senate, Oklahoma: 7, 15, 19, 36, 60–63, 69–77, 83, 87, 91, 104–15, 126–30, 134, 167, 169–70, 173–75, 177–78, 183–84, 186–87, 193–98, 201–10, 220; qualifications, responsibilities, compensation, 8–9, 68; officers, 9–11, 14; party membership, 20–22; reapportionment, 46–49; turnover, 78

Senate rules study guide: 247–59

Simple resolutions: 111

Socioeconomic levels: 49, 55, 137, 139, 158, 225, 246; shift, 50–51

Speaker, House of Representatives: 9–10, 14, 17, 37, 45, 126–27, 130–31, 134; and committee appointments, 122–23

State Election Board: 15

State Regents for Higher Education: 7

Supreme Court, Oklahoma: 15, 47, 102, 147

Supreme Court, United States: 42, 46–47

Supreme Court Reporter: 101

Taxation: 6, 36–37, 140, 151, 236, 246; voting on, 145, 157–58

Tax Commission, Oklahoma: 103

Teachers retirement system report: 98

Tennessee legislature: 61, 77, 181, 229

Tenth Circuit Court of Appeals: 42

Tenure and turnover, legislative: 77–81, 121

Texas: 140

34th Legislature: 83

33rd Legislature: 146

Tulsa County: 22, 37–41

Tulsa, Oklahoma: 36–37, 47

Turnpike Authority, Oklahoma: 7

"Unwritten rules of the game": *see* legislative norms

Urbanism: 35–40, 50; and urban legislators, 145, 152, 155

U. S. Lawyer's Edition: 101

U. S. Reports: 101

Variables: 140, 158, 160, 162

Vermont legislature: 151

Veterans of Foreign Wars: 212

Veto: 116–17; pocket, 7, 109, 119; item, 119–120; and partisan considerations, 120

Virginia legislature: 229

West Virginia legislature: 229

Whips: 14

Wisconsin legislature: 166